Surveys in
Economic Dynamics

Surveys in Economic Dynamics

Donald A. R. George,
University of Edinburgh

Les Oxley,
University of Waikato

and

Simon Potter,
Federal Reserve Bank of New York

BLACKWELL
Publishers

British Library Cataloguing in Publication Data has been applied for

Library of Congress Cataloging in Publication Data has been applied for

ISBN 0-631-22036-4 (pbk)

Typeset by Mathematical Composition Setters Ltd, Salisbury, Wiltshire
Printed and bound in Great Britain
by MPG Books Ltd, Bodmin, Cornwall

This book is printed on acid-free paper

CONTENTS

PREFACE

This is the second book in the series *Surveys of Recent Research in Economics*: its theme is economic dynamics. The first book in the series dealt with cointegration and the third will be on Political Economy.

It is now widely known that nonlinear dynamic modelling raises some vital and fascinating issues for economists. These include multiple equilibria, statistical inference, stability, robustness, chaos and undecidability. Many economists still find the nonlinear dynamic economy such a weird and distressing place that they seek to suppress its interesting features by appeal to techniques such as linearisation. The Editors hope that this volume will convince the reader that the use of nonlinear modelling techniques can significantly enhance our understanding of a wide range of important economic behaviour.

The contributions to the book discuss recent work on economic dynamics from the theoretical and empirical points of view; they have all been selected to be accessible to the technically competent non-specialist. Our thanks to all those at Blackwells who have helped pilot the book through the production process.

Donald A. R. George, Les Oxley and Simon Potter

1

NONLINEAR TIME SERIES MODELLING: AN INTRODUCTION

Simon M. Potter

1. Introduction

It is now ten years since Jim Hamilton's seminal paper on nonlinear modelling of U.S. output was published. This ten years has witnessed an explosion of interest amongst econometricians in the testing, estimation, specification and properties of nonlinear models. The purpose of this chapter is to give a non-technical survey of the main developments and some observations on the difficulties of successful nonlinear modelling in macroeconomics.[1] It is useful to begin by giving some motivation for the need for nonlinear modelling.

The 1970s and 1980s saw economists adopt many of the time series techniques introduced by Box and Jenkins. The basis for such modelling approaches was the Wold Representation: any covariance stationary time series can be expressed as moving average function of present and past innovations:

$$Y_t = \sum_{i=0}^{\infty} \theta_i U_{t-i}, \quad \text{with } \sum \theta_i^2 < \infty, \ \theta_0 = 1,$$

where

$$E[U_t U_{t-i}] = 0 \quad \text{for all } i \neq 0 \text{ and } E[U_t^2] = \sigma_u^2$$

This infinite moving average can nearly always be well approximated by low order autoregressive processes perhaps with some moving average components. Further, the dynamics of the time series could be 'read off' from

I would like to thank Gary Koop for numerous helpful discussions. The views expressed in this chapter are those of the author and do not necessarily reflect the views of the Federal Reserve Bank of New York or the Federal Reserve System.

the Wold Representation since θ_i represents the impulse response function at horizon i.

It might appear at first that there is no need for nonlinear modelling given the Wold Representation. However, as well illustrated in the appropriately titled 'Forecasting White Noise', by Clive Granger, lack of autocorrelation in a time series does not imply that the time series cannot be predicted. Indeed some perfectly predictable time series have zero autocorrelations at all lags.[2]

Further, while the Wold Representation gives the impulse response function directly it imposes some strong restrictions on it. First, the impulse response function does not depend on the recent history of the time series. Thus, for example, the response to a positive innovation of 1% is the same whether last period's growth rate was 8% or -8%. Second, the response to innovations is restricted to be homogeneous of degree 1. That is, once the response to a shock of size 1 has been found all other shocks are given by simple scalings of this response.

Successful nonlinear time series modelling would improve forecasts and produce a richer notion of business cycle dynamics than linear time series models allow. For this to happen two conditions are necessary. First, economic time series must contain nonlinearities. Second, we need reliable statistical methods to summarize and understand these nonlinearities suitable for time series of the typical macroeconomic length. Unfortunately the second condition is needed to evaluate the veracity of the first condition and as we shall see it is not clear that we have yet found reliable statistical methods.

The organization of the chapter is as follows: I start by describing three types of models most widely used in the economics literature and Classical and Bayesian estimation techniques in simple cases; the testing problem is then discussed with respect to these three models; finally simulation of the conditional expectations is described and its use in the construction of forecasts and impulse response functions.

2. Three models

In this section I discuss the three types of models that have most commonly be used in nonlinear modelling particularly for aggregate output measures and unemployment. I will use a common notation across all models. Y_t will be a univariate covariance stationary time series, $y^t = (Y_1, Y_2, ..., Y_t)$ will be the history of the time series up to time t. V_t will be a sequence of independent and identically distributed random variables with unit variance. When likelihood based methods are discussed one can assume that V_t has a standard normal distribution. The Greek letters α, ϕ, σ will respectively refer to the intercepts, autoregressive coefficients and the scaling of the time series innovation. $\phi(L)$ is a polynomial in the lag operator of the form:

$$\phi_1 L + \phi_2 L^2 + \cdots + \phi_p L^p.$$

Below we will make use of the fact that if $V_t \sim N(\mu, 1)$ and the prior belief on μ is flat over the line then the posterior belief about μ after observing a sample of size T is

$$\mu \sim N\left(\frac{1}{T}\sum_{t=1}^{T} v_t, \frac{1}{T}\right).$$

2.1. Markov switching

It is best to begin with Hamilton's model from *Econometrica* 1989. His original motivation was to model long swings in the growth rate of output but instead he found evidence for discrete switches in the growth rate at business cycle frequencies. Output growth was modelled as the sum of a discrete Markov chain and a Gaussian autoregression:

$$Y_t = Z_t + X_t,$$

where

$$Z_t = \alpha_0 + \alpha_1 S_t, \quad S_t = 0 \quad \text{or} \quad 1$$

and

$$X_t = \phi_1 X_{t-1} + \phi_2 X_{t-2} + \phi_3 X_{t-3} + \phi_4 X_{t-4} + \sigma V_t,$$

and $P[S_t = 1 \mid S_{t-1} = 1] = p$, $P[S_t = 0 \mid S_{t-1} = 0] = q$, $V_t \sim N(0, 1)$.

The major estimation difficulty with the model is the lack of separate observability of Z_t and X_t. A simple variation on the model is:

$$Y_t = Z_t + \phi(L)Y_{t-1} + \sigma V_t,$$

where only S_t is now unobservable. Note that the original model can also be written in this form by multiplying both sides by $(1 - \phi(L))$ we have:

$$Y_t = (1 - \phi(L))Z_t + \phi(L)Y_{t-1} + \sigma V_t. \tag{1}$$

Expanding out the term $(1 - \phi(L))Z_t$ using the lag operator we see that the two state Markov chain is transformed into a tightly parameterized 32 state chain.

A slightly different model is produced by allowing all of the parameters to switch with the Markov chain:

$$Y_t = \alpha^{s(t)} + \phi^{s(t)}(L)Y_{t-1} + \sigma^{s(t)}V_t \tag{2}$$

Three approaches to estimating the model have been taken.[3] In Hamilton's original article he developed a nonlinear filter to evaluate the likelihood function of the model and then directly maximized the likelihood function. Hamilton (1990) constructed an EM algorithm that is particularly useful for the case where all the parameters switch. Finally, Albert and Chib (1993) developed a Bayesian approach to estimation that was later refined using results due to Chang-Jin Kim. The recent monograph by Kim and Nelson (1999) contains an excellent discussion of both Classical and Bayesian estimation of Markov switching models. The idea behind all three approaches can be illustrated in the following simple model:

$$Y_t = \alpha_0(1 - S_t) + \alpha_1 S_t + V_t, \quad t = 1, 2, \ldots T.$$

For simplicity suppose we know that $S_0 = 1$, then entering the next period the $P[S_1 = 1 \mid S_0 = 1] = p$. The observation Y_1 is either drawn from a normal distribution with mean α_0 and variance 1 or a normal distribution with mean α_1 and variance 1 and the likelihood is given by

$$f(y_1; \alpha_0, \alpha_1, p, q, s_0 = 1) = \frac{p \exp(-0.5(y_1 - \alpha_1)^2) + (1 - p)\exp(0.5(y_1 - \alpha_0)^2)}{\sqrt{2\pi}}$$

Assume for the moment the two mean parameters are known, then given the realization of Y_1 Bayes rule can be used to update the probability $S_1 = 1$, denote this by b_1:

$$P[S_1 \mid Y_1, S_0 = 1, \alpha_0, \alpha_1, p, q] = b_1$$

$$= \frac{\exp(-0.5(y_1 - \alpha_1)^2)p}{\exp(-0.5(y_1 - \alpha_1)^2)p + \exp(-0.5(y_1 - \alpha_0)^2)(1 - p)}.$$

Now b_1 can be used to produce a prediction of the state next period denote this by $\hat{b}_2$:

$$P[S_2 \mid Y_1, S_0 = 1, \alpha_0, \alpha_1, p, q] = \hat{b}_2 = pb_1 + (1 - q)(1 - b_1).$$

Using this prediction we can weight together the two possible likelihood functions depending on the state to produce a likelihood function that averages out over the value of S_2:

$$f(y_2 \mid y_1; \alpha_0, \alpha_1, p, q, s_0 = 1)$$

$$= \frac{\hat{b}_2 \exp(-0.5(y_2 - \alpha_1)^2) + (1 - \hat{b}_2)\exp(-0.5(y_2 - \alpha_0)^2)}{\sqrt{2\pi}}$$

and so on. This process then continues up through the last observation T to obtain the overall the likelihood function:

$$f(y_1, \ldots, y_T; \alpha_0, \alpha_1, p, q, s_0 = 1)$$

$$= \prod_{t=1}^{T} \frac{\hat{b}_t \exp(-0.5(y_t - \alpha_1)^2) + (1 - \hat{b}_t)\exp(-0.5(y_t - \alpha_0)^2)}{\sqrt{2\pi}}$$

Numerical optimization techniques can be used to find the maximum with respect to α_0, α_1, p, q. Further, one can also treat the probability that initial state $s_0 = 1$ as a parameter to be estimated.

For both the EM algorithm and the Bayesian analysis and inference about the unobserved Markov chain one needs to 'smooth' the estimate of the Markov state b_t so that it contains information from the whole sample. Only the last probability b_T contains information on the whole observed time series. Using the Markov property and the exogeneity of the Markov chain we know that conditional on observing tomorrow's state s_{t+1} all future realizations of the observed time series $\{Y_s : s > t\}$ are not relevant for the estimate of today's state. Using this restriction and ignoring the dependence on estimated parameters we have:

$$P[S_{T-1} = 1, S_T = 1 \mid Y^T]$$
$$= P[S_{T-1} = 1 \mid S_T = 1, Y^{T-1}]P[S_T = 1 \mid Y^T]$$
$$= P[S_{T-1} = 1 \mid S_T = 1, Y^{T-1}]b_T$$
$$= p\,\frac{b_{T-1}}{\hat{b}_T}\,b_T, \tag{3}$$

since

$$P[S_{T-1} = 1 \mid S_T = 1, Y^{T-1}]$$
$$= \frac{P[S_{T-1} = 1, S_T = 1 \mid Y^{T-1}]}{P[S_T = 1 \mid Y^{T-1}]}$$
$$= \frac{P[S_{T-1} \mid Y^{T-1}]P[S_T = 1 \mid S_{T-1} = 1]}{\hat{b}_T}$$
$$= \frac{b_{T-1}p}{\hat{b}_T}. \tag{4}$$

Thus denoting the smoothed probability by $\tilde{b}_{T-1}$ we need to average out the value of S_T in (3) by performing a similar calculation for the case that $S_T = 0$:

$$\tilde{b}_{T-1} = b_{T-1}\left(p\,\frac{\tilde{b}_T}{\hat{b}_T} + (1-q)\,\frac{1 - \tilde{b}_T}{1 - \hat{b}_T} \right).$$

This process continues until we arrive at time 1 or 0 depending on the assumption made on the initial condition. In the EM algorithm the smoothed probabilities are used to produce estimates of the unknown parameters as follows:

$$\hat{\alpha}_0^i = \sum_{t=1}^{T} y_t(1 - \tilde{b}_{t+1}), \quad \hat{\alpha}_0^i = \sum_{t=1}^{T} y_t\tilde{b}_{t+1}$$

and using (3):

$$\hat{p}^i = \frac{\sum_{t=1}^T P[S_{t-1}=1, S_t=1 \mid Y^T]}{\sum_{t=1}^T P[S_{t-1}=1 \mid Y^T]} = \hat{p}^{i-1} \frac{b_{t-1}}{\hat{b}_t} \frac{\tilde{b}_t}{\hat{b}_{t-1}},$$

$$\hat{q}^i = \frac{\sum_{t=1}^T P[S_{t-1}=0, S_t=0 \mid Y^T]}{\sum_{t=1}^T P[S_{t-1}=0 \mid Y^T]} = \hat{q}^{i-1} \frac{(1-b_{t-1})}{(1-\hat{b}_t)} \frac{(1-\tilde{b}_t)}{(1-\hat{b}_{t-1})}.$$

Thus, the intercepts are estimated by weighting observations by the likelihood they are in regime 0 or 1 and the transition probabilities by a pseudo count of the number of times the Markov chain stayed in the same state.

These updated parameter values are then used to re-run the filter and smoother on the observed data. This produces new parameter values and the iteration continues until a fixed point is achieved. This fixed point will be a local maxima of the likelihood function. By considering different starting parameter values for the algorithm one can check which of one local maxima is the global one. Of course one local maximum occurs at the least squares estimate of the mean of the time series with no transitions amongst states and is easy to discard (but we shall see later it causes inference problems). Consider the case of the EM algorithm where all the smoothed probabilities were 1 or 0 and there were some transitions amongst states. Then in this case the smoother would have correctly identified the movement of the Markov chain and the data would be grouped in the appropriate manner. The Bayesian approach works off this intuition by using the filter probabilities to generate realizations of the Markov chain.

Starting from b_T a value of s_T is drawn using standard inversion techniques (that is, generate a uniform random number, if it is less than or equal to b_T, $s_T=1$, otherwise $s_T=0$). Then using (4) if $S_T=1$ is drawn (or its obvious complement if $S_T=0$ is drawn), a value of S_{T-1} is drawn and this process continues until the whole sequence of the realization of the Markov chain has been drawn, $\{s_t^i\}$. Using this sequence of values for the Markov chain it is possible to split the observed data directly into two regimes. That is,

$$\hat{\alpha}_0^i = \frac{1}{T_0^i} \sum_{t=1}^T y_t(1-s_t^i), \quad T_0^i = \sum_{t=1}^T (1-s_t^i),$$

$$\hat{\alpha}_1^i = \frac{1}{T_1^i} \sum_{t=1}^T y_t s_t^i, \quad T_1^i = \sum_{t=1}^T s_t^i.$$

In the case that flat independent priors are used for α_0, α_1, their posterior densities are normal with means $\hat{\alpha}_0^i, \hat{\alpha}_1^i$ and variances $1/T_0^i, 1/T_1^i$ respectively. These posterior distributions can then be used to draw realizations of α_0, α_1.

The posterior of the transition parameters can also be simply found under the assumption that the priors are independent Beta distributions:

$$f(p) \propto p^{\delta_1 - 1}(1 - p)^{\delta_2 - 1}, f(q) \propto q^{\eta_1 - 1}(1 - q)^{\eta_2 - 1},$$

where $\delta_1, \delta_2, \eta_1, \eta_2$ are all strictly positive and a standard uniform prior is obtained for $\delta_1 = \delta_2 = \eta_1 = \eta_2 = 1$. Given the Beta prior the posterior will also have a Beta form with parameters:

$$\delta_1^i = \delta_1 + \hat{p}^i \sum_{t=1}^{T} P[S_{t-1} = 1 \mid Y^T], \delta_2^i = \delta_2 + (1 - \hat{p}) \sum_{t=1}^{T} P[S_{t-1} = 1 \mid Y^T]$$

$$\eta_1^i = \eta_1 + \hat{q}^i \sum_{t=2}^{T} P[S_{t-1} = 0 \mid Y^T], \eta_2^i = \eta_2 + (1 - \hat{q}^i) \sum_{t=2}^{T} P[S_{t-1} = 0 \mid Y^T],$$

where $\hat{p}^i$, $\hat{q}^i$ are defined in the same manner as in the EM algorithm. Again it is easy to draw from these posterior densities to obtain the realization p^i, q^i. Combined with the realization for the intercepts the new values can be used to run the nonlinear filter and smoother again and obtain a fresh draw of the Markov chain.

This is a Gibbs sampling algorithm for the Markov switching model. One important issue is how to initialize the algorithm. A good choice is the maximum likelihood estimates. Unlike the EM algorithm the output of the Gibbs sampler is a collection of draws from the posterior of the Markov switching model. In addition to draws of the parameters this also includes the draws of the full sample smoother. Features of the posterior distribution can then be found by averaging. For example, the estimate of the path of the Markov chain would be obtained by averaging the draws of the full sample smoother:

$$P[S_t = 1 \mid Y^T] = \frac{1}{I} \sum_{i=1}^{I} \tilde{b}_t^i.$$

2.2. Threshold models

Threshold autoregressive (TAR) models are perhaps the simplest generalization of linear autoregressions. They were introduced to the time series literature by Howell Tong (see his 1983 and 1990 monographs for descriptions and extensive background on nonlinear time series).[4] Various different threshold models have been successfully applied to US GDP/GNP by Beaudry and Koop (1993), Potter (1995) and Potter and Pesaran (1997). The general form is as follows

$$Y_t = \alpha^{j(t)} + \phi^{j(t)}(L)Y_{t-1} + \sigma^{j(t)}V_t,$$

where $j(t) = 1$ if $Y_{t-d} < r_1, j(t) = 2$ if $r_1 \leqslant Y_{t-d} < r_2, ..., j(t) = J$ if $r_{J-1} \leqslant Y_{t-d}$, and it is possible that the length of the autoregression varies across the regimes. The parameters r_j are called the thresholds and d is called the delay.

Although this model looks very similar to the Markov switching one in (2) there is a crucial difference. In the threshold model regimes are defined by the past values of the time series itself, in the Markov switching case regimes are defined by the exogenous state of the Markov chain. Filardo (1994) constructed an intermediate case where the transition probabilities of the Markov chain vary with the history of the observed time series.

Suppose $\{r_j\}$, $\{p_j\}$, d were known then the model can be estimated by separating the data into groups by regime and finding the least squares estimates for the parameters in each regime. Unfortunately these parameters are not known and standard nonlinear least squares algorithms are not useful since the sum of squares function is not differentiable with respect to these parameters. For the discrete parameters of the delay and order of autoregressive lags it is easy to repeat the least squares estimation for each choice. In the case of the threshold parameters one needs to estimate the sum of squares for a finite number of choices.

Estimation can be illustrate in a similar simplified model to the Markov switching:

$$Y_t = \alpha_0 1(Y_{t-1} < r) + \alpha_1 1(Y_{t-1} \geqslant r) + V_t,$$

where $1(Y_{t-1} < r) = 1$ if the inequality holds and is zero otherwise.

The first step is to organize data into the matrix:

$$\begin{bmatrix} Y_1 & Y_0 \\ Y_2 & Y_1 \\ \vdots & \vdots \\ Y_T & Y_{T-1} \end{bmatrix},$$

then sort this matrix from smallest to largest according to the values in the second column:

$$\begin{bmatrix} Y_t^{\{1\}} & Y_{t-1}^{\{1\}} \\ Y_t^{\{2\}} & Y_{t-1}^{\{2\}} \\ \vdots & \vdots \\ Y_t^{\{T\}} & Y_{t-1}^{\{T\}} \end{bmatrix}.$$

Now note that if $r < Y_{t-1}^{\{1\}}$ then all the data are in regime 1 ($\hat{\alpha}_1$ would be the sample average, α_0 is not identified) or if $r > Y_{t-1}^{\{T\}}$ then all of the data are in regime 0 ($\hat{\alpha}_0$ would be the sample average, a_1 is not identified). If $Y_{t-1}^{\{1\}} \leqslant r < Y_{t-1}^{\{2\}}$ then

$$\hat{\alpha}_0^{\{1\}} = Y_t^{\{1\}}, \quad \hat{\alpha}_1^{\{1\}} = \frac{1}{T-1} \sum_{s=2}^{T} Y_t^{\{s\}},$$

and we have the (least squares) recursion:

$$\hat{\alpha}_0^{\{i+1\}} = \frac{T_0^{\{i\}}}{T_0^{\{i+1\}}} \hat{\alpha}_0^{\{i\}} + \frac{1}{T_0^{\{i+1\}}} Y_t^{\{i+1\}}, \ T_0^{\{i+1\}} = i+1$$

$$\hat{\alpha}_i^{\{i+1\}} = \frac{T_1^{\{i\}}}{T_1^{\{i+1\}}} \hat{\alpha}_0^{\{i\}} - \frac{1}{T_1^{\{i+1\}}} Y_t^{\{i+1\}}, \ T_1^{\{i+1\}} = T-i-1$$

These estimates give the sum of squared errors function in terms of the threshold:

$$SSE_0^{\{i\}} = \sum_{s=1}^{T_0^{\{i\}}} (Y_t^{\{s\}} - \hat{\alpha}_0^{\{i\}})^2, \ SSE_1^{\{i\}} = \sum_{s=T_0^{\{i\}}+1}^{T} (Y_t^{\{s\}} - \hat{\alpha}_i^{\{i\}})^2$$

The obvious least squares estimate of r is the interval associated with the smallest sum of square errors (this is also the case when the delay is estimated). Note that any estimate within this interval is equally valid. Under the assumption of Gaussianity of the errors this would also be the maximum likelihood estimate. Chan (1993) showed that the estimate of the threshold (and delay) converges at a sufficiently fast rate that conditioning on the least squares/maximum likelihood estimate of the threshold, one could ignore its sampling variability in the asymptotic inference about the other parameters.

The Bayesian approach to estimating the threshold model (under the assumption of Gaussian errors) is similar in terms of the regime coefficients. Continuing with our simple example and assuming flat independent priors on the two intercepts, conditional on the threshold, the intercepts would have Normal distributions centered at the least squares estimates $\hat{\alpha}_0^{\{i\}}, \hat{\alpha}_1^{\{i\}}$ with variances $1/T_0^{\{i\}}, 1/T_1^{\{i\}}$ respectively. In order to find the marginal posterior of the threshold consider the case of a flat prior on the thresholds. Then the joint posterior is proportional to the likelihood function.

$$p(\alpha_0, \alpha_1, r \mid Y^T) \propto \frac{1}{\sqrt{2\pi}^{T_0^{\{i\}}}} \exp\left(-0.5 \sum_{s=1}^{T_0^{\{i\}}} (Y_t^{\{s\}} - \alpha_0)^2\right)$$

$$\times \frac{1}{\sqrt{2\pi}^{T_1^{\{i\}}}} \exp\left(-0.5 \sum_{s=T_0^{\{i\}}+1}^{T} (Y_t^{\{s\}} - \alpha_1)^2\right).$$

Subtracting and adding the least squares estimates of the intercepts in each squared function and re-arranging using the orthogonality of least squares estimates we have:

$$p(\alpha_0, \alpha_1, r \mid Y^T) \propto \exp\left(-0.5\left[\sum_{s=1}^{T_0^{\{i\}}} (Y_t^{\{s\}} - \hat{\alpha}_0^{\{i\}})^2 + \sum_{s=T_0^{\{i\}}+1}^{T} (Y_t^{\{s\}} - \hat{\alpha}_1^{\{i\}})^2\right]\right)$$

$$\times \exp(-0.5[T_0^{\{i\}}(\hat{\alpha}_0^{\{i\}} - \alpha_0)^2 + T_1^{\{i\}}(\hat{\alpha}_1^{\{i\}} - \alpha_1)^2]).$$

Now integrating out over α_0, α_1 we have:

$$p(r \mid Y^T) \propto \frac{1}{\sqrt{T_0 T_1}} \exp(-0.5[SSE_0^i + SSE_1^i])(Y_{t-1}^{\{i\}} - Y_{t-1}^{\{i-1\}}), \qquad (5)$$

for $i = 2, ..., T$. Where the intervals $(Y_{t-1}^{\{i\}} - Y_{t-1}^{\{i-1\}})$ represent the fact that there is no information on the threshold between data points.

The Bayesian modal estimate of the threshold is not likely to be the same as the classical one (i.e., the same interval) even under the assumption of a flat prior on the thresholds. Although the exponential term will be maximized at the same threshold value as the total sum of square errors, the lead term involving the inverse of the square roots of the sample size in each regime will affect the location of the maximum. Further, the mean and median of the posterior distribution of the threshold are very unlikely to be at the mode unless T is very large and the sum of squared errors terms dominates.

Marginal inference about the regime coefficients is very different than in the classical case (see Hansen 1999 for a method to improve the classical approach). In the Bayesian case inference about the intercepts would be based on weighting the individual normal distributions by the posterior probability of the particular threshold interval and threshold uncertainty would affect inference about individual regime coefficients.

2.3. Smooth transition autogressions

For many the abrupt regime changes in the threshold model are unrealistic. Consider the case where one is forecasting US GDP and the initial release his slightly below the threshold but the subsequent revision is above the threshold. A threshold model would imply large changes in the forecast of the future for this small change initial conditions. Further, the difficulties of the non-standard likelihood/least squares functions are a distraction.

As originally suggested by Chan and Tong (1986) and subsequently developed by Timo Teräsvirta and his various co-authors (see for example, his 1993 monograph with Clive Granger) if one introduces smooth transitions between regimes standard nonlinear estimation techniques can be used. Since smooth transition models have a more traditional structure, Teräsvirta has been able to implement a model specification, estimation and diagnostic cycle very similar to the Box and Jenkins approach (see his 1994 *JASA* paper). The models were successfully applied to a wide range of industrial production series by Teräsvirta and Anderson (1992).

In the simple threshold model above imagine changing from the indicator function to a smooth cumulative distribution function:

$$Y_t = \alpha_0(1 - F(Y_{t-1}; \gamma, r)) + \alpha_1 F(Y_{t-1}; \gamma, r) + V_t,$$

where $F(-\infty; \gamma, r) = 0$, $F(\infty; \gamma, r) = 1$.

The simplest smooth transition function is of a logistic type:

$$F(Y_{t-1}; \gamma, r) = \frac{1}{1 + \exp(-\gamma(Y_{t-1} - r))},$$

where the parameter $\gamma > 0$ determines the abruptness of the transition at r. For example, for very large γ the smooth transition model might effectively be the same as a threshold model for certain values of r since for the pair observations of Y_{t-1} either side of r the transition might be complete. On the other hand, if $\gamma \simeq 0$ then the logistic function hardly varies away from 0.5 and there is really only one regime.

Once again if r and γ were known ex-ante, simple least squares methods could be used to estimate the remaining parameters. Thus, one can concentrate the least squares function/likelihood function with respect to r and γ and use standard nonlinear optimizers to estimate these parameters. In practice because of numerical instability issues it makes some sense to limit the variation in one of these two parameters. One choice favored by Teräsvirta is to normalize $(Y_{t-1} - r)$ by the standard deviation of the delay variable. Another is to examine a finite set of thresholds, as in the Threshold autoregression case, thus leaving only γ to be directly estimated by the nonlinear optimizer.[5]

A more general version of the model is as follows:

$$Y_t = \alpha_1 + \phi_1(L)Y_{t-1} + (\alpha_2 + \phi_2(L)Y_{t-1})F(Y_{t-d}; r, d, \gamma) + \sigma V_t \qquad (6)$$

One difference to the other two models is that less attention is focused on possible changes in the variance of the innovations across regimes. In addition to the logistic smooth transition function there has also been considerable attention paid to the possibility of symmetric transitions away from the threshold:

$$F^s(Y_{t-1}; \gamma, r) = 1 - \exp(-\gamma(Y_{t-1} - r)^2).$$

Lubrano (1999) discusses Bayesian estimation of smooth transition autoregressions. As in the threshold autoregression case one can integrate out the intercept, autoregressive coefficients and variance. This leaves a 3-dimensional posterior distribution. One dimension is the delay parameter and is discrete, the other two involve the threshold and speed of transition. One choice is to find their posterior using standard numerical techniques. Another choice is to use a Metropolis–Hastings algorithm.

3. Testing

Perhaps the greatest theoretical progress in the last ten years has been in our understanding of testing for nonlinearity in economic time series. On the other hand, perhaps the least empirical progress has been made in finding evidence for nonlinearity in economic time series given the new theoretical tools available. For example, a range of statistical tests have been applied to aggregate output in the United States. At first the results were encouraging but as shown by Hansen

(1992, 1996a) some of the encouragement was of the wishful thinking variety. First, direct tests of the Hamilton's Markov switching model suggested that it was not statistically significant. Subsequent searches over different Markov switching specifications (Chib 1995, Hansen 1992) were motivated by this failure and their success should be qualified. Second, direct tests of threshold models also indicate that the nonlinear terms are not highly statistically significant. Tests for smooth transition models usually do not take into account the effects of searching over different values of the delay parameter. These classical statistical results have also been supported by the Bayesian analysis of Koop and Potter (1999a). Overall there is probably less evidence for nonlinearity in US output at the end of the 1990s then researchers thought at the start of the decade but still considerable evidence that the behavior of output in at business cycle turning points is not well captured by linear models.[6]

In Hamilton's (1989) paper he was careful to point out that testing the null hypothesis of a linear model against his particular nonlinear model was not standard and appeared to be very difficult. There were two main problems. First, under the null hypothesis the transition parameters of the Markov chain in the alternative hypothesis were not pinned down. Consider the likelihood value from above:

$$f(y_1; \alpha_0, \alpha_1, p, q, s_0 = 1) = \frac{p \exp(-0.5(y_1 - \alpha_1)^2) + (1 - p)\exp(-0.5(y_1 - \alpha_0)^2)}{\sqrt{2\pi}}$$

In the case that $\alpha_1 = \alpha_0$ the value of p has no effect on the likelihood function.

Second, the likelihood function for the nonlinear model has a local maximum at the parameter values for the linear model with p set at the boundary value of 1 since this implies all the realizations of the Markov chain will be in state 1 given that this is the initial condition.

The first problem is common to nearly all nonlinear models with the notable exception of the smooth transition class where the following reparametrization is available:

$$F^*(Y_{t-1}; r, \gamma) = \frac{1}{1 + \exp(-\gamma(Y_{t-d} - r))} - 0.5.$$

Now testing for nonlinearity can be undertaken by allowing γ to take on all real values under the alternative and fixing the delay at a particular value. The null hypothesis of linearity is captured by the restriction $\gamma = 0$. As described in Teräsvirta (1994) a Lagrange Multiplier test can be developed. However, in the general case where the delay is unknown the problem crops up again.

In the general case the imposition of the null hypothesis of linearity leaves some of the parameters describing the nonlinear model free. In statistics it is called the Davies' problem. In order to understand the seriousness of the Davies' problem consider that under the null hypothesis for a fixed choice of the parameters the likelihood ratio will have a Chi-squared distribution in large samples. But one can vary these 'free' parameters to find a largest and smallest likelihood ratio. Again under the null hypothesis these are both draws from the same Chi-squared distribution. Obviously if the minimum value still exceeds the critical value rejection of the null hypothesis is warranted. Such an outcome is possible in the case where some restrictions are placed on the parameters present only under the alternative. For example, in the threshold case if each regime must have at least 15% of the data or in the Markov switching case where one rules out boundary values for the transition probabilities and defines them on a closed subset of the unit interval. One solution is to choose the nuisance parameters at random. Another more powerful one is to examine the properties of the maximum across the parameter space as described in the accompanying article by Bruce Hansen.

All of the previous solutions ignored some information in the behavior of the test statistic as the parameters describing the nonlinear model are varied. In a large enough sample it is safe to do this and concentrate on the most powerful tests involving the largest test statistic. However, in a typical macroeconomic application where the likelihood function might have many local maxima such an approach can be dangerous. One obvious solution would be to examine some average of the test statistics. This intuition was formalized by Andrews and Ploberger (1994) who showed that under certain conditions averaged test statistics were the most powerful.

In order to illustrate these ideas I will work with the simple threshold autoregression as the alternative nonlinear model.

$$Y_t = \alpha_0 1(Y_{t-1} < r) + \alpha_1 1(Y_{t-1} \geq r) + V_t$$

and the sequence of observed data $y_0 = -0.2$, $y_1 = 2$, $y_2 = -0.1$, $y_3 = -1.9$. The initial observation will be treated as fixed and for both linear and nonlinear models the innovation variance is assumed to be 1. For the linear model we have a sample average of 0 and a resulting sum of squared errors of $2^2 + 0.1^2 + 1.9^2 = 7.62$.

For the threshold model we shall assume *a priori* that the threshold value is in the interval $[-1, 1]$. Thus we have 3 possible sum of squared error functions:

1. If $-1 \leq r \leq -0.2$, then the same sum of squared error function is the same as the linear model since all the observations are drawn from the same regime.
2. If $-0.2 < r \leq -0.1$ then observations 2 and 3 are drawn from the upper regime and observation 1 is drawn from the lower regime. Thus, $\hat{\alpha}_0 = 2$, $\hat{\alpha}_1 = (-0.1 + -1.9)/2 = -1$ and the sum of squared errors is $0^2 + 0.9^2 + 0.9^2 = 1.62$.
3. If $-0.1 < r \leq 1$ then observations 1 and 3 are drawn from the lower regime and observation 2 is drawn from the upper regime. Thus, $\hat{\alpha}_0 = (2 + -1.9)/2 = 0.05$, $\hat{\alpha}_1 = -0.1$ and the sum of squared errors is $1.95^2 + 0^2 + 1.95^2 = 7.605$.

We have three log likelihood ratio statistics: $0, 6, 0.03$ (in this example the log likelihood ratio is just the difference in the sum of squared errors). Clearly, an estimate of r in the interval $-0.2 < r \leq -0.1$ is the maximum likelihood estimate and the associated test statistic of 6 is large relative to a Chi-squared distribution with one degree of freedom that one would use to measure statistical significance in large samples. On the other hand the minimum statistic of 0 is obviously not significant compared to a Chi-squared distribution. If we average the test statistics against a uniform distribution for the threshold in the given interval the value is $0.4 \times 0 + 0.05 \times 6 + 0.55 \times 0.03 = 0.317$. This is also the expected value of a randomized test but such a test would have considerable variability depending on which interval was chosen.

Hansen (1996a) provides a general method of calculating sampling distributions under the null hypothesis for such operations on the family of test statistics. The procedure in this case works as follows (note in this special case the procedure gives an exact small sample result, this is not true in general). Generate 3 standard normal random variables and without loss of generality assume they are ordered: $V_1 \leqslant V_2 < V_3$. The likelihood ratio statistic considered by plugging in the maximum likelihood estimate of the threshold is equivalent to the following minimization problem:

$$\tfrac{4}{9}(V_1^2 + V_2^2 + V_3^2) - \tfrac{1}{4}\min\{V_1^2 + V_2^2, V_2^2 + V_3^2\}$$

The 95th percentile of this distribution is approximately 2.9 thus on this measure there is significant evidence of the threshold effect (the p-value for the observed statistic is 0.1%). This give significance at a better than 1% level. However, if we consider the average likelihood ratio statistic using the observed frequency of likelihood ratios different than zero:

$$0.6[\tfrac{4}{9}(V_1^2 + V_2^2 + V_3^2) - \tfrac{1}{4}(V_1^2 + V_2^2) - \tfrac{1}{4}(V_2^2 + V_3^2)],$$

the 95th percentile is approximately 1.4. Thus, on this measure the threshold effect is not statistically significant.

An alternative to the classical approach is to use Bayes factors to compare the linear and nonlinear models (see Koop and Potter, 1999a). The Bayes factor in this case is ratio of the average value (over prior distribution of parameters) of the likelihood function for the nonlinear model against the average value (over the prior distribution of parameters) of the likelihood function for the linear model. In order for the Bayes factor to be useful, informative priors on the parameters are required. In this simple case we shall assume that the prior on the mean for the linear model is uniform over $[-m, m]$ and that the prior on the nonlinear model is uniform and independent for both intercepts over the same interval of length $2m$. Then using our previous result on the posterior for the threshold and the numbers for differences in sum of squared errors form above we have:

$$\frac{\sqrt{2\pi}}{2m}\left[0.4 \times 1 + 0.05 \times \frac{\sqrt{3}}{\sqrt{2}}\exp(3) + 0.55 \times \frac{\sqrt{3}}{\sqrt{2}}\exp(0.015)\right]$$

$$= \frac{1.2533}{m}2.314 \quad \text{if } m \geqslant 2.$$

Here to keep things simple I have assumed that the prior is sufficiently flat that boundary value problems do not occur. The interpretation of the Bayes factor is different to classical statistical tests. In this case it is giving (assuming linear and nonlinear models were equally likely *ex ante*) the posterior odds in favor of the nonlinear model. Notice that if $2 \leqslant m < 1.253 \times 2.314 = 2.899$ they are favorable. For an ignorant prior ($m \to \infty$) the Bayes factor would always favor the simpler linear model. The highest posterior odds for the nonlinear model are obtained at $m = 2$ and are equal to about 1.45, that is about 60% of the posterior weight is placed on the nonlinear model and about 40% on the linear model.

Obviously the main drawback of the Bayesian approach is its sensitivity to the prior distributions on the parameters. For example, if the prior on the threshold had been uniform on $[-10, 10]$ then the Bayes factor would be

$$\frac{\sqrt{2\pi}}{2m} \left[\frac{9.8}{20} \times 1 + \frac{0.1}{20} \times \frac{\sqrt{3}}{\sqrt{2}} \exp(3) + \frac{10.1}{20} \times \frac{\sqrt{3}}{\sqrt{2}} \exp(0.015) \right]$$

$$= \frac{1.253}{m} 1.241 \quad \text{if } m \geqslant 2.$$

and at best ($m = 2$) the posterior odds in favor of nonlinearity would be 44%. The benefit of the drawback is that the Bayes factor has a very big penalty for more complicated models something that classical models are unable to do. For example, in the case that both the threshold and intercepts are assumed to uniformly distributed over a wide interval we are placing most of the ex-ante weight on very strong forms of nonlinearity. Suppose $m = 10$ and $r \sim U[-10, 10]$ then most threshold models produced would have bimodal distributions with modes very far apart and values like $y_2 = -0.1$ are improbable.

Bayesian methods have a strong advantage when it comes to finding tests for Markov switching models. Hansen (1992, 1996b) provides a bounds test that deals with the both the Davies' problem and the zero scores problem. However, this is a very computationally intensive test and it only provides a bound on the size. Garcia (1998) adopts the approach of Andrews and Ploberger (1994)and Hansen (1996a) by ignoring the zero scores problem. His simulation results suggest that zero scores might not be a problem in practice. In contrast, Bayesian testing of the Markov switching models is simple and direct. In order to illustrate consider the simple Markov switching model:

$$Y_t = \alpha_1 S_t + V_t.$$

Here linearity is given by the restriction that $\alpha_1 = 0$. As discussed in Koop and Potter (1999a) the Bayes factor in this Markov switching case can be written as the ratio of the posterior density to the prior density for α_1 evaluated at zero, i.e.,

$$\frac{b(\alpha_1 = 0)}{p(\alpha_1 = 0 \mid Y^T)}.$$

Once again suppose that α_1 has a uniform prior on the interval $[-m, m]$ and using our previous results we have a conditional Bayes factor of:

$$\frac{b(\alpha_1 = 0)}{p(\alpha_1 = 0 \mid Y^T, \{s_t^i\}, p^i, q^i)} = \frac{\sqrt{T_1^i}}{2m\sqrt{2\pi}} \exp[-0.5 T_1^i (\hat{\alpha}_1^i)^2].$$

The overall Bayes factor is found by replacing the conditional posterior density with its average across posterior draws:

$$p(\alpha_1 = 0 \mid Y^T) = \frac{1}{I} \sum_{i=1}^{I} \frac{\sqrt{T_1^i}}{\sqrt{2\pi}} \exp[-0.5 T_1^i (\hat{\alpha}_1^i)^2],$$

which requires minimal changes to existing computer code.

Once again if the initial ignorance about α_1 is high (large values of m) there is less chance of finding evidence of nonlinearity. Or alternatively if the priors on p and q lead to most runs of $\{s_t^i\}$ consisting of zeros there is also little chance of finding nonlinearity. Chib (1995) discusses a slightly more computationally intensive method of constructing the average likelihood for the Markov switching model that is easier to implement when all the parameters of the model switch with the Markov variable as in (2).

4. Constructing conditional expectations

Once a final nonlinear model is arrived at there remains the issue of understanding the estimated dynamics and forecasting capabilities. Since the primary objective of nonlinear modelling is to obtain the true conditional expectation function there is still a substantial task remaining.

The task is easiest for the Markov switching models. As an illustration consider Hamilton's original model in the form given in (1). We introduce the following notation: $\mathbf{P}$ represents the transition matrix of the 32 state Markov chain, $\mathbf{b}_t$ is a vector representing the filter probabilities for each of the 32 individual states, $\mathbf{s}^*$ is a vector containing the 32 possible values of $(1 - \phi(L))Z_t$.

$$E_t[Y_{t+h}] = E_t[Z_{t+h}^*] + E_t[\phi(L)Y_{t+h-1}].$$

The second term on the LHS can be evaluated using standard linear recursions. The first term on the LHS requires more care. Assume for the moment that S_t^* was in the information set at time t. Then one could find $E_t[S_{t+h}^*]$ using the estimated probability transition matrix as follows:

$$E[S_t^* \mid S_t^* = s_j] = \mathbf{s}^{*\prime} \mathbf{P}^{h\prime} \mathbf{e}_j,$$

where $\mathbf{e}_j$ is a vector of zeros except for the jth row which contains 1. Of course the state of the Markov chain is not known at time t but one can replace $\mathbf{e}_j$ with filter probabilities over the states of the Markov chain at time t,

$$E[S_t^* \mid S_t^* = s_j] = \mathbf{s}^{*\prime} \mathbf{P}^{h\prime} \mathbf{b}_t.$$

For the TAR and STAR models obtaining the conditional expectation nearly always requires the use of simulation once the forecast horizon exceeds the length of the delay lag. If the horizon is less than the delay lag then the conditional expectation is given by iterating on the nonlinear difference equation. For example, in the simple model:

$$Y_t = -1(Y_{t-4} < 0) + 1(Y_{t-4} \geqslant 0) + V_t,$$

the conditional expectation function up to horizon 4 is given by

$$E[Y_{t+h} | Y^t] = -1(Y_{t+h-4} < 0) + 1(Y_{t+h-4} \geqslant 0), \quad \text{if } h \leqslant 4.$$

Suppose the conditional expectation of Y_{t+1} at time t was 1 (i.e., $Y_{t-3} > 0$). It would be incorrect to use this value in the indicator function to forecast $Y_{t+5} = 1$ since V_{t+1} is standard normal there is non-zero probability that $Y_{t+1} < 0$. Continuing with this example, there is approximately a 16% probability that $Y_{t+1} < 0$. Thus,

$$E[Y_{t+5} | Y_{t-3} > 0] = -P[Y_{t+1} < 0 | Y_{t-3} > 0] + P[Y_{t+1} \geqslant 0 | Y_{t-3} > 0]$$
$$= -0.16 + 0.84 = 0.68.$$

Similar results would be available up to forecast horizon 8 where things become more complicated:

$$E[Y_{t+9} | Y_{t-3} > 0] = -P[Y_{t+5} < 0 | Y_{t-3} > 0] + P[Y_{t+5} \geqslant 0 | Y_{t-3} > 0].$$

In order to evaluate the probabilities on the RHS one can iterate forward the distribution for Y_{t+5} using the fact that Y_{t+1} is drawn from a $N(1, 1)$ with probability 0.84 and from a $N(-1, 1)$ with probability 0.16.

Notice that forecasts after horizon 4 were crucially dependent on the assumption on the innovations were Gaussian and the size of their variance, unlike the linear case. Further the calculations were greatly simplified by the fact there were no autoregressive lags. Consider another simple model:

$$Y_t = 0.5 Y_{t-1} 1(Y_{t-1} \geqslant 0) + V_t.$$

We have $E[Y_{t+1}[Y^t] = 0.5 Y_t 1(Y_t \geqslant 0)$ and at horizon 2

$$E[Y_{t+2} | Y^t] = 0.5 E[Y_{t+1} 1(Y_{t+1} \geqslant 0) | Y^t],$$

which can be evaluated using the fact the $Y_{t+1} 1(Y_{t+1} \geqslant 0)$ is a (conditional) truncated normal with parameters $0.5 Y_t 1(Y_t \geqslant 0)$ and 1 to obtain

$$E[Y_{t+2} | Y^t] = 0.25 Y_t 1(Y_t \geqslant 0) + 0.5 \left[\frac{\varphi(-0.5 Y_t 1(Y_t \geqslant 0))}{1 - \Psi(-0.5 Y_t 1(Y_t \geqslant 0))} \right],$$

where $\varphi(z)$ and $\Psi(z)$ are the standard normal density and cumulative distribution functions respectively. Notice that for $Y_t \gg 0$ the forecasts are very similar to a first order linear autoregression with zero intercept and autoregressive coefficient of

0.5. For smaller values of Y_t the forecasts are very different from such a linear autoregression. However,

$$E[Y_{t+3} \mid Y^t] = 0.5E[Y_{t+2}1(Y_{t+2} \geqslant 0) \mid Y^t],$$

is much less tractable since Y_{t+2} does not have a conditional normal distribution.

Instead of directly attempting to calculate this expectation consider using the time series model to simulate a large number of time series for each particular history. Thus, we know that $Y_{t+1} \sim N(0.5Y_t 1(Y_t \geqslant 0), 1)$ and this fact can be used to generate K realizations from this distribution. Now take this realizations and generate K realizations of Y_{t+2} using K draws of V_{t+2} and the equation:

$$y_{t+2}^k = 0.5y_{t+1}^k 1(y_{t+1}^k \geqslant 0) + v_{t+2}^k.$$

We can then approximate $E[Y_{t+3} \mid Y^t]$ by:

$$\frac{1}{K} \sum_{k=1}^{K} 0.5y_{t+2}^k 1(y_{t+2}^k \geqslant 0)$$

which by the Law of Large Numbers will converge to the conditional expectation as $K \to \infty$.

For both the Threshold and Smooth Transition Models dynamic simulation of time series paths allows one to calculate good approximations to the conditional expectation function for a wide range of specifications.

4.1. Forecasting with known parameters

Given a method to calculate the conditional expectation function and a model with no unknown parameters the production of forecasts is straightforward. The comparison of these forecasts with those from linear models is less straightforward. First, in out of sample comparisons it is important that the nonlinear feature found in the historical sample is present. For example, many of the nonlinear models of U.S. output focus on the dynamics entering and recovering from recessions. The last recession in the United States ended in early 1991, thus it has been difficult to verify the nonlinearities out of sample.

This lack of variation in the out of sample period can be compensated for by various experiments within the sample. In particular, unlike linear models useful information can be generated by considering in sample multistep ahead prediction. Consider first a linear first order autoregression with zero intercept and estimated first order coefficient $\hat{\phi}$ and residuals $\{\hat{U}_t\}$. We have the following identities:

$$Y_{t+1} = \hat{\phi}Y_t + \hat{U}_{t+1},$$

$$Y_{t+2} = \hat{\phi}Y_{t+1} + \hat{U}_{t+2} = \hat{\phi}^2 Y_t + \hat{\phi}\hat{U}_{t+1} + \hat{U}_{t+2}, \dots,$$

$$Y_{t+H} = \hat{\phi}Y_{t+H-1} + \hat{U}_{t+H} = \hat{\phi}^H Y_t + \sum_{h=0}^{H-1} \hat{\phi}^h \hat{U}_{t+H-h}.$$

Thus, for large sample size the in sample one-step ahead forecast variance is $\hat{\sigma}^2$, the two-step ahead is $\hat{\sigma}^2(1 + \hat{\phi}^2)$, and h-step ahead by $\hat{\sigma}^2(\sum_{h=0}^{H-1} \hat{\phi}^{2h})$.

For nonlinear models such a recursion does not exist. In fact it is not even possible to show that the RMSE of a forecasts grows monotonically with the horizon as in a linear model for all histories. This cost in terms of computational complexity is a benefit in terms of model evaluation since simulation of h-step ahead conditional expectation function in sample can provide a diagnostic check on the nonlinear model. By definition, for any forecast horizon, the variance of the forecast error using the best linear predictor has to be greater than or equal to the variance of the forecast error using the true conditional expectation function, Thus, a good diagnostic check on the estimated nonlinear model is whether this is true in the observed sample.

There are two ways to formalize the notion of the best linear predictor. One is to use the linear model used in the testing phase and iterate it as above to obtain multi-step predictions. In this case it might prove useful to adjust for the loss of observations as the steps ahead of the prediction increase. For Markov switching models this is an easy check since no simulation is required. For the other models it becomes more computationally intensive once the forecast horizon exceeds the delay lag of the threshold variable.

Using the iterated properties of a linear model is only a weak check since if nonlinearity is present the model will only produce the best linear forecasts for one step ahead. A stronger one in the case where nonlinearity is present but not necessarily of the type estimated, is to estimate different linear models for each prediction horizon. If the true nonlinearity is different from that estimated then such adaptive linear models should start to outperform the nonlinear model.

4.2. *Forecasting with parameter uncertainty*

It is typical in linear time series forecasting applications to provide some measure of the effect on the forecast of parameter uncertainty. There are a two main ways of doing this using classical statistical methods. One can use asymptotic approximations for functions of the parameters of the model or one can simulate random draws from the approximately normal sampling distributions of the parameters and construct the forecasts from the draws. These methods are only directly applicable to the STAR model. Even in this case the situation is far more complicated than the linear one, since we need to calculate the conditional expectation function, as described above, for each set of parameter values.

In the case of the threshold model, the threshold estimates and delay are converging at faster rates than the other parameters, hence in a large enough sample they can be ignored. Unfortunately, the adequacy of this large sample approximation in time series of the typical length in macroeconomics is very much open to question. Further, unlike the mild effects that a poor approximation might have in a linear model the effects in threshold models can be drastic. Consider the case where the threshold variable in the information set for the forecast is close to the estimate of the threshold. By treating the threshold and

delay as known the forecast will be very different depending on which side of the
threshold the observed data is. However, this is a false precision since the value of
the threshold or delay is not known with certainty.

Dacco and Satchell (1999) find that the regime misclassification introduced can
lead to a nonlinear model having inferior forecast performance to a linear model
even when the nonlinear model is true and all parameters but the threshold are
known. This issue can be illustrated using the simple intercept shift threshold
autoregression under the assumption that α_0, α_1 are known. In this case the
posterior distribution for the threshold is given by:

$$p(r \mid Y^T) \propto \exp(-0.5[SSE_0^i + SSE_1^i])(Y_{t-1}^{\{i\}} - Y_{t-1}^{\{i-1\}}).$$

Denoting the cumulative distribution function of the posterior of r by G we have
for the one step ahead forecast:

$$E_T[Y_{T+1}] = \alpha_0 + (\alpha_1 - \alpha_0)G(y_T).$$

Obviously as the sample size increases $G(y_T)$ will start to get closer to an indicator
function but in typical macroeconomic samples it will contain considerable
uncertainty about the true location of the threshold.

One implication of the above analysis is that for forecasting Bayesian
estimation of threshold models has a distinct advantage (although it might be
possible to adapt some of results of Hansen 1999 to reproduce a classical analog).
This is also true for the Markov switching models. In this case the difficulty is that
the estimate of the current Markov state is dependent on the whole set of
parameter estimates. Any change in the parameter estimates would affect the
estimate of the Markov state. One could simulate from the asymptotic
distribution of the parameter estimates and then rerun the filter at these
parameter values to obtain some feeling for how the estimate of the current state
would change. But this is an inconsistent approach: the new filter values would
imply different parameter estimates (by definition only maxima in the likelihood
function will not have this problem, see the discussion of the EM algorithm
above). The Bayesian solution to the forecasting problem is to use the output of
the Gibbs sampler. Recall that for each complete draw from the Gibbs sample we
have draws of the unknown parameter values and the value of the filter
probability of the most recent state. These values can be used to form a forecast.
Repeating this exercise across all the draws from the posterior and averaging will
produce the conditional expectation allowing for parameter uncertainty.

4.3. Impulse response functions

Once one is satisfied with the nonlinear model there is the remaining question of
describing how its dynamics differ from that of linear models fit to the same time
series. Since most economists describe the dynamics of linear models using
impulse response functions it is important to generalize impulse response
functions to nonlinear time series. As described in the introduction the linear
dynamics of a time series are given by the Wold Representation. The coefficients

in the Wold Representation can be thought of as producing the same answer to the following four questions:

1. What is the response to a unit impulse today when all future shocks are sent to zero?
2. What is the response to a unit impulse today when all future shocks are integrated out?
3. What is the derivative of the predictor of the future?
4. How does the forecast of the future change between today and yesterday?

For nonlinear models there will be different answers to each question. To illustrate consider the simple threshold model:

$$Y_t = -1(Y_{t-1} < 0) + 1(Y_{t-1} \geqslant 0) + V_t$$

and the case of a positive unit impulse for the first two questions.

1. If $Y_t \geqslant 0$ then the response is 0 for all horizons, if $-1 \leqslant Y_t < 0$ then response is 2 for all horizons since this permanently moves the time series into the upper regime given the assumption of no future shocks, if $Y_t < -1$ then the response is 0 for all horizons.
2. At horizon 1 the response is the same as the answer to question 1 but as the horizon increases we have the difference:

$$E[Y_{t+h} \mid Y_t = y_t + 1] - E[Y_{t+h} \mid Y_t = y_t],$$

which must converge to zero by the stationarity of the underlying time series.
3. The derivative is either 0 or not defined if $Y_t = 0$.
4. Consider the case where $E_{t-1}[Y_t] = 1$ and the realized value of $Y_t = 1$. Then the initial shock is 0 but

$$E_t[Y_{t+1}] - E_{t-1}[Y_{t+1}] = 1 - 0.68 = 0.32.$$

Or the case where $E_{t-1}[Y_t] = 1$ and the realized value of $Y_t = 5$. Then the initial shock is 4 but the $E_t[Y_{t+1}] - E_{t-1}[Y_{t+1}]$ is still equal to 0.32.

It should be immediately apparent that questions 1 and 3 are not particularly useful questions to ask for a nonlinear time series. This leaves a choice between the more traditional definition of the impulse response function defined by the answer to question 2 and the forecasting revision function defined by the answer to question 4. In order to choose between the two possibilities observe that both the initial condition and the magnitude and sign of the impulse is important in describing the dynamics of nonlinear models. This is problematic since one can chose values of the initial condition or shock that produce atypical responses. In answering question 4 the properties of the impulse are defined directly by the time series model, that is:

$$E_t[Y_t] - E_{t-1}[Y_t],$$

or σV_t in our examples. Further, in order to define the initial conditions one can use the history of the time series or random draws from its simulated distributions. In answering question 2 there is no direct way of defining the relevant set of perturbations away from the initial condition using the properties of the time series model. Note that using the time series innovation to define the perturbation is not correct since this innovation represents the unforcastable change between time $t-1$ and t.

Koop, Pesaran and Potter (1996) and Potter (1999) call the forecast revision function a generalized impulse response function and develop its properties. Of particular importance is the fact that the generalized impulse response function is a random variable on the same probability space as the time series. Thus, in order to measure the size of a response at a particular horizon one needs to measure the size of a random variable. In the cases where the response averages to zero (the standard one for the forecast revision function) one can use the concept of second order stochastic dominance. Some other experiments lead to responses with non-zero means where size can be measured by the mean. Perhaps the most interesting nonlinear feature found from impulse response functions has been a lower level of persistence of negative shocks in recessions than expansions (see Beaudry and Koop 1993).

In the linear time series literature there is a considerable literature on inference for impulse response functions. As the previous discussion of forecasting under parameter uncertainty would indicate such inference is more difficult for nonlinear time series models. Koop (1996) develops a Bayesian approach to the analysis of generalized impulse response functions that allows directly for parameter uncertainty. Koop and Potter (1999b) combine this analysis of impulse response functions under parameter uncertainty with Bayesian measures of model uncertainty (see the discussion at the end of Section 3) to present impulse response functions that are less reliant on particular model specifications.

5. Concluding remarks

Three basic nonlinear time series models have been reviewed. Both Classical and Bayesian approaches to estimation and inference have been described. The focus has been on univariate time series models. The three basic models do generalize to the multiple time series case but some of the difficulties concerning inference highlighted in this chapter are compounded in higher dimensions. Given the difficulties of interpreting test statistics for linearity vs. nonlinearity discussed, it seems important to shift the focus to differences in forecasting and dynamics that allow for both parameter and model uncertainty.

Acknowledgements

I would like to thank Gary Koop for numerous helpful discussions. The views expressed in this chapter are those of the author and do not necessarily reflect the views of the Federal Reserve Bank of New York or the Federal Reserve System.

Notes

1. There is also a vast literature in finance. While many of the developments and problems are similar, the higher frequency of observation of financial time series has allowed a much greater emphasis on flexible non-parametric methods. An excellent example of such methods is in Gallant, Rossi and Tauchen (1993).
2. The classic example is Brock and Chamberlain's 1984 working paper which like Granger's paper has a title that gives the result. In the late 1980s nonlinear modeling was strongly associated with the study of chaotic systems. Such systems are less amenable to statistical techniques than the nonlinear time series models considered here.
3. Links to software for all three types of estimation can be found at *http://weber.ucsd.edu/~jhamilto/sofware.htm#Markov*
4. Software for classical estimation and inference of threshold autoregressions can be obtained from *www.ssc.wisc.edu/~bhansen*. Software for Bayesian estimation and inference can be obtained from *http://emlab.Berkeley.EDU/Software/abstracts/potter0898.html*.
   These latter algorithms make heavy use of recursive least algorithms that can produce big speed ups in estimation time.
5. Smooth transition autoregressions can be estimated using standard econometric packages with nonlinear estimation options. In addition there will be a website available soon with Gauss software available implementating the full approach taken by Teräsvirta.
6. For a review of earlier testing approaches see Brock and Potter (1993).

References

Albert, J. and Chib, S. (1993) Bayesian inference via Gibbs sampling of autoregressive time series subject to Markov mean and variance shifts. *Journal of Business and Economic Statistics*, 11, 1–15.

Andrews, D. and Ploberger, W. (1994) Optimal tests when a nuisance parameter is present only under the alternative. *Econometrica*, 62, 1383–1414.

Beaudry, P. and Koop, G. (1993) Do recessions permanently change output. *Journal of Monetary Economics*, 31, 149–163.

Brock, W. and Chamberlain G. (1984) Spectral Analysis cannot tell a macroeconometrician whether his time series came from a stochastic economy or a deterministic economy. *SSRI WP* 8419, University of Wisconsin Madison.

Brock, W. and Potter, S. (1993) Nonlinear time series and macroeconometrics. In G. S. Maddala *et al.* (eds), *Handbook of Statistics*, Amsterdam: North Holland.

Chan, K.S. (1993) Consistency and limiting distribution of the least squares estimator of a threshold autoregression. *Annals of Statistics*, 21, 520–5.

Chan, K. S. and Tong, H. (1986) On estimating thresholds in autoregressive models. *Journal of Time Series Analysis*, 7, 178–190.

Chib, S. (1995) Marginal likelihood from the Gibbs output. *Journal of the American Statistical Association*, 90, 1313–1321.

Dacco R. and Satchell, S. (1999) Why do regime-switching models forecast so badly, *Journal of Forecasting*, 18, 1–16.

Filardo, A. (1994) Business cycle phases and their transitional dynamics. *Journal of Business and Economic Statistics*, 12, 299–308.

Gallant, A. R., Rossi, P. E. and Tauchen, G. (1993) Nonlinear Dynamic Structures. *Econometrica*, 61, 871–908.

Garcia, R. (1998) Asymptotic null distribution of the likelihood ratio test in Markov switching models. *International Economic Review*, 39, 763–788.

Granger, C. W. J. (1983) Forecasting white noise. In *Applied Time Series Analysis of Economic Data*, Proceedings of the Conference on Applied Time Series Analysis of Economic Data, edited by A. Zellner, U.S. Government Printing Office.

Granger, C. W. J. and Teräsvirta, T., *Modelling Nonlinear Economic Relationships*. Oxford: Oxford University Press.

Hamilton, J. (1989) A new approach to the economic analysis of nonstationary time series and the business cycle. *Econometrica*, 57, 357–384.

Hamilton, J. (1990) Analysis of time series subject to changes in regime. *Journal of Econometrics*, 45, 39–70.

Hansen, B. (1992) The likelihood ratio test under non-standard conditions: testing the Markov switching model. *Journal of Applied Econometrics*, 7, S61–S82.

Hansen, B. (1996a) Inference when a nuisance parameter is not identified under the null hypothesis. *Econometrica*, 64, 413–430.

Hansen, B. (1996b) Erratum. *Journal of Applied Econometrics*, 11, 195–198.

Hansen B. (1999) Sample splitting and threshold estimation. *Econometrica*, forthcoming.

Judge, G., Griffiths, W., Hill, R. C. and Lee, T.-C. (1985) *The Theory and Practice of Econometrics, second edition*. New York: John Wiley and Sons.

Kim, C.-J. and Nelson, C. (1999) *State-Space Models with Regime Switching: Classical and Gibbs-Sampling Approaches with Applications*, Cambridge: MIT Press.

Koop, G. (1996) Parameter uncertainty and impulse response analysis. *Journal of Econometrics*, 72, 135–149.

Koop, G., Pesaran, M. H. and Potter, S. M. (1996) Impulse response analysis in nonlinear multivariate models. *Journal of Econometrics*, 74, 119–148.

Koop, G. and Potter, S. M. (1999a) Bayes factors and nonlinearity: evidence from economic time series. *Journal of Econometrics*, forthcoming.

Koop, G. and Potter, S. M. (1999b) Asymmetries in US Unemployment. *Journal of Business and Economic Statistics*, forthcoming.

Lubrano, M. (1999) Bayesian analysis of nonlinear time series models with a threshold to appear in *Nonlinear Econometric Modelling*, William Barnett *et al.* (ed.), Cambridge: Cambridge University Press.

Pesaran, M. H. and Potter, S. (1997) A floor and ceiling model of US output. *Journal of Economic Dynamics and Control*, 21, 661–695.

Poirier, D. (1995). *Intermediate Statistics and Econometrics*, Cambridge: The MIT Press.

Potter, S. (1995) A nonlinear approach to US GNP. *Journal of Applied Econometrics*, 10, 109–125.

Potter, S. (1999) Nonlinear impulse response functions. *Journal of Economic Dynamics and Control*, forthcoming.

Priestley, M. B. (1988) *Non-Linear and Non-Stationary Time Series*, New York: Academic Press.

Teräsvirta, T. and Anderson, H. (1992) Characterising nonlinearities in business cycles using smooth transition autoregressive models. *Journal of Applied Econometrics*, S119–S136.

Teräsvirta, T. (1994) Specification, estimation and evaluation of smooth transition autoregressive models. *Journal of the American Statistical Association*, 89, 208–218.

Tong, H. (1983) Threshold models in non-linear time series analysis. Lecture Notes in Statistics, No. 21, Heidelberg: Springer.

Tong, H. (1990), *Non-linear Time Series: A Dynamical System Approach*. Oxford: Clarendon Press.

2

ROBUSTNESS AND LOCAL LINEARISATION IN ECONOMIC MODELS

Donald A. R. George

and

Les Oxley

1. Introduction

Economics, like the mediaeval Church, is riddled with schisms. Most concern such pressing issues as how many equilibria can dance on a manifold which is compact in the Slobolev 3 topology. But, by contrast, there is at least one important and interesting distinction, namely that between the equilibrium and the dynamic outlooks. The two approaches are apparently bridged by appeal to disequilibrium and stability analysis, the best-known example of which is undoubtedly the Samuelsonian adjustment process of orthodox general equilibrium theory. Walras' famous (but entirely fictional) auctioneer adjusts prices according to the dynamic relationship:

$$\dot{\mathbf{p}} = aZ(\mathbf{p}) \tag{1}$$

where $\mathbf{p}$ is the price vector, Z the excess demand function and a is a constant. (The 'dot' notation will denote time derivatives throughout.) If all goods in the economy are weak gross substitutes, the process of equation (1) demonstrates global stability. That is the economy will converge to an equilibrium from any initial conditions. Without the (highly implausible) assumption of weak gross substitutes even the seemingly innocuous equation (1) can generate extremely weird behaviour. In fact Sonnenschein (1972) and others have shown that **any** (reasonable) excess demand function Z can be thought of as arising from the maximisation of standard utility and profit functions. There arises the possibility, elaborated below, that the hitherto peaceful Samuelsonian/Walrasian economy might easily be overwhelmed by chaos.

So awkward has the disequilibrium approach become that orthodox game theorists have dumped it altogether. This point is easily illustrated by appeal to the standard textbook Cournot duopoly model. It is depicted in Figure 1 which shows two 'reaction curves', intersecting in a single (Nash) equilibrium, and a step-like path to equilibrium. Is this a picture of 'disequilibrium game theory'? Not if we take the Nash equilibrium concept seriously. In that case the duopoly model would have to be re-written to include a new Nash equilibrium concept covering the firms' decisions in every period. No 'stability analysis' is required because everything is an (Nash) equilibrium.

Econometricians evidently share the theorists' enthusiasm for equilibrium, as can be seen in the current emphasis on cointegration (see, for example, *Journal of Economic Surveys* vol. 12 no. 5). Given time series data, the objective is to locate a long-run equilibrium relationship in those data. The possibility that there may be no such relationship, or that it may be too complicated for easy mathematical representation, is usually taken as a counsel of despair. An alternative approach would be to look for evidence of chaos in time series data, and to try to fit a simple, fully deterministic, model to those data. The first aspect of this project is illustrated in Section 5 below, in which we report the outcome of a research project using high-frequency data from financial markets.

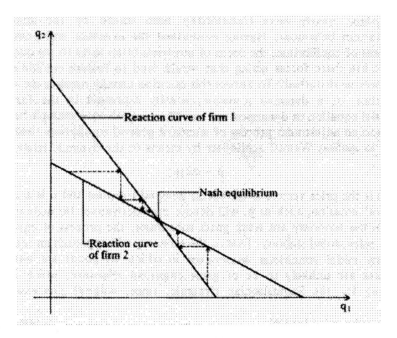

Figure 1. The textbook Cournot model.

The interesting dynamics which are the focus of this chapter (and most of this issue of the *Journal*) cannot arise in a linear dynamical system. Let the vector $\mathbf{x}$ represent the deviations (possibly in logs) of economic variable from their equilibrium values and A an $n \times n$ matrix. Then the equation:

$$\dot{\mathbf{x}} = A\mathbf{x} \tag{2}$$

represents a linear dynamical system. Any solution path of (2) either:

- converges to the origin (corresponding to equilibrium of the underlying model) or
- diverges to infinity or
- is a cyclical path surrounding the origin (the phase portrait is a centre).

This last possibility is structurally unstable in the sense that arbitrarily small perturbations of the matrix A will cause the solution paths to transmute into either divergent or convergent paths. Thus regular and persistent cycles cannot occur in a linear model in a structurally stable way. We return to structural instability below.

When nonlinear models are admitted the dynamic possibilities become much more interesting. Suppose (2) is replaced by:

$$\dot{\mathbf{x}} = F(\mathbf{x}) \tag{3}$$

where F is any (reasonable but possibly nonlinear) function. The dynamic behaviour of (3) includes the following possibilities:

- convergence to points
- divergence to infinity
- convergence to limit cycles
- convergence to strange (fractal) attractors.

The last of these occurs in chaotic systems, and plays an important role in Section 5 below, which is concerned with empirical chaos.

At this stage it is worthwhile drawing the important distinction between *structural stability* and *robustness*. The former is a property of *whole phase portraits*: a structurally stable system is one whose phase portrait transmutes into a qualitatively equivalent (homeomorphic) phase portrait in response to arbitrarily small parameter perturbations. The latter is a property of *individual solution paths*: a robust path is one which transmutes into another path with the same limiting behaviour (as $t \to \infty$) in response to arbitrarily small parameter perturbations (where parameters now include boundary conditions). The closed orbit (centre) phase portrait of a linear model is structurally unstable. Saddlepoint models of the type discussed in Sections 2 and 3 below are structurally stable, and in such a model divergent paths are robust, while convergent paths are not. It will be argued in Section 3 that non-robust paths are unobservable and thus, for scientific purposes, can be ignored.

Clearly the economic world is nonlinear, so it would appear that focusing on linear dynamics is of limited interest. However economists have found nonlinear models to be so tiresome and intractable that they have adopted the technique of linearisation to deal with them. Thus linear dynamics have retained a role in economic analysis. Section 2 below deals with the technique of linearisation and examines its shortcomings. Section 3 develops the notion of robustness and uses it to show that many conventional macroeconomic models can be rejected on methodological grounds alone. Both sections use a simple 'money and growth' model to illustrate the argument. This model has certain implications for hyperinflation which are examined empirically in Section 4. Section 5 turns to the question of chaos and reports the results of research on the detection of chaos in financial data. Section 6 concludes.

2. Local v. global analysis

Most economic models are inherently nonlinear but, as mentioned in the Introduction, economists have typically found nonlinear dynamics to be intractable and have, accordingly, resorted to the method of local linearisation. This approach relies on a theorem due to Hartman which provides a local linear approximation to a dynamical system such as equation 3 above. The theorem tells us that, provided the phase portrait of equation 3 is not a centre, it will be *locally* homeomorphic to the phase portrait of its linearisation (which can be located by evaluating the matrix of first partial derivatives of $F(\mathbf{x})$). The two vital aspects of this result are:

- The equivalence of phase portraits is *topological* (homeomorphic) only. This equivalence preserves only topological properties, not, for example, distances, angles, curvature or rates of change.
- The equivalence is *local*. It holds only in an arbitrarily small neighbourhood of the point at which the linearisation is calculated. (This could be any point, but in economic models is usually taken to be an equilibrium, i.e. a point $\mathbf{x}^*$ such that $F(\mathbf{x}^*) = 0$.) Outside such an arbitrarily small neighbourhood the equivalence might easily break down.

Both these features of the linearisation process can be misleading when it is applied to economic models, which in many cases, require global rather than local analysis. In this section we develop a simple perfect foresight, market clearing 'money and growth' model due originally to Burmeister and Dobell (1971). We compare the local and global dynamics of this model. Local linearisation generates the standard saddlepoint dynamics with a unique long run equilibrium possessing familiar macroeconomic properties. Global analysis reveals that the model has two long run equilibria, a saddlepoint and a stable equilibrium. Convergence to the latter is robust, while convergence to the former is non robust.

Assume a constant returns to scale production function:

$$Y = F(K, L) \tag{4}$$

where $Y=$ output, $K=$ capital stock, $L=$ labour. This may be written in intensive form:

$$y = f(k) \tag{5}$$

where $y = Y/L$ and $k = K/L$. A simple proportionate consumption function is assumed:

$$C = cY \quad (0 < c < 1) \tag{6}$$

giving a goods market equilibrium condition:

$$Y = cY + \dot{K} + \delta K \quad (0 < \delta < 1) \tag{7}$$

where $\delta =$ depreciation rate. The goods market is assumed to clear continually and thus equation (7) is permanently satisfied. From equations (4) to (7) it is easy to derive the following differential equation:

$$\dot{k} = sf(k) - (\delta + n)k \equiv B(k) \tag{8}$$

where $s = 1 - c$ and $n =$ (exponential) growth of labour force.

Turning now to the money market, a constant exogenous growth rate (θ) is assumed for the nominal money supply (M):

$$\dot{M} = \theta M \tag{9}$$

A standard demand for money function is assumed:

$$m \equiv M/L = P.G(y,r) \tag{10}$$

where $P =$ price level, $r =$ nominal interest rate and we assume:

$$G_y > 0 \quad \text{and} \quad G_r < 0 \tag{11}$$

Equation (10) can be rewritten as:

$$x \equiv m/p = G(y,r) \tag{12}$$

where $x =$ per capita real money balances. The money market is assumed to clear continually and the conditions of the implicit function theorem are assumed to hold for equation (12). We may then write:

$$r = H(y, x) \tag{13}$$

for some function H. There are in effect only two assets in the model, money and physical capital. The nominal interest rate may therefore be identified with the expected money yield on physical capital. Assuming the rate of inflation is perfectly foreseen, we may write:

$$r = f'(k) - \delta + \dot{P}/P \tag{14}$$

Equation (14) effectively identifies the real rate of interest with the marginal product of capital, net of depreciation.

From equations (9) to (14) it is easy to derive the following differential equation in x:

$$\dot{x} = x(f'(k) + \theta - \delta - n - H(f(k), x)) \equiv D(k, x) \tag{15}$$

Equations (8) and (15) together constitute a dynamical system in k and x, though note that (8) can be solved independently of (12) since the former equation does not involve x. Local linearisation of this model reveals the existence of an equilibrium (k^*, x^*) such that $k^*, x^* > 0$ and:

$$B(k^*) = 0, \qquad D(k^*, x^*) = 0 \tag{16}$$

In the neighbourhood of this equilibrium dynamics take the saddlepoint form, as illustrated in Figure 2. Paths starting on the stable branch converge to equilibrium. All other paths are divergent and thus treated as economically

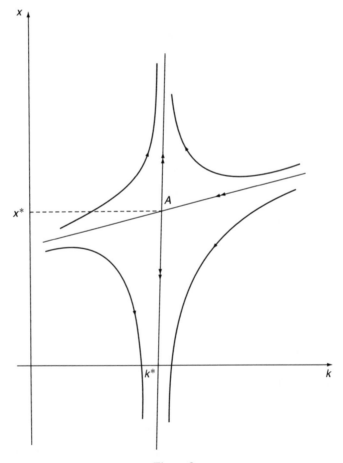

Figure 2.

meaningless (we return to this point in Section 3 below, where the 'transversality condition' is discussed). Note, however, that *all* solution paths satisfy the perfect foresight and market clearing conditions. In long run equilibrium the level of per capita real money balances is constant and hence the steady state rate of inflation is equal to the (exogenous) rate of money growth minus the (exogenous) rate of population growth. Thus controlling money growth is necessary and sufficient for the (long run) control of inflation.

The global dynamics of this model are quite different from the local dynamics (see Figure 3). In addition to the saddlepoint discussed above (point A in Figure 3), there is a globally stable equilibrium, $(k^*, 0)$ (point B in Figure 3). Note that Hartman's Theorem does indeed hold in the neighbourhood of point A. Paths with initial conditions lying above the stable branch entail real per capita money diverging to infinity and might therefore be rejected. However, paths with initial conditions lying below the stable branch entail real per capita money tending to zero. There is no reason to reject these paths: they all satisfy the market

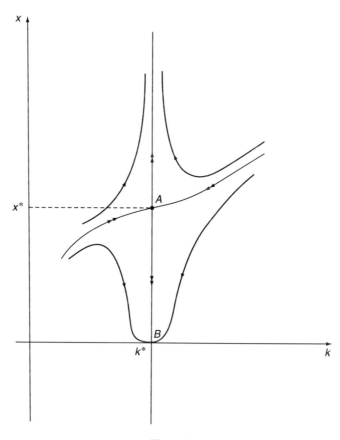

Figure 3.

clearing and perfect foresight conditions and (as will be discussed below) most transversality conditions. Since real per capita money tends to zero along such a path, the price level must eventually grow faster than the rate of growth of nominal money minus the population growth rate. Using standard functional forms for the production function and demand for money function, it is easy to show that the inflation rate diverges to infinity along such a path, and hence the control of the nominal money supply is *not* sufficient for the control of inflation. These paths represent hyperinflationary bubbles, but they are wholly rational, equilibrium bubbles, with no inbuilt tendency to burst. In Section 3 below we argue that they represent the major scientifically valid implication of the model.

The model developed above illustrates clearly the dangers of local linearisation. Hartman's theorem only holds locally, so that treating the linearisation as globally valid can lead to to the neglect of dynamics which may have important economic implications. Thus a global approach to dynamics is essential in most economic applications.

3. Robustness

It is widely accepted that the demarcation between scientific and non-scientific assertions should be based on the requirement that a scientific assertion be susceptible, at least in principle, to refutation by empirical data. An observation which refutes an implication of a theory also refutes at least one of that theory's underlying assumptions. It follows that the underlying assumptions of a scientific theory need not be open to empirical test, provided that testable implications can be drawn from them. In practice it is generally the case that the assumptions underlying a theory cannot be *exactly* true, but rather, it is to be hoped, are close approximations to reality. Under these circumstances it is essential that the implications of a theory are robust to small variations in its underlying assumptions. Without this property, empirical testing of a theory is impossible.

Consider, for example, a chemical theory which predicts the outcome of a particular chemical reaction under conditions of constant ambient temperature. Whatever care the experimental chemist takes, he will not be able to hold the ambient temperature *exactly* constant: it is bound to fluctuate slightly during the course of the experiment. Suppose now that the outcome of the experiment is substantially different from what the theory predicted. Is the theory refuted? The theoretical chemist can always reply that the ambient temperature was not *exactly* constant as her theory required, and that the experiment does not, therefore, constitute a refutation of her theory. This defence would not be possible if the robustness property were required *ab initio*.

Referring to linear difference equation models of the trade cycle, Baumol (1958) remarks that:

> 'But our statistics are never fine enough to distinguish between a unit root and one which takes values so close to it ... it is usually possible to show that a slight amendment in one of the simplifying assumptions will eliminate the unit

roots and so have profound qualitative effects on the system. As Solow has pointed out, since our premises are necessarily false, good theorising consists to a large extent in avoiding assumptions ... (with the property that) ... a small change in what is posited will seriously affect the conclusions'.

We go further than this, and claim that non-robust implications of a theory are scientifically meaningless and should be ignored. It is a necessary (though possibly not sufficient) condition for scientific validity that a theory make robust predictions.
    We may define robustness more precisely as follows:

DEFINITION. *Any property of a model will be called robust if the set of parameter values for which it occurs is of strictly positive Lebesgue measure.*

A non-robust property is one which occurs for a parameter set of zero Lebesgue measure and can thus be thought of as having a zero probability of occurring. Of course it is a well-known conundrum of probability theory that although a non-occurring event has probability zero, the converse does not hold. An event with zero probability could occur, but we consider it appropriate to label such events as 'unobservable'. Note that it is not enough for robustness that the relevant paramater set is dense, because dense sets can easily have zero measure. For example, the set of rational numbers is dense in the set of real numbers, but it is countable, and therefore certainly of measure zero.
    For the case of dynamic models, the definition of robustness given in the Introduction is a special case of the definition above, where the property at issue is the limiting behaviour of a solution path as $t \to \infty$. In a saddlepoint model, such as the linearised model of Section 2, convergence is non-robust while divergence is robust. Since the 'monetary control of inflation' result depends upon convergence, it too is non-robust, and must therefore be considered an unobservable event. In the global version of the model convergence to the saddlepoint equilibrium (point A) is non-robust, while convergence to the stable equilibrium (point B) is robust and hence so are the hyperinflationary bubbles that this latter convergence entails, According to the global dynamics of the model then, the 'monetary control of inflation' property is unobservable, while hyperinflationary bubbles are obser-vable. In general we conclude that *any* assertion which depends upon convergence in a saddlepoint model can be safely dismissed as non-scientific. Thus a large part of macrodynamics can be dismissed on methodological grounds alone.
    A favourite technique for avoiding the non-robustness problem in saddlepoint models is to add auxiliary assumptions to the model in an attempt to rule out divergent paths. Suppose, for example, that the economy is controlled by an agent choosing per capita consumption (z) to maximise a utility function such as:

$$\int_0^\infty U(z, x)e^{(n - \rho)t}dt \tag{17}$$

subject to the constraints of equations (8) and (15). To ensure convergence of the integral, take $n < \rho$, and leave aside the question as to why money should appear in the utility function. Applying Pontryagin's Maximum Principle to this problem yields the transversality condition:

$$\lambda k + \mu x \to 0 \qquad \text{as} \qquad t \to \infty \qquad\qquad (18)$$

where λ and μ are the costate variables for equations (8) and (15) respectively. In the linearised saddlepoint model of Section 2, only convergent paths satisfy this transversality condition. Hence the addition of a utility maximising assumption shrinks the set of solution paths down to the set of convergent paths, thus avoiding the non-robustness problem.

There are a number of difficulties with this argument:

1. Short of a centrally planned economy it is hard to see exactly who the controlling agent is supposed to be. The utility maximising approach seems to involve teleology (i.e. attributing intention to the economy as a whole rather than to an individual agent).
2. The transversality condition is *not*, in general, a necessary condition for the solution of the Pontryagin problem. (e.g. see Halkin, 1974)
3. In the global version of the model in Section 2, the transversality condition (18) is satisfied on paths converging to the stable equilibrium (point B), for a wide class of utility functions U.
4. In the linearised version of the model, it is not clear how the economy is supposed to get on to the stable branch if it should become displaced from it (for example by a shift in policy parameters).

Problem no. 4 is 'solved' by appeal to the notion of a 'jump variable'. If the price level jumps by exactly the right amount, real per capita balances can jump by just the amount required to place the economy on the stable branch, and thus ensure convergence. Again, short of a centrally planned economy, it is hard to see what mechanism is supposed to bring this jump about.

In summary then, the non-robustness problem which necessarily arises with saddlepoint dynamics, can be avoided by (a) imposing a transversality condition and (b) appealing to the notion of a 'jump variable'. As discussed above both are unsatisfactory assumptions, and both take the model a long way from its (relatively) innocuous origins in perfect foresight and market clearing.

We propose that the robustness property be required of any model claiming scientific status, and that *ad hoc* auxilliary assumptions, designed to ensure robustness, be disallowed. On this basis, virtually all the macroeconomics based on saddlepoint dynamics can be rejected on methodological grounds alone.

In the next two sections we will pursue the issue of empirical observability and support for nonlinear models via two different examples. The first, in Section 4, will consider several modern hyperinflations and consider their dynamics in relation to the theoretical model developed in Section 2 above. In Section 5 we investigate the existence of chaos using 16 127 daily observations from the Standard & Poor's Composite Price Index. To anticipate, in both cases we find support for nonlinear explanations of economic events and data.

4. The empirics of hyperinflations

The global version of the model described in Section 2 suggests that an economy operating a fixed money growth rule is likely to experience inflationary bubbles. While the model is clearly too simple to provide an adequate explanation of inflationary or hyperinflationary experience, it might provide the basis for an explanatory model. It is therefore of interest to consider, albeit briefly, the empirical evidence for the existence of inflationary bubbles.

The seminal paper by Flood and Garber (1980) tests for the presence of bubbles in the general price level using German data, but fails to locate any. Subsequent work by Burmeister and Wall (1982) applies Kalman filtering techniques to the German hyperinflation and concludes that rational bubbles in the general price level do occur. This conclusion is confirmed by Flood, Garber and Scott (1984) who use multi-country tests. There are several studies which locate bubbles in particular markets such as the foreign exchange market (see e.g. Woo, 1987). An excellent survey of the literature is provided by Camerer (1989).

The global version of the model described in Section 2 above implies the existence of time periods when:

$$\dot{P}/P > \dot{M}/M$$

or alternatively, $M/P \to 0$ as $t \to \infty$. Further, the model predicts that high nominal interest rates will be associated with high inflation rates.

In this part of the chapter we will present data from a number of high/hyperinflation episodes. The particular events considered are the classic European hyperinflation episodes, which occurred in Germany, Greece and Hungary. The more recent Latin American and Israeli cases are also briefly investigated.

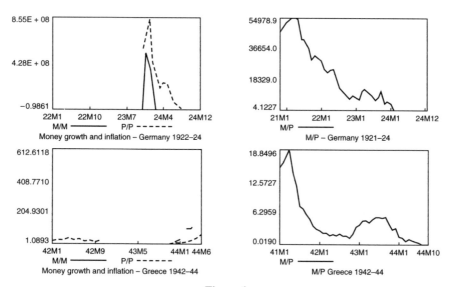

Figure 4.

4.1. *Germany, Greece and Hungary*

The data taken from Sargent (1986) for the German and Polish cases and Anderson
et al. (1988), for Hungary and Greece, are presented as Figures 4 and 5 below.
  Firstly, for all the countries considered periods where

$$\dot{P}/P > \dot{M}/M$$

clearly exist. That they tend to be short in the main is probably due to government
attempts to 'cure' the hyperinflation, i.e. change the initial conditions to shift the
economy to a different trajectory. The tendency for $M/P \rightarrow 0$ as $t \rightarrow \infty$ is
exhibited for all the countries and is illustrated as Figures 4 and 5.

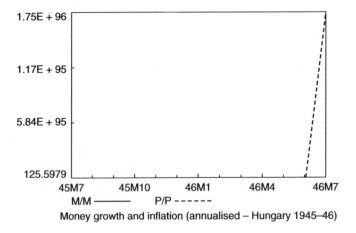

Money growth and inflation (annualised – Hungary 1945–46)

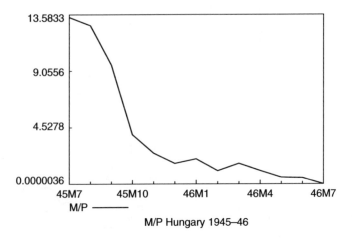

M/P Hungary 1945–46

Figure 5.

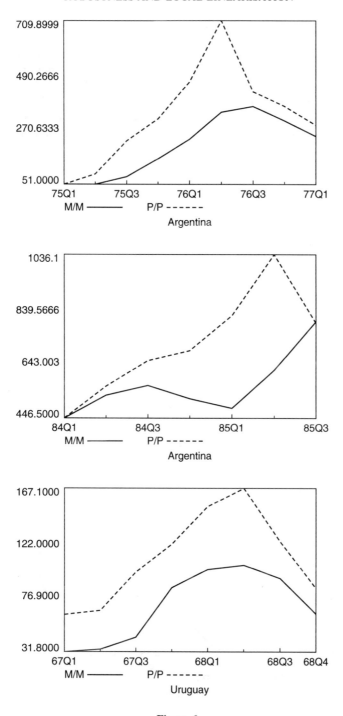

Figure 6.

4.2. *Argentina, Mexico and Uruguay*

The data used in these cases is drawn from the International Monetary Fund (IMF) International Financial statistics. All data relate to a common measure of 'money' and the units are annual rates of change of M and P, presented as quarterly observations. Such data is presented as Figures 6 and 7 below. The rates of change of M and P on most measures would not constitute periods of hyperinflation, except perhaps Argentina. However, the data does not refute the implication that periods when

$$\dot{P}/P > \dot{M}/M$$

exist, even for less extreme episodes of inflation.

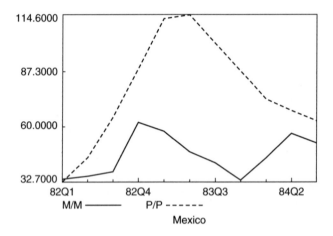

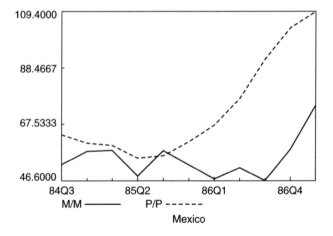

Figure 7.

4.3. *Nominal interest rate data*

A further implication of the model is the association of high nominal interest rates and high $\dot{P}/P$. Again utilising IMF data sources, some support for the implication is presented as Table 1 below. The data below does not refute this possibility for the recent cases of high inflation experienced in Argentina, Brazil, Mexico and Israel.

To summarise, a preliminary investigation of actual data lends support to the qualitative and quantitative predictions of the model. Clearly, this does not rule out observationally equivalent alternative traditional models which may well predict similar events. This was never the intention of either the modelling section nor the data conformability exercise. However, it does offer some support for a more extensive modelling and data evaluation study, including the simulation of $\dot{P}/P$ based upon actual money growth rates. Further, the implications of allowing $\dot{M}/M$ to be endogenously determined with a government budget constraint, needs to be investigated.

As the empirical data suggest, bubbles (i.e. $\dot{P}/P > \dot{M}/M$) do exist. They do not, however, seem to last longer than about two years. We suggest that this is probably due to successful efforts by governments to change initial conditions, P and/or M, in order to influence the actual trajectory followed. That this is an option open to governments should not be in doubt. Even 'hardline' RE theorists, for example, Patrick Minford, accept that governments may want to influence macro-dynamics. He chooses, however, to put the burden on to terminal conditions, (Minford, 1988), to quote:

> ... given a policy-maker's desperate problems with non-unique economies, they certainly have a strong incentive to give guarantees that underlie these *terminal* conditions. (Minford, 1988) (emphasis added).

Table 1. Nominal Interest rates (% per annum)

Year	Argentina	Brazil	Mexico	Israel
1977	142.1	—	—	—
1978	125.2	33	10.5	—
1979	99	35	15.02	—
1980	88	38	22.5	89
1981	122.7	49	30.8	177
1982	166.2	49	45.8	170
1983	407.8	156	59	140
1984	558	215	49	186
1985	520.3	219	63	823
1986	61.2	50	88	503
1987	—	391	103	60

Source: IMF International Financial Statistics, various issues.

5. Chaos in the S&P 500

Chaos is widely found in the fields of physics and other natural sciences, however, the existence of chaos in economic data is still an open question. Various contributions have been made to this economic literature, including Barnett *et al.* (1994), Barnett and Chen (1988), Chen (1996), Brock and Sayers (1989), and Ramsey, Sayers and Rothman (1990). In addition, a new international journal, which is exclusively devoted to, and entitled, *Studies in Non-linear Dynamics and Econometrics*, has recently been founded which is testimony to the interest in this area. The research reported in this section was carried out jointly with R.G. Harison, Dejuin Yu and Weiping Lu.

Some of the main problems, which pervade the area of economic time series evidence on chaos, are the effects of noise, trend, and more general structural change. Of these noise and time evolution appear to be the most problematic with the latter often modelled via ARCH/GARCH processes that allow changing means and variances. These problems are frequently compounded by the paucity of available data. In attempting to answer questions relating to the existence of nonlinearities and chaos in economic data, researchers have normally used either the Hinich bispectrum test, the BDS test of Brock, Dechert and Scheinkman (1996), White's (1989), test or more recently Kaplan's test, to identify nonlinearities and, when considering chaos, have used tools based on phase space reconstruction developed and used successfully in the physical sciences. The most commonly used of these chaos tests are the Lyapunov exponents test and the Grassberger-Procaccia (GP) correlation dimension test. While these tests have revealed an abundance of previously unexplained non-linear structure and yielded a deeper understanding of the dynamics of many different economic time series, the case of deterministic chaos in these types of series is yet to be clarified. The main problem we identify in this study is that of noise which degrades these measurement techniques. The use of conventional filtering methods such as low pass filtering using Fourier transforms, moving averages etc., and also singular spectrum analysis based on singular value decomposition commonly used in economics, can lead to distortion of the dynamics.

5.1. *The testing approach*

Before economic data can be analysed for the existence of deterministic chaos, the twin problems of growing time trends and noise require consideration. The main contribution of this chapter will be to the latter where new non-linear noise reduction (NNR), techniques will be applied to the data. However, the following general methodology will be followed. Firstly, the (log) data will be adjusted to remove systematic calendar effects and trend effects by differencing, following Nelson and Plosser (1982).

Secondly, in order to reconstruct a chaotic attractor in phase space, two basic parameters, the embedding dimension m, and delay time h, must be correctly determined. The embedding theorem ($m = 2d + 1$, where d is correlation dimension) provides a sufficient condition for reconstructing an attractor from a scalar time series. An efficient method to determine an acceptable minimum m, from experimental time series is the so-called *false nearest neighbour* (FNN), recently developed using a geometrical construction. It monitors the behaviour of near neighbours under changes in the embedding dimension from $m \to m+1$. When the number of the false nearest neighbours arising through projection is zero in dimension m, the attractor has unfolded in this embedding dimension m. This technique is robust to the noise and a correct region of the embedding dimension can be determined in the presence of noise, which is important for the type of data used here. An estimate of the value of the delay time h, is provided by the autocorrelation function (ACF).

The Lyapunov exponents test and the Grassberger-Procassia correlation dimension method are well-documented methods used in the quantitative analysis of time series data as tests for chaos; see for example, Abarbanel *et al.* (1993). Here we concentrate on the latter.

The geometrical features of an attractor can be specified using the Grassberger-Procaccia correlation *dimension*. Suppose we have a scalar time series x_i $(i = 1, 2, \dots N)$ of a dynamical variable sampled at an equal time interval Δt from which the K vectors $\mathbf{Y}_j$ $(j = 1, 2, \dots K)$ in the m-dimensional phase space can be reconstructed using the time delay technique. Then the *correlation dimension D_2* is defined and calculated as:

$$D_2 = \lim_{\varepsilon \to 0} \frac{\log_2 C_m(\varepsilon)}{\log_2 \varepsilon}, \tag{19}$$

where $C_m(\varepsilon)$ is known as the correlation integral and can be computed as

$$C_m(\varepsilon) = \lim_{K \to \infty} \frac{1}{K(K-1)} \sum_{ij}^{K} \theta(\varepsilon - \| \mathbf{Y}_i - \mathbf{Y}_j \|), \tag{20}$$

Where $\theta(x)$ is the Heaviside step function and $\| \mathbf{Y}_i - \mathbf{Y}_j \|$ is the distance between the vectors $\mathbf{Y}_i$ and $\mathbf{Y}_j$. Thus, the sum $\sum_{ij}^{K} \theta(\varepsilon - \| \mathbf{Y}_i - \mathbf{Y}_j \|)$ is equal to the number of pairs (i, j) whose distance $\| \mathbf{Y}_i - \mathbf{Y}_j \|$ in the reconstructed phase space is less than the distance ε. For a chaotic attractor, D_2 is a non-integer, the value of which determines whether the system is low- or high dimensional.

The use of this approach must, however, be applied with caution since it describes a kind of scaling of behaviour in the limit as the distance between points on the attractor approaches zero and therefore is sensitive to the presence of noise. Indeed our numerical experiments have shown that a noise level as small as $2 \sim 5\%$ of the time series content can make these measurements inaccurate and inconclusive. Moreover, noise can also prevent precise prediction. Here we use NNR algorithms based on finding and extracting the approximate trajectory, which is close to the original clean dynamics in reconstructed phase space from the observed time series. The implementation of the algorithms involves three basic steps: i) to reconstruct the underlying attractor from the observed series, ii) to estimate the local dynamical behaviour choosing a class of models and fitting the parameters statistically, and iii) to adjust the observations to make them consistent with the clean dynamics. The technique can reduce noise by about one order of magnitude. If some standard techniques are employed to pre-process the data, such as band-pass filtering, filtered embedding and singular value decomposition, significantly larger amounts of noise can be reduced since the local dynamics are enhanced.

These non-linear noise reduction algorithms have been developed under the assumption that the noise is additive rather than dynamic. In practice, the two may not be distinguishable, being based on data only and both of them can be reduced, as long as the exact dynamics can be reconstructed. However, in the following cases, the algorithms will fail: i) where the data are purely stochastic, ii) where the deterministic dynamics are so weak that the data are uncorrelated, and iii) where the dynamic noise has driven the trajectories far from the exact dynamics of the non-linear system, which becomes a shadowing problem. These methods are applied to the data prior to the application of the quantitative measurements for chaos.

While the correlation dimension measurement is often accepted as 'proof' of chaos, it is not a definitive test against time series data with certain types of coloured noise. This issue will be resolved using *surrogate* techniques. The correlation dimension method must be applied together with a surrogate technique to reliably discriminate between chaos and noise from a time series, so as to avoid claims of chaos when simpler explanations (such as linearly correlated noise) are adequate. The consideration of surrogate data is based on the following. 1) Statement of a null hypothesis that shall be tested for consistency with the recorded original data. 2) Generation of a number of *surrogate* data sets; an algorithm is to randomise the phase of the raw data so that the surrogated set has the same Fourier spectra as the original. 3) Calculation of the value of interest, e.g., correlation dimension, Lyapunov exponents etc., for the original and all the surrogates. 4) Calculate mean and spread of the results obtained from the surrogates to determine whether the difference to the original, if any, is statistically significant.

5.3 *Some results based upon the Standard and Poor's Composite Price Index*

Although several economic data sets have been considered, we will report only one based upon the Standard and Poor's Composite Price Index, which comprises 16 127 daily observations on the logarithmic price change $x_t = 100[log(p_t) - log(p_{t-1})]$. For details of the data set see Gallant *et al.* (1993). The time series x_t has been adjusted to remove systematic calendar and trend effects and is taken to be jointly stationary. A representative window of the raw series taken after 1947 is shown as Figure 8(a).

Our analysis, based upon the GP correlation dimension measurement, in conjunction with the non-linear noise reduction filtering and surrogate technique provides strong evidence in favour of chaos in this data. Some results are detailed

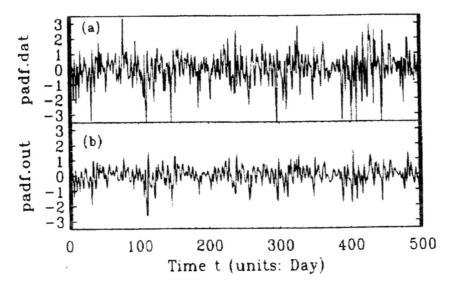

Figure 8. Two time series of $x(t)$ (a) raw data and (b) data after NNR.

below. As shown in Figure 8(c) (open squares), the raw data gave no saturated correlation dimension on increasing embedding dimension, suggesting that the data may be noise-dominated.

Figure 9(b) presents the data after NNR of the raw data. Comparison of this with the raw data shows that the effect of noise is manifested as relatively large amplitude random fluctuations, masking the overall deterministic patterns in which the noise level is estimated to be $\sim 90\%$ of the clean signal. Correlation dimension analysis of this noise-filtered data revealed a clear (scaling) saturation

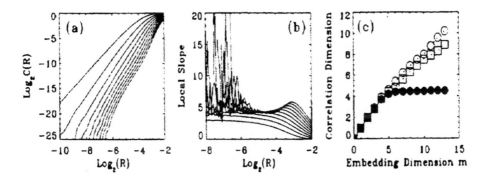

Figure 9. (a) Logarithmic plot of correlation function $C_m(R)$ versus correlation distance R for embedding dimension $m = 3, 4, ..., 13$, (b) Local slope as a function of $\mathrm{Log}_2(R)$ derived from (a), and (c) Correlation dimension D_2 versus embedding dimension m: $\square$ — data before NNR, $\bullet$ — data after NNR, and $\bigcirc$ — surrogate set from the data after NNR.

region on increasing the embedding dimension as shown in Figure 9 (solid circles in (c)), indicative of deterministic chaos.

In confirming that the convergent correlation dimension is a result of chaotic dynamics, both the raw and noise-filtered series were surrogated to randomise the phase and so destroy the deterministic structure. The results show the dimension to diverge as shown in Figure 9(c) (open circles), consistent with stochastic behaviour, from which we confirm that the saturated correlation dimension of the noise-filtered data in Figure 9(c) arises from an endogenous deterministic mechanism. The accuracy of these results improves with the increase in the number of recording points and the length of the time series, 5000 data points being sufficient to identify deterministic dynamics. A particularly interesting finding is the overriding prevalence of stochastic behaviour in the first 5000 data points corresponding to the period 1928–1946, beyond which the data, analysed in either sets of 5000 data points or as a whole, displayed the deterministic chaotic dynamics with a correlation dimension $D_2 \sim 4.5$. These characterisations may be a consequence of the economic and social shocks caused by the Great Depression and subsequent Second World War.

Using the Standard and Poor's Composite Price Index comprising 16 127 daily observations from 1928–1987, we have identified the existence of deterministic chaos. Furthermore, the pre-WW2 period appears to be more volatile than the post-war period. Nonlinear noise reduction methods appear crucial in the removal of noise and this may transpire to be a general issue in the identification of chaotic dynamics in economic data.

6. Conclusions

This chapter had several aims. Firstly, we wish to emphasise the need to consider nonlinearities in economic models and to this end highlight some of the dangers of linearisation and using 'tricks' to force behaviours on models which, in general cases, do not arise. Via a standard money and growth model we highlight the important differences between local and global solutions which arise in many macroeconomic models — differences which unfortunately are typically ignored by many authors. Nonlinear models typically produce a much richer palette of dynamical behaviours, but sometimes at the cost of technical simplicity and simple analytical solutions.

Secondly, we argue in favour of 'robustness' being considered a necessary property of economic models and make the important distinction between structural stability and robustness. On another level, models which do not possess the robustness property might simply be regarded as 'unscientific' as they propose outcomes which have measure zero in terms of likelihood of observability.

Finally, we consider two examples which consider the role of nonlinearities in economic behaviour. In the first, which considers several recent hyperinflations, the theoretical distinctions between local and global analysis discussed in Section 2, is illustrated with data for Germany, Greece, Hungary, Argentina,

Mexico, Uruguay and Israel. The second example considers whether evidence of deterministic chaos exists in the Standard and Poor's Composite Price Index. When the noise is removed via nonlinear noise reduction techniques, evidence of deterministic chaos is, in fact, found.

Nonlinear models and nonlinear methods have a major role to play in economics and econometrics and although they may involve more sophisticated modelling and estimation techniques, the rewards are enormous.

References

Abarbanel, H., Brown, R., Sidorowich, J. and Tsimring, L. (1993) The analysis of observed chaotic dynamics in physical systems. *Review of Modern Physics*, 65, 1331–92.

Barnett, W. and Chen, P. (1988) The aggregation-theoretic monetary aggregates are chaotic and have strange attractors: An econometric application to mathematical chaos. In W. Barnett, E. Berndt and H. White, (eds), *Dynamic Econometric Modelling*. Cambridge: Cambridge University Press.

Barnett, W., Gallant, R., Hinich, M., Jungeilges, J., Kaplan, D. and Jensen, M. (1994) A single-blind controlled competition among tests for nonlinearity and chaos, *Working Paper 190*, Washington University, St. Louis, Missouri.

Baumol, W. J. (1958) Topology of second-order linear difference equations with constant coefficients. *Econometrica*, 26, 258–287.

Brock, W., Dechert, W. and Scheinkman, J. (1996) A test for independence based on the correlation dimension. *Econometric Reviews*, 15, 197–235.

Brock, W. and Sayers, C. Is the business cycle characterised by deterministic chaos? *Journal of Monetary Economics*, 22, 71–80.

Burmeister, E. and Dobell, R. (1971) *Mathematical Theories of Economic Growth*. London: Macmillan.

Burmister, E. and Wall, K. D. (1982) Kalman filtering estimation of unobserved rational expectations with an application to the German hyperinflation. *Journal of Econometrics*, 20, 255–84.

Camerer, C. (1989) Bubbles and fads in asset prices. *Journal of Economic Surveys*, 3, 3–42.

Chen, P. (1993) Study of chaotic dynamical systems via time-frequency analysis. *Proceedings of IEEE-SP International Symposium on Time-Frequency and Time-Scale Analysis* (IEEE, pp. 357–60). New Jersey: Piscataway.

Chen, P. (1996) A random walk or color chaos on the stock market? Time frequency analysis of S&P index. *Studies in Nonlinear Dynamics and Econometrics*, 1, 87–123.

Flood, R. P. and Garber, P. M. (1980) Market fundamentals versus price-level bubbles: the first tests. *Journal of Political Economy*, 88, 745–70.

Flood, R. P., Garber, P. M. and Scott, L. O. (1984) Multi-country tests for price level bubbles. *Journal of Economic Dynamic & Control*, 8, 329–40.

Halkin (1971) Necessary conditions for optimal control problems with infinite horizons. *Econometrica*, 42, 267–272.

Minford, P. (1988) Review of: Pesaran, M. H. (1987). *The Limits of Rational Expectations*. Blackwell. *Economic Journal*, 98, 1204–06.

Nelson, C. and Plosser, C. (1982) Trends and random walks in macroeconomic time series, some evidence and implications. *Journal of Monetary Economics*, 10, 139–62.

Ramsey, J., Sayers, C. and Rothman, P. (1990) The statistical properties of dimension calculations using small data sets: Some economic applications. *International Economic Review*, 31, 991–1020.

Sargent, T. J. (1986) *Rational Expectations and Inflation*. New York: Harper & Row.

Sonnenschein (1972) Market excess demand functions. *Econometrica*, 40.

White, H. (1989) An additional hidden unit test for neglected nonlinearity in multilayer feed forward networks. *Proceedings of the International Joint Conference on Neural Networks*, Washington DC, vol. 2, 451–5.

Woo, W. T. (1987) Some evidence of speculative bubbles in the foreign exchange market. *Journal of Money, Credit & Baking*, 19, 499–514.

3

TESTING FOR LINEARITY

Bruce E. Hansen

1. Introduction

If a researcher proposes a non-linear time series model, the question will invariably arise: Is the non-linear specification superior to a linear model? The statistical analog is: Can you reject the hypothesis of linearity in favor of the non-linear model? This question is quite central to the analysis of self-exciting threshold autoregressive (SETAR) models. More generally, we are interested in determining the number of thresholds or regimes in a SETAR model, and hypothesis tests are useful tools in this determination.

In this chapter we describe the least-squares (LS) approach to estimation and inference in SETAR models. LS methods are conceptually and computationally straightforward. As the SETAR models are nested, testing is based on classic F statistics which are computationally straightforward to calculate. Inference is complicated, however, as the asymptotic distributions of the tests are non-standard due to the presence of nuisance parameters which are only identified under the alternative hypothesis. As a result, simulation-based methods are necessary for correct inference. Luckily, with the advancement in computing power, simulation-based inference is relatively easy to implement on modern personal computers.

The SETAR model, which is a particular class of piecewise linear autoregressions, is attributed to Tong (1978). For detailed reviews see Tong (1983, 1990). The subject of testing for non-linearity in the context of threshold models has been studied by Tsay (1989), Chan (1990, 1991), Chan and Tong (1990), Hansen (1996, 1997), and Caner and Hansen (1998). The testing problem is algebraically quite similar to the issue of testing for structural change of unknown timing, which dates back to Quandt (1960). Tests for single

The author's web page is: www.ssc.wisc.edu/~bhansen

47

structural change in stationary models has been studied by Andrews (1993) and
Andrews and Ploberger (1994), and in the context of non-stationary models by
Hansen (1992, 1999a), Seo (1998), and Kuo (1998). Tests for multiple
structural change have been studied by Bai (1997) and Bai and Perron
(1998), and similar techniques have been applied to threshold models by
Hansen (1999b). Both testing problems fall in the class of tests in the presence
of unidentified nuisance parameters, which have been studied by Davies (1977,
1987), Andrews and Ploberger (1994), Hansen (1996), and Stinchcomb and
White (1998).

The class of SETAR models is a restriction on the class of smooth transition
autoregression (STAR) models, considered by Chan and Tong (1986), Luukkonen, et al. (1988), and extensively reviewed in Granger and Terasvirta (1993) and
Terasvirta, et al. (1994). The testing issues which apply to SETAR models also
apply to STAR models, and the methods discussed in this chapter could easily be
extended to cover STAR models as well.

SETAR and STAR models may be viewed as parsimonious approximations to
general nonlinear autoregressions. While linear autoregressions dominate the
empirical modeling of time series, there is no compelling a priori reason to
presume that the true dynamic structure is linear. The primary argument for
linearity is simplicity (estimation, interpretation, forecasting), yet current research
is showing that the analysis of SETAR and STAR models is reasonably
straightforward. Furthermore, there is no compelling theoretical reason to focus
exclusively on linear models. Models derived from first-principles (utility and
production functions) will only have linear dynamics under narrow functional
form restrictions. Non-linearities becomes especially important in the presence of
asymmetric costs of adjustment, irreversibilities, transactions costs, liquidity
constraints, and other forms of rigidities.

Non-linear autoregressions been used in several economic applications,
including: Industrial production (Terasvirta and Anderson (1992), Granger and
Terasvirta (1993); GNP (Granger, Terasvirta, and Anderson (1993), Potter (1995),
Hansen (1996), Galbraith (1996), Koop and Potter (1999)): Unemployment
(Rothman (1991), Burgess (1992), Hansen (1997), Montgomery, et al. (1998),
Caner and Hansen (1998); Stock volatilities (Cao and Tsay (1992). See also Brock
and Potter (1993) for a review.

The organization of this chapter is as follows. In Section 2 we introduce the
SETAR model, and discuss the general principle of least-squares estimation and
testing within the class of SETAR models. In Section 3 we introduce two time-
series which will serve to illustrate the methods for the remainder of the chapter.
Section 4 discusses estimation methods. Explicit methods to estimate one-regime,
two-regime, and three-regime SETAR models are presented. Section 5 discusses
testing the SETAR(1) model against the SETAR(2) model. Asymptotic and
bootstrap approximations are described, allowing both for homoskedastic and for
heteroskedastic errors. Part of the purpose of this section is to show how inference
can be sensitive to the assumptions and methods employed. Section 6 discusses

testing SETAR(1) against SETAR(3), and Section 7 discusses testing SETAR(2) against SETAR(3). A conclusion follows.

GAUSS programs which replicate the empirical work can be downloaded from the author's webpage.

2. SETAR model classes

Let Y_t be a univariate time series and let $X_{t-1} = (1\ Y_{t-1} Y_{t-2} \ldots Y_{t-p})'$, a $k \times 1$ vector with $k = 1 + p$. A SETAR(m) model[1] takes the form

$$Y_t = \alpha_1' X_{t-1} I_{1t}(\gamma, d) + \cdots + \alpha_m' X_{t-1} I_{mt}(\gamma, d) + e_t, \tag{1}$$

where $\gamma = (\gamma_1, \ldots, \gamma_{m-1})$ with $\gamma_1 < \gamma_2 < \cdots < \gamma_{m-1}$, and $I_{jt}(\gamma, d) = I(\gamma_{j-1} < Y_{t-d} \leqslant \gamma_j)$, where $I(\cdot)$ is the indicator function[2] and we use the convention $\gamma_0 = -\infty$ and $\gamma_m = \infty$. The parameters γ_j are called the thresholds, and d is called the delay parameter. The latter may be any strictly positive integer less than some upper bound $\bar{d}$, where typically $\bar{d} = p$.

The error e_t in (1) is a uniformly square integrable martingale difference sequence, hence

$$E(e_t \mid \mathfrak{I}_{t-1}) = 0, \tag{2}$$

where $\mathfrak{I}_t$ denotes the natural filtration,[3] and $\sigma^2 = E e_t^2 < \infty$.

A SETAR(m) model has m 'regimes', where the jth regime occurs when $I_{jt}(\gamma, d) = 1$. Our interest in this chapter is the determination of the number of regimes m. The class of SETAR(m) models is strictly nested, with $m = 1$ being the most restrictive. Hence it is conceptually convenient to consider the sequence of SETAR(m) models as a sequence of nested hypotheses, which lends itself readily to hypothesis testing.

The class SETAR(1) is the class of (linear) autoregressions, which can be written as

$$Y_t = \alpha_1' X_{t-1} + e_t. \tag{3}$$

Thus testing for linearity (within the SETAR class of models) is a test of the null hypothesis of SETAR(1) against the alternative of SETAR(m) for some $m > 1$. Similarly, we can test the null hypothesis of the SETAR(2) model

$$Y_t = \alpha_1' X_{t-1} I_{1t}(\gamma, d) + \alpha_2' X_{t-1} I_{2t}(\gamma, d) + e_t, \tag{4}$$

against the alternative of a SETAR(m) for some $m > 2$.

Note that we are implicitly assuming that there are no additional constraints placed on the vectors α_j, while in some applications it may be desirable to impose constraints (such as exclusion restrictions). We will not consider such constraints in our analysis, but the following should be noted. If the same constraints are imposed on all vectors α_j, then there are no complications. If different constraints are imposed on the different vectors α_j, then the SETAR(m) classes are no longer strictly nested, so the testing problem concerns non-nested hypotheses which are more delicate to handle.

The parameters of (1) may be collected as $\theta = (\alpha_1, \alpha_2, ..., \alpha_m, \gamma, d)$. Under assumption (2) the appropriate estimation method is least-squares (LS). The LS estimator $\hat{\theta}$ solves the minimization problem

$$\hat{\theta} = \underset{\theta}{\text{argmin}} \sum_{t=1}^{n} (Y_t - \alpha_1' X_{t-1} I_{1t}(\gamma, d) - \cdots - \alpha_m' X_{t-1} I_{mt}(\gamma, d))^2. \qquad (5)$$

We discuss computational solutions to this problem in Section 4. Collect the LS residuals into the $n \times 1$ vector $\hat{e}_m$. Then the sum of squared residuals is $S_m = e_m' \hat{e}_m$, a natural by-product of LS estimation.

The natural LS test of the hypothesis of SETAR(j) against SETAR(k) $(k > j)$ is to reject for large values of

$$F_{jk} = n \left(\frac{S_j - S_k}{S_k} \right). \qquad (6)$$

This is the likelihood ratio test when the errors e_t are independent $N(0, \sigma^2)$. It is also the conventional F (or Wald) test, and is equivalent to the conventional Lagrange multiplier (or score) test. These observations suggest that this test is likely to have excellent power relative to alternative tests.

One important testing issue is that it is necessary to restrict the thresholds γ_j so that each regime contains a minimal number of observations. Let

$$n_j = \sum_{t=1}^{n} I_{jt}(\gamma, d),$$

be the number of sample observations in the jth regime. The asymptotic theory suggests that we should constrain the thresholds so that as $n \to \infty$, $n_j/n \geq \tau$ for some $\tau > 0$. While there is no clear choice for τ, a reasonable value (which we use in our applications) is $\tau = 0.1$.

3. Data

We illustrate our methods with applications to two univariate time series. The first is annual sunspot means for the time period 1700–1988. The numbers are well known, ours are taken from Appendix 3 of Tong (1990). We follow Ghaddar and Tong (1981) and make a square-root transformation $N_t = 2(\sqrt{1 + N_t^*} - 1)$, where N_t^* denotes the raw sunspot series. The series N_t is displayed in Figure 1.

Many authors have analyzed this series. In particular, Tong and Lim (1980) estimated a constrained SETAR(2) with $p = 11$ for the period 1700–1920, and Ghaddar and Tong (1981) fit a similar specification for the period 1700–1979. We follow their lead and set $p = 11$ for our applications.

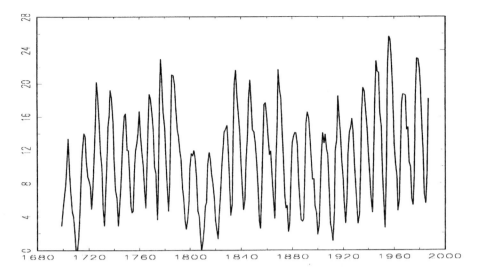

Figure 1. Annual sunspot means, 1700–1988.

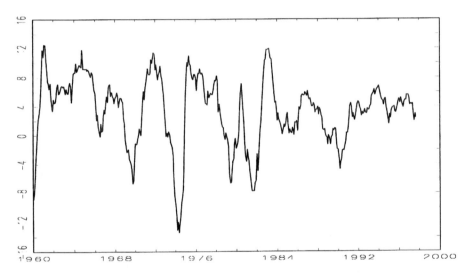

Figure 2. U.S. Monthly industrial production annual growth, 1960–1998.

The second application is to U.S. monthly industrial production for the period 1960.01 through 1998.09. Smooth SETAR models have been used to model quarterly industrial production by Terasvirta and Anderson (1992). See also Section 9.1 of Granger and Terasvirta (1993). SETAR models have been fit to a similar series (U.S. GNP) by Potter (1995) and Hansen (1996). We transform the series to approximate stationarity by taking annualized growth rates setting

$Q_t = 100 * (\ln(IP_t) - \ln(IP_{t-12}))$, where IP_t denotes the raw industrial production series. The series Q_t is displayed in Figure 2. Some experimentation with a baseline SETAR(1) model suggested that $p = 16$ is sufficient to reduce the errors to white noise.

4. Estimation

4.1. SETAR(1) model

The SETAR(1) is the linear autoregression (3). The solution to the LS problem (5) is ordinary least squares (OLS):

$$\hat{\alpha}_1 = (X'X)^{-1}(X'Y),$$

where X is the $n \times k$ matrix whose ith row is X'_{t-1} and Y is the $n \times 1$ vector whose ith element is y_t. The residual vector is $\hat{e}_1 = Y - X\hat{\alpha}_1$ and the sum of squared errors is $S_1 = \hat{e}'_1\hat{e}_1$. Table 1 reports the OLS estimates of SETAR(1) models fit to our two data series. The reported standard errors (here and throughout the chapter) are computed as in White (1980) to be robust to heteroskedasticity of unknown form.

As in many testing contexts, the sampling distribution of the test statistics F_{12} and F_{13} will depend upon the conditional variance properties of the error e_t. To

Table 1. Least squares estimates of SETAR(1) models.

	Annual sunspots		Industrial production	
	$\hat{\alpha}_1$	s.e.	$\hat{\alpha}_1$	s.e.
Const.	1.39	(0.45)	0.22	(0.07)
y_{t-1}	1.22	(0.07)	1.22	(0.06)
y_{t-2}	−0.48	(0.12)	−0.13	(0.08)
y_{t-3}	−0.15	(0.12)	0.01	(0.07)
y_{t-4}	0.27	(0.10)	−0.05	(0.06)
y_{t-5}	−0.24	(0.10)	−0.14	(0.06)
y_{t-6}	0.01	(0.09)	−0.04	(0.06)
y_{t-7}	0.16	(0.09)	0.13	(0.06)
y_{t-8}	−0.21	(0.10)	0.03	(0.07)
y_{t-9}	0.30	(0.10)	−0.02	(0.07)
y_{t-10}	0.02	(0.10)	0.03	(0.06)
y_{t-11}	−0.02	(0.06)	−0.04	(0.07)
y_{t-12}			−0.49	(0.08)
y_{t-13}			0.57	(0.09)
y_{t-14}			−0.13	(0.08)
y_{t-15}			0.15	(0.07)
y_{t-16}			−0.16	(0.05)
S_1	1135		362	
n	278		437	
$\hat{\sigma}_1^2$	4.08		0.817	

assess the presence of conditional heteroskedasticity, we regressed the squared residual on squares of the regressors, and tested the joint significance of the regressors using a Wald statistic. For the sunspot series N_t, the statistic was 58, which is highly significant with a p-value near zero (based on the $\chi^2(11)$ distribution). For the industrial production series Q_t, the statistic was 15, with an asymptotic p-value (based on the $\chi^2(16)$ distribution) of 0.52. This difference will turn out to be important in the inference procedures we discuss later.

4.2. SETAR(2) model

In the SETAR(2) model, $\gamma = \gamma_1$, so we let $I_{1t}(\gamma, d) = I(Y_{t-d} \leqslant \gamma)$ and $I_{2t}(\gamma, d) = I(\gamma < Y_{t-d})$. Let $\alpha = (\alpha_1' \alpha_2')'$ and

$$X_{t-1}(\gamma, d) = \begin{pmatrix} X_{t-1} I_{1t}(\gamma, d) \\ X_{t-1} I_{2t}(\gamma, d) \end{pmatrix}.$$

Let $X(\gamma, d)$ be the $n \times 2k$ matrix whose ith row is $X_{t-1}(\gamma, d)'$.
  Observe that the minimization problem (5)

$$S_2 = \min_{d, \gamma, \alpha} (Y - X(\gamma, d)\alpha)'(Y - X(\gamma, d)\alpha)$$

can be solved sequentially through concentration. That is, for given (d, γ), minimization over α is an OLS regression of Y on $X(\gamma, d)$. We can write the solution as

$$\hat{\alpha}(\gamma, d) = (X(\gamma, d)'X(\gamma, d))^{-1}(X(\gamma, d)'Y). \tag{7}$$

Let

$$S_2(\gamma, d) = (Y - X(\gamma, d)\hat{\alpha}(\gamma, d))'(Y - X(\gamma, d)\hat{\alpha}(\gamma, d))$$

be the residual sum of squared errors for given (d, γ). Then

$$(\hat{\gamma}_1, \hat{d}) = \operatorname*{argmin}_{\gamma, d} S_2(\gamma, d). \tag{8}$$

Once the solution to (8) is found, we find $\hat{\alpha}$ through (7), vis $\hat{\alpha} = \hat{\alpha}(\hat{\gamma}_1, \hat{d})$, and then obtain $S_2 = S_2(\hat{\gamma}_1, \hat{d})$ and $F_{12} = n((S_1 - S_2)/S_2)$ as natural by-products.
  Now observe that

$$S_2(\gamma, d) = Y'(I - X(\gamma, d)(X(\gamma, d)'X(\gamma, d))^{-1}X(\gamma, d)')Y \tag{9}$$

involves $X(\gamma, d)$ only through a projection, so the result is invariant to linear reparameterizations of $X(\gamma, d)$, and in particular, we can redefine $X(\gamma, d) = [X \ X(\gamma, d)]$, where $X(\gamma, d)$ is the matrix whose ith row is $X_{t-1} I_{1t}(\gamma, d)$. Noting the identity $Y = X\hat{\alpha}_1 + \hat{e}_1$, and since X lies in the space spanned by $X(\gamma, d)$, this means that we can replace Y in (9) by $\hat{e}_1$. Since $X'\hat{e}_1 = 0$, standard partitioned matrix inversion calculations and the fact that $X_1(\gamma, d)'X = X_1(\gamma, d)'X_1(\gamma, d)$ show that

$$S_2(\gamma, d) = \hat{e}_1'\hat{e}_1 - \hat{e}_1'X_1(\gamma, d)M_n^*(\gamma, d)^{-1}X_1(\gamma, d)'\hat{e}_1$$
$$= S_1 - f_2(\gamma, d)$$

where

$$M_n^*(\gamma, d) = X_1(\gamma, d)'X_1(\gamma, d) - (X_1(\gamma, d)'X_1(\gamma, d))(X'X)^{-1}(X_1(\gamma, d)'X_1(\gamma, d))$$
(10)

and

$$f_2(\gamma, d) = \hat{e}_1'X_1(\gamma, d)M_n^*(\gamma, d)^{-1}X_1(\gamma, d)'\hat{e}_1.$$ (11)

We thus see that the minimization (8) can be equivalently achieved through maximization of $f_2(\gamma, d)$. It is also interesting to observe that we can rewrite the linearity test statistic as

$$F_{12} = n\left(\frac{f_2(\hat{\gamma}_1, \hat{d})}{S_1 - f_2(\hat{\gamma}_1, \hat{d})}\right).$$ (12)

The maximization (11) is best solved through a grid search, noting that the argument d is discrete and that the function $f_2(\gamma, d)$ is typically a highly erratic function of γ. Since the parameter γ only arises through the indicator functions $I(Y_{t-d} \leqslant \gamma)$, there is no loss in restricting the search to the observed values of Y_{t-d}. The requirement that $n_1 \geqslant n\tau$ and $n_2 \geqslant n\tau$ further restricts the search to values of Y_{t-d} lying between the τth and $(1-\tau)$th quantiles. For the bootstrap methods we discuss latter, when n and p are large a full grid search can prove too costly for all but the most patient researchers. A close approximation can be achieved by restricting the search to N values of γ lying on a grid between the τth and $(1-\tau)$th quantiles of Y_{t-d}. If $\bar{d} = p$, then a joint search over (d, γ) will require pN function evaluations. For the empirical work we report here, we set $N = 100$. Since we set $p = 11$ in the sunspot application (and $p = 16$ in the industrial production application), this means that the maximization (11) requires a grid search over 1100 (respectively 1600) pairs of (γ, d). While this may seem like an intensive search, it only takes a few seconds on a personal computer. For example, a GAUSS program running on a 400 Mhz Pentium II computes the SETAR(2) model for the sunspot series in 2.5 seconds, and for the industrial production series in 7.6 seconds.

We report in Table 2 our estimates of the SETAR(2) models for our two data sets. For the sunspot series N_t, we find $\hat{d} = 2$ and $\hat{\gamma}_1 = 7.42$. For the industrial production series Q_t, we find $\hat{d} = 6$ and $\hat{\gamma}_1 = 0.226$. For both series, we find the F_{12} statistic for the test of SETAR(1) against SETAR(2) equals 70. The sampling distribution of F_{23}, the test for SETAR(2) versus SETAR(3), will depend on whether the SETAR(2) errors e_t are conditionally heteroskedastic. We assessed this through an OLS regression of the squared LS residual on the squares of the

Table 2. Least squares estimates of SETAR(2) models.

	Annual sunspots				Industrial production			
	$N_{t-2} \leqslant 7.4$		$N_{t-2} > 7.4$		$Q_{t-6} \leqslant 0.23$		$Q_{t-6} > 0.23$	
	$\hat{\alpha}_1$	s.e.	$\hat{\alpha}_2$	s.e.	$\hat{\alpha}_1$	s.e.	$\hat{\alpha}_2$	s.e.
Const.	−0.58	(0.90)	2.32	(0.55)	−0.07	(0.13)	0.10	(0.11)
Y_{t-1}	1.22	(0.10)	0.95	(0.08)	1.34	(0.11)	1.04	(0.06)
Y_{t-2}	−0.97	(0.26)	−0.03	(0.11)	−0.37	(0.18)	0.03	(0.08)
Y_{t-3}	0.49	(0.29)	−0.48	(0.10)	−0.01	(0.13)	0.07	(0.07)
Y_{t-4}	−0.19	(0.26)	0.32	(0.09)	−0.07	(0.13)	−0.05	(0.07)
Y_{t-5}	−0.14	(0.28)	−0.21	(0.08)	0.06	(0.12)	0.21	(0.07)
Y_{t-6}	0.12	(0.26)	−0.04	(0.08)	−0.22	(0.11)	0.04	(0.07)
Y_{t-7}	0.13	(0.21)	0.18	(0.08)	0.16	(0.12)	0.16	(0.07)
Y_{t-8}	−0.22	(0.23)	−0.22	(0.09)	0.13	(0.11)	−0.02	(0.06)
Y_{t-9}	0.46	(0.26)	0.19	(0.09)	−0.11	(0.11)	0.02	(0.07)
Y_{t-10}	−0.07	(0.20)	−0.02	(0.09)	0.03	(0.14)	0.03	(0.06)
Y_{t-11}	−0.07	(0.12)	0.12	(0.07)	0.04	(0.19)	−0.04	(0.06)
Y_{t-12}					−0.88	(0.19)	−0.37	(0.09)
Y_{t-13}					0.95	(0.12)	0.40	(0.09)
Y_{t-14}					−0.32	(0.16)	−0.07	(0.08)
Y_{t-15}					0.25	(0.16)	0.16	(0.07)
Y_{t-16}					−0.25	(0.12)	−0.15	(0.05)
n_j	86		192		96		341	
S_2	907				312			
F_{12}	70				70			

lagged dependent variable, and on dummy variables indicating the regime. These results are reported in Table 3. The F statistic for the exclusion of all variables other than an intercept (F_{hetero}) is highly significant for the sunspot series, but not for the industrial production series.

4.3. SETAR(3) model

The SETAR(3) model is

$$Y_t = \alpha_1' X_{t-1} I_{1t}(\gamma, d) + \alpha_2' X_{t-1} I_{2t}(\gamma, d) + \alpha_3' X_{t-1} I_{3t}(\gamma, d) + e_t, \qquad (13)$$

where $\gamma = (\gamma_1, \gamma_2)$. In principle, this model can be estimated using the same techniques described in the previous section, namely conditional on (γ, d), the parameters $(\alpha_1, \alpha_2, \alpha_3)$ may be estimated by OLS, and then a grid search over (γ, d) yields the LS estimates. The difficulty is that if N points are evaluated at each of γ_1 and γ_2, then this search involves $p \times N^2$ OLS regressions. While such estimation is feasible, it does not lend itself easily to bootstrap evaluation of the test statistics. (Estimation would take about 12 minutes for the industrial production series, and 1000 bootstrap replications would take about 200 hours.)

Table 3. Least squares estimates of SETAR(2) conditional variance.

	Annual sunspots		Industrial production	
I_{1t}	3.765	(0.880)	0.761	(143)
I_{2t}	1.858	(0.698)	0.504	(0.084)
y_{t-1}^2	0.001	(0.005)	−0.007	(0.006)
y_{t-2}^2	−0.000	(0.006)	0.017	(0.008)
y_{t-3}^2	−0.005	(0.007)	−0.011	(0.006)
y_{t-4}^2	0.008	(0.008)	0.004	(0.005)
y_{t-5}^2	−0.011	(0.009)	−0.004	(0.005)
y_{t-6}^2	0.022	(0.010)	0.004	(0.005)
y_{t-7}^2	−0.028	(0.011)	0.000	(0.006)
y_{t-8}^2	0.027	(0.013)	−0.003	(0.005)
y_{t-9}^2	−0.005	(0.009)	−0.002	(0.005)
y_{t-10}^2	−0.005	(0.008)	0.014	(0.006)
y_{t-11}^2	0.000	(0.004)	−0.011	(0.007)
y_{t-12}^2			−0.000	(0.009)
y_{t-13}^2			0.003	(0.007)
y_{t-14}^2			0.001	(0.007)
y_{t-15}^2			−0.008	(0.006)
y_{t-16}^2			0.008	(0.004)
F_{hetero}	48.1		20.8	

Fortunately, a computational short-cut was proposed by Bai (1997) and Bai and Perron (1998) in the change-point literature. Arguments analogous to those suggested by these authors show that if the true model is (13), but the (misspecified) SETAR(2) model (4) is actually estimated, the least-squares estimate $\hat{d}$ will be consistent for d and $\hat{\gamma}_1$ will be consistent for one of the pair (γ_1, γ_2). They show further that if $\gamma = (\gamma_1, \gamma_2)$ is estimated by least-squares on (13), enforcing the constraint that $d = \hat{d}$ and that one element of γ equals $\hat{\gamma}_1$, then the second-stage estimate $\hat{\gamma}_2$ will be consistent for the remaining element of the pair (γ_1, γ_2). Thus this two-step method yields consistent estimation of $\hat{d}$ and $\hat{\gamma} = (\hat{\gamma}_1, \hat{\gamma}_2)$. Furthermore, Bai (1997) shows that these estimates can be made asymptoticaly efficient, in the sense of having the same asymptotic distribution as estimates obtained from joint estimation of (13), if this method is iterated at least once. That is, $\gamma = (\gamma_1, \gamma_2)$ is estimated by least-squares on (13), enforcing the constraint that $d = \hat{d}$ and that one element of γ equals $\hat{\gamma}_2$, yielding a refined estimate $\hat{\gamma}_1$. Further iteration does not affect the asymptotic distribution, but may yield finite-sample improvements.

This 'one-step-at-a-time' approach yields enormous computational savings. Rather than pN^2 function evaluations, it involves approximately $pN + 2N$ function evaluations, which is only a minor increase over the requirements for estimation of the SETAR(2) model.

It is important to impose the requirement that all three regimes have at least $n\tau$ observations. In addition to the restrictions imposed on the search discussed in

Table 4. Least squares estimates of SETAR(3) models.

	Annual sunspots						Industrial production					
	$N_{t-2} \leqslant 5.3$		$5.3 < N_{t-2} \leqslant 8.0$		$N_{t-2} > 8.0$		$Q_{t-6} \leqslant -2.5$		$-2.5 < Q_{t-6} \leqslant 0.35$		$Q_{t-6} > 0.35$	
	$\hat{\alpha}_1$	s.e.	$\hat{\alpha}_2$	s.e.	$\hat{\alpha}_3$	s.e.	$\hat{\alpha}_1$	s.e.	$\hat{\alpha}_2$	s.e.	$\hat{\alpha}_3$	s.e.
Const.	0.037	(1.14)	9.08	(2.99)	2.31	(0.55)	0.28	(0.29)	-0.06	(0.20)	0.11	(0.11)
y_{t-1}	1.57	(0.12)	1.09	(0.10)	0.91	(0.07)	1.03	(0.16)	1.53	(0.12)	1.04	(0.06)
y_{t-2}	-1.18	(0.33)	-1.10	(0.39)	-0.02	(0.11)	-0.13	(0.22)	-0.52	(0.18)	0.04	(0.08)
y_{t-3}	0.62	(0.37)	-0.11	(0.36)	-0.44	(0.09)	-0.03	(0.17)	-0.02	(0.14)	0.08	(0.07)
y_{t-4}	-0.57	(0.28)	0.00	(0.29)	0.27	(0.08)	0.15	(0.19)	-0.31	(0.18)	-0.05	(0.07)
y_{t-5}	0.36	(0.24)	-1.11	(0.38)	-0.17	(0.08)	0.03	(0.16)	0.31	(0.17)	-0.21	(0.07)
y_{t-6}	-0.31	(0.26)	0.70	(0.41)	-0.05	(0.08)	-0.28	(0.17)	-0.36	(0.22)	-0.05	(0.07)
y_{t-7}	0.43	(0.22)	0.11	(0.28)	0.16	(0.08)	0.11	(0.13)	0.34	(0.21)	0.16	(0.07)
y_{t-8}	-0.30	(0.24)	0.58	(0.25)	-0.21	(0.09)	0.14	(0.16)	0.09	(0.17)	-0.03	(0.06)
y_{t-9}	0.30	(0.26)	-0.48	(0.27)	0.17	(0.09)	-0.37	(0.19)	0.03	(0.11)	0.03	(0.07)
y_{t-10}	-0.02	(0.24)	0.33	(0.26)	0.03	(0.09)	0.24	(0.23)	-0.12	(0.15)	0.03	(0.06)
y_{t-11}	-0.02	(0.13)	-0.32	(0.15)	0.12	(0.06)	0.11	(0.28)	-0.10	(0.18)	-0.04	(0.06)
y_{t-12}							-0.96	(0.26)	-0.65	(0.20)	-0.36	(0.09)
y_{t-13}							0.74	(0.31)	0.97	(0.13)	0.39	(0.09)
y_{t-14}							-0.17	(0.31)	-0.34	(0.16)	-0.07	(0.08)
y_{t-15}							0.27	(0.31)	0.25	(0.14)	0.15	(0.07)
y_{t-16}							-0.16	(0.18)	-0.30	(0.10)	-0.15	(0.05)
n_j	58		36		184		46		53		338	
S_2	769						294					
F_{13}	132						101					
F_{23}	50						27					

Section 4.2, we need to impose the requirement in the second- and third-stage searches that at least $n\tau$ observations lie in the regime where $\gamma_1 \leqslant Y_{t-d} \leqslant \gamma_2$ (or $\gamma_2 \leqslant Y_{t-d} \leqslant \gamma_1$ if $\gamma_2 < \gamma_1$).

In Table 4 we report the least-squares estimates of the SETAR(3) models for our two time-series. For the sunspot series, the two thresholds are 5.32 and 8.04. We find that the F_{13} statistic for the test of SETAR(1) against SETAR(3) is 132 and the F_{23} statistic for the test of SETAR(2) against SETAR(3) is 50.

For the industrial production series, the two thresholds are -2.53 and 0.348. The F_{13} statistic is 101 and the F_{23} statistic is 27.

5. Testing SETAR(1) against SETAR(2)

5.1. *Homoskedasticity*

While the standard theory of hypothesis testing suggests that a good test of the SETAR(1) model against the SETAR(2) alternative is to reject for large values of the statistic F_{12}, the test cannot be implemented unless we know the distribution of F_{12} under the null hypothesis, as this is the only way to control the Type I error of the test.

We start by imposing the assumption of conditional homoskedasticity

$$E(e_t^2 \mid \Im_{t-1}) = \sigma^2 \tag{14}$$

and consider the general case of conditional heteroskedasticity in the next section.

In most testing contexts, test statistics such as F_{12} can be expected to have an asymptotic $\chi^2(k)$ distribution under (14). In the present context, however, this is not the case. This can perhaps best be seen by examining the form of the statistic F_{12} as defined in (11) and (12) Let

$$F_{12}(\gamma, d) = n\left(\frac{f_2(\gamma, d)}{S_1 - f_2(\gamma, d)}\right),$$

which is a monotonically increasing function of $f_2(\gamma, d)$. Since $F_{12} = F_{12}(\hat{\gamma}_1, \hat{d})$ and $(\hat{\gamma}_1, \hat{d})$ maximize $f_2(\gamma, d)$, it follows that

$$F_{12} = \max_{\gamma, d} F_{12}(\gamma, d). \tag{15}$$

Now $F_{12}(\gamma, d)$ is a fairly conventional test statistic. It is equivalent to the test for the exclusion of $X_1(\gamma, d)$ (with (γ, d) fixed) from a regression of Y on X and $X_1(\gamma, d)$. If the data are weakly stationary and satisfy standard regularity conditions, we can show that for any fixed (γ, d), $F_{12}(\gamma, d)$ has an asymptotic $\chi^2(k)$ distribution. Now the problem is that the maximization (15) involves not just a single value of (γ, d), but a very large number of values. Our proposed implementation involves maximization over pN values of (γ, d) (which is 1100 for the sunspot application), so we are taking the maximum of pN distinct asymptotic chi-square random variables. Thus the distribution of F_{12} is distinctly greater than the $\chi^2(k)$. Thus if F_{12}

is not significant when compared to the $\chi^2(k)$, it will be certainly not significant when compared to the correct asymptotic distribution. In most applications this will not be a helpful bound, however, as typically the observed value of F_{12} will be very 'significant' when compared to the $\chi^2(k)$ distribution.

Thus it is not helpful to think of the statistic $F_{12}(\gamma, d)$ for fixed values of (γ, d). Instead, we need to think of $F_{12}(\gamma, d)$ as a random function of the arguments (γ, d), and view F_{12} (as defined in (15)) as the random maximum of this random function. To develop an asymptotic distribution theory for this statistic, we therefore need an asymptotic theory appropriate for random functions, which is known as empirical process theory. A good review can be found in Andrews (1994). For the stationary SETAR model under (14), Hansen (1996) has shown that the asymptotic distribution of the empirical process $F_{12}(\gamma, d)$ is

$$F_{12}(\gamma, d) \Rightarrow T(\gamma, d)$$

where

$$T(\gamma, d) = G(\gamma, d)' M^*(\gamma, d)^{-1} G(\gamma, d)$$

$$M^*(\gamma, d) = M(\gamma, d) - M(\gamma, d) M^{-1} M(\gamma, d),$$

$$M = E(X_{t-1} X'_{t-1})$$

$$(16)$$

$$M(\gamma, d) = E(X_{t-1} X'_{t-1} I_{1t}(\gamma, d))$$

and $G(\gamma, d)$ is a mean-zero Gaussian process with covariance kernel

$$E[G(\gamma, d)G(\gamma', d')'] = E(X_{t-1} X'_{t-1} I_{1t}(\gamma, d) I_{1t}(\gamma', d')) - M(\gamma, d) M^{-1} M(\gamma', d').$$

$$(17)$$

That is, for fixed (γ, d) the distribution of $G(\gamma, d)$ is multivariate normal with covariance matrix $M^*(\gamma, d)$, and all pairs $(G(\gamma, d), G(\gamma', d'))$ are jointly normal with covariance given in (17). Thus $G(\gamma, d)$ is a random function with arguments (γ, d).

Note that for fixed (γ, d) the random variable $T(\gamma, d)$ is $\chi^2(k)$. Thus for fixed (γ, d), $F_{12}(\gamma, d) \to_d \chi^2(k)$. The statistic F_{12} is the maximum of this random function, so coverges in distribution to the maximum of this random limit function, or

$$F_{12} \xrightarrow{d} T = \max_{\gamma, d} T(\gamma, d).$$

While for fixed (γ, d), $T(\gamma, d)$ is $\chi^2(k)$, the distribution of T is less easy to characterize. Its distribution depends to a great extent on the degree of dependence between the random variables $T(\gamma, d)$ for distinct values of (γ, d), which is determined through the covariance functional (17), and thus by moments of the regressors X_{t-1} and the threshold variables Y_{t-d}. Since the distribution of T depends upon these moments (which are application-specific), the distribution T cannot be tabulated for general use. Rather, critical values and p-values must be calculated for each and every application.

Hansen (1996) describes an algorithm to calculate the asymptotic distribution.[4] It can be described as follows. In the formula for the asymptotic distribution T given in (16), replace all population moments by sample counterparts (e.g., replace M by $M_n = n^{-1}X'X$) to define a random variable T_n. Since the sample moments are consistent estimates of the population moments, T_n is the asymptotic approximation of interest. An *exact* draw from the asymptotic distribution T_n can be made by letting u denote a random $N(0, I_n)$ vector, $\hat{u} = u - X(X'X)^{-1}X'u$, and then setting

$$T_n = \max_{\gamma, d} \hat{u}'(\gamma, d)M_n^*(\gamma, d)^{-1}X_1(\gamma, d)'\hat{u} \tag{18}$$

where $M_n^*(\gamma, d)$ is defined in (10). This is similar (and asymptotically equivalent), to a bootstrap replication where u is treated as the dependent variable, and the regressors X_{t-1} and threshold variables Y_{t-d} are held fixed at their sample values. To calculate the distribution of T_n, a large number (we use 2000) of independent draws are made from (18). Then critical values may be calculated from the quantiles of these draws, or better yet, a p-value may be calculated by counting the percentage of the draws which exceed the observed F_{12}.

This is similar to a bootstrap, but it should not be confused with a bootstrap distribution. The distribution T_n is the asymptotic distribution of the test statistic, and simply the fact that a simulation is used to compute the p-value does not make it more accurate than any other asymptotic approximation. The main advantage of the calculation of this asymptotic distribution is that it is computationally less costly than a bootstrap calculation. Since most of the computational work in implementing (18) comes through the matrix inversion of

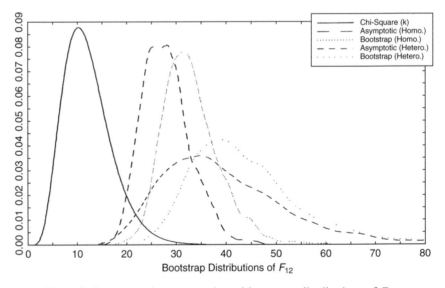

Bootstrap Distributions of F_{12}

Figure 3. Sunspot series asymptotic and bootstrap distributions of F_{12}.

$M_n^*(\gamma, d)$, and these are constant across draws of T_n, computational savings may be made if the matrices $M_n^*(\gamma, d)^{-1}$ are stored, and not re-calculated for each draw. The computational savings are such that this algorithm takes only one-quarter the time of the bootstrap method to be described next.

The asymptotic distributions (18) were calculated using 2000 independent draws for each of our two time-series. Estimates[5] of the density functions are plotted (long dashes) in Figures 3 and 4, and labeled 'Asymptotic (Homo.)'. The $\chi^2(k)$ density is also plotted (solid line) for reference. It is clear that the $\chi^2(k)$ distribution is highly misleading relative to the asymptotic distribution. Still, the observed value of the test statistic F_{12} is 70 for each application, which is in the far right tail of the asymptotic distribution, so the observed value appears to be highly significant. In Table 5 we report the asymptotic p-value, which is 0.000 in both applications, since none of the 2000 simulations exceeded the test statistic in the observed sample.

Since a fair amount of computation is involved in calculating the asymptotic p-value, one might ask: Why not make a little extra effort and calculate the p-values using a bootstrap approximation? There is a considerable body of statistical theory (e.g. Hall (1992), Shao and Tu (1995), Davison and Hinkley (1997)) that the bootstrap is a better approximation to finite sample distributions than first-order asymptotic theory. Under certain technical conditions (such as the existence of an Edgeworth expansion), the bootstrap distribution of an asymptotically pivotal statistic achieves a higher rate of convergence to the sampling distribution than the first-order asymptotic approximation. These conditions have not been verified for the SETAR model (and may in fact not hold) so it is unclear if the boostrap will achieve an accelerated rate of convergence.

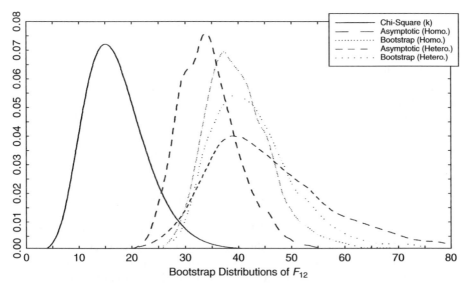

Figure 4. Industrial production asymptotic and bootstrap distributions of F_{12}.

Table 5. Asymptotic and bootstrap tests of SETAR(1) against SETAR(2).

	F_{12}	Homoskedastic p-values		Heteroskedastic p-values	
		Asymptotic	Bootstrap	Asymptotic	Bootstrap
Sunspots	70	0.000	0.000	0.030	0.031
Industrial production	70	0.000	0.001	0.047	0.010

An argument in favor of the bootstrap is that it appears to work globally in the parameter space. While the asymptotic approximation of Hansen (1996) outlined above requires that the process Y_t be stationary, excluding unit roots or near unit roots, Caner and Hansen (1998) show that the bootstrap achieves a good approximation even if there is a unit root or near unit root.

While there is no Monte Carlo study comparing the bootstrap and asymptotic approximations in the context of testing for SETAR models, Diebold and Chen (1996) present an analogous study of the Andrews structural change test in the AR(1) model. They find that the bootstrap yields an excellent approximation, a certain improvement over the asymptotic distribution.

There is no free lunch, and the downside to any bootstrap implementation is that it requires taking a position on the distribution of the errors e_t. This requires the imposition of more structure on the model than might be desirable. For example, the bootstrap algorithm that we now describe imposes the condition that the errors e_t are independent of $\Im_{t-1}$, which is considerably stronger than the martingale difference assumption (2) and the homoskedasticity condition (14).

An appropriate bootstrap distribution will calculate the distribution of the statistic F_{12} under the assumption that the data satisfy the SETAR(1) hypothesis and the parameters are calibrated to match the observed data. The natural method to do this is to use the SETAR(1) estimates and add an auxiliary assumption on the errors e_t. The assumption we make is that the errors e_t are independent over time, and estimate the distribution of the errors by the empirical distribution of the SETAR(1) residuals $\hat{e}_t$. The bootstrap distribution also depends on how the initial conditions ($y_0, y_{-1}, y_{-2}, ..., y_{-p+1}$) are modeled. We take the simple approach of conditioning on the observed values, so hold these values fixed in repeated samples.

Thus the algorithm is as follows. Generate a random sample e_t^*, $t = 1, ..., n$ by sampling (with replacement) from the OLS residuals from the SETAR(1) model. Then using the fixed initial conditions ($y_0, y_{-1}, y_{-2}, ..., y_{-p+1}$), recursively generate a sample y_t^*, $t = 1, ..., n$ using the SETAR(1) model (3) with the parameter $\hat{\alpha}_1$ taken from the SETAR(1) estimates. On this simulated series y_t^*, calculate the statistic F_{12}^* using the same methods as to calculate F_{12} on the actual series. Repeat this a large number of times. (We make 2000 replications.) The bootstrap p-value is the percentage of simulated F_{12}^* which exceed the observed F_{12}.

Estimated density functions for this bootstrap distribution of F_{12}^* are displayed using dotted lines (closely spaced) in Figures 3 and 4, labeled 'Bootstrap (Homo.)'. In both applications, the bootstrap distribution takes a similar shape to the asymptotic distribution, but is noticeably shifted to the right and has a thicker right tail. There is no simple explanation for this phenomenon, but it suggests that for many potential values of F_{12}, the asymptotic distribution and bootstrap distribution would give contrary results. In our applications, the value of F_{12} is sufficiently high that there is no meaningful difference between the asymptotic and bootstrap p-values reported in Table 5.

5.2. Heteroskedasticity

The previous section evaluated the distribution of F_{12} under homoskedasticity of the error term. This might seem innocuous, but is actually quite powerful. As we discussed in Section 4.1, there is strong evidence that this assumption is violated for at least the sunspot series. We now turn to sampling approximations which do not impose (14).

Hansen (1996) has shown how to calculate the asymptotic distribution for the case of stationary data with possibly heteroskedastic error terms. It is identical to (16), except that $G(\gamma, d)$ is a mean-zero Gaussian process with covariance kernel

$$E[G(\gamma, d)G(\gamma', d')'] = E\left(X_{t-1}X_{t-1}'I_{1t}(\gamma, d)I_{1t}(\gamma', d')\frac{e_t^2}{\sigma^2} \right)$$

$$- M(\gamma, d)M^{-1}E\left(X_{t-1}X_{t-1}'I_{1t}(\gamma', d')\frac{e_t^2}{\sigma^2} \right)$$

$$- E\left(X_{t-1}X_{t-1}'I_{1t}(\gamma, d)\frac{e_t^2}{\sigma^2} \right)M^{-1}M(\gamma', d')$$

$$- M(\gamma, d)M^{-1}E\left(X_{t-1}X_{t-1}'\frac{e_t^2}{\sigma^2} \right)M^{-1}M(\gamma', d'). \quad (19)$$

Let T^H denote the distribution (16) under this alternative covariance kernel. There is no clear relationship between T and T^H, so it is not clear what is the bias if one is calculated instead of the other.

Hansen (1996) has provided an algorithm which allows the calculation of this asymptotic distribution. Let T_n^H denote the distribution (16) with covariance kernel (19), where population moments are replaced by sample moments. For example,

$$E\left(X_{t-1}X_{t-1}'I_{1t}(\gamma, d)I_{1t}(\gamma', d')\frac{e_t^2}{\sigma^2} \right)$$

is estimated by

$$\frac{1}{n}\sum_{t=1}^{n}\left(X_{t-1}X'_{t-1}I_{1t}(\gamma,d)I_{1t}(\gamma',d')\frac{\hat{e}_t^2}{\hat{\sigma}^2}\right).$$

Then an exact draw from T_n^H can be made by letting u denote a random $N(0, I_n)$ vector, setting $\eta = u \odot \hat{e}/\hat{\sigma}$ (element-by-element multiplication), $\hat{\eta} = \eta - X(X'X)^{-1}X'\eta$, and then setting T_n^H as in (18). Computationally this is not more complicated that the calculation of T_n. The advantages of this asymptotic approximation are that it is easy to implement, and is asymptotically robust to heteroskedasticity of unknown form.

Estimated densities of the distributions of T_n^H are plotted in short dashes in Figures 3 and 4 for the two time-series, labeled 'Asymptotic (Hetero.)'. In both cases, there is a striking distinction between the two asymptotic distributions, with that for the null of linear/heteroskedastic being dramatically shifted to the right relative to that for linear/homoskedasticity. Not surprisingly, the p-values are quite different as well. For the sunspot series, the p-value is 0.03, and for the industrial production series it is 0.047. What is evident from this calculation is that the allowance for heteroskedasticity dramatically moderates the evidence in favor of the SETAR(2) model.

We found in our analysis of the homoskedastic model that there was a large distinction between the asymptotic and bootstrap distributions, and there is good reason to expect this distinction to be even larger in the heteroskedastic case. It is therefore desirable to calculate a bootstrap distribution of F_{12} allowing for the possibility of general heteroskedasticity. The difficulty is that there is not a well-accepted bootstrap method which is appropriate in the present context. Block resampling schemes are inappropriate because they do not impose the null hypothesis. On the other hand, any model-based bootstrap will require a parametric model for the conditional variance, and the validity of the bootstrap method will depend upon the validity of the selected conditional variance functional. While this calls for careful selection of an empirically-determined conditional variance function, the presumption must be that the results will not be overly sensitive to misspecification of the conditional variance.

For our conditional variance function, we specify that $\sigma_{t-1}^2 = E(e_t^2 | \mathfrak{I}_{t-1})$ is a linear function in the squares of the regressors. Hence, let Z_{t-1} be the $k \times 1$ vector of the squared regressors (e.g., $Z_{t-1} = X_{t-1} \odot X_{t-1}$), so that $\sigma_{t-1}^2 = Z'_{t-1}\beta$ for some vector β. Then $e_t^2 = Z'_{t-1}\beta + \xi_t$ with $E(\xi_t | \mathfrak{I}_{t-1}) = 0$, so β can be estimated by OLS regression of $\hat{e}_t^2$ on Z_{t-1}, where $\hat{e}_t$ is the OLS residual from the SETAR(1) model. We calculate the fitted values $\hat{\sigma}_{t-1}^2 = Z'_{t-1}\hat{\beta}$ and the rescaled residuals $\hat{\varepsilon}_t = e_t/\hat{\sigma}_{t-1}$ (with the convention that $\hat{\varepsilon}_t = 0$ if $\hat{\sigma}_{t-1}^2 \leqslant 0$).

Our heteroskedastic bootstrap method assumes that the rescaled errors $\varepsilon_t = e_t/\sigma_{t-1}$ are independent over time, and works similarly to the homoskedastic bootstrap in Section 5.1 except how the errors e_t^* are generated. We fix the initial conditions $X_0^* = (y_0, y_{-1}, y_{-2}, ..., y_{-p+1})$ and now describe the recursion $X_{t-1}^* \rightarrow y_t^*$.

Let $\sigma_{t-1}^{*2} = \max(Z_{t-1}^{*\prime} \hat{\beta}, 0)$ where $Z_{t-1}^{*} = X_{t-1}^{*} \odot X_{t-1}^{*}$. Let ε_t^{*} be an independent draw from the empirical distribution of $\{\hat{\varepsilon}_t\}$, set $e_t^{*} = \sigma_{t-1}^{*} \varepsilon_t^{*}$, and $y_t^{*} = \hat{\alpha}_1^{\prime} X_{t-1}^{*} + e_t^{*}$. This recursion creates simulated time-series y_t^{*} with the desired conditional mean and variance functions. On this sample, we calculate the test statistic F_{12}^{*}, and repeat a large number of times to find the bootstrap distribution.

Estimated densities of the bootstrap distributions are displayed using dotted lines in Figures 3 and 4, with the label 'Bootstrap (Hetero.)'. In both cases, the heteroskedastic bootstrap distributions are considerably different from both the asymptotic distributions and the homoskedastic bootstrap distribution. In both cases, the heteroskedastic bootstrap distribution is shifted more to the right than the homoskedastic bootstrap. It is interesting to observe, however, that for the sunspot series the heteroskedastic bootstrap is more shifted to the right than the asymptotic distribution allowing heteroskedasticity, while in the industrial production application these rankings are reversed.

The heteroskedastic bootstrap p-values are reported in Table 5. In both applications, the F_{12} test appears to be statistically significant.

In summary, examining the displays in Figures 3 and 4, we can make the following general recommendations. In the presence of conditional heteroskedasticity, distributions calculated under the assumption of homoskedasticity can be quite misleading. Since it is unknown whether or not there is meaningful conditional heteroskedasticity (tests are helpful but not decisive), this suggests that the preferred distributions are those which allow for conditional heteroskedasticity. There can be large discrepancies, however, between asymptotic and bootstrap approximations, suggesting that inference be made in practice using carefully selected bootstrap distributions which account for the error heteroskedasticity.

For example, in the sunspot example, there is very strong evidence for conditional heteroskedasticity. Thus the more appropriate p-value is the heteroskedastic bootstrap, which is 0.031. This is marginally significant, leading us to lean towards rejecting the SETAR(1) model in favor of the SETAR(2) model, but reserving some hesitations. In the industrial production example, there is no strong evidence for heteroskedasticity, so it is less clear whether we should prefer the homoskedastic bootstrap (p-value of 0.001) or the heteroskedastic bootstrap (p-value of 0.010). Since both are highly significant, we feel safe in concluding that the evidence allows us to reject the SETAR(1) model in favor of the SETAR(2) for this series.

6. Testing SETAR(1) against SETAR(3)

As discussed in Section 2, the natural test for SETAR(1) against SETAR(3) is to reject for large values of $F_{13} = n(S_1 - S_3)/S_3$. As discussed in the previous section, the statistic has a non-standard asymptotic distribution under the SETAR(1) hypothesis, so conventional critical values (such as the $\chi^2(2k)$) are not appropriate. An asymptotic approximation similar to (16) can be developed, and can be calculated using methods similar to those described in Section 4. As we

argued in Section 4, however, the asymptotic distributions appear to be quite
different from bootstrap distributions, and we expect the latter to provide better
approximations. In addition, there is no obvious short-cut which enables faster
computation of the asymptotic distribution relative to the bootstrap distribution.[6]
Since there are no clear computational advantages, it appears advisable to simply
focus on bootstrap distributions.

There are no additional complications in calculating the bootstrap distribution
of F_{13} relative to calculating that of F_{12}. Both are calculated under the same null
hypothesis (the SETAR(1) model) so the same technique is used. For either the
homoskedastic (or heteroskedastic) bootstrap, simulated time-series are generated
as described in Section 4.1 (or Section 4.2) and the F_{13} statistic is calculated on
this simulated data. Through repeated replication (we use 2000), the bootstrap
distribution is uncovered.

We display the bootstrap distributions (both homoskedastic and heteroskedastic) for the sunspot series in Figure 5. The conventional $\chi^2(2k)$ is plotted
also for reference. The distributions, as expected, are noticeably different
from the chi-square, and are also noticeably different from one another, with
the heteroskedastic bootstrap distribution shifted out more to the right. The
bootstrap p-values are presented in Table 6, and are both highly significant. We
are able to easily reject the hypothesis of the SETAR(1) in favor of the
SETAR(3).

In Figure 6 we display the bootstrap distributions for the industrial production
data, and report the bootstrap p-values in Table 6. The evidence suggests the
rejection of the SETAR(1) model, but the rejection is not as strong as the rejection
from the previous section.

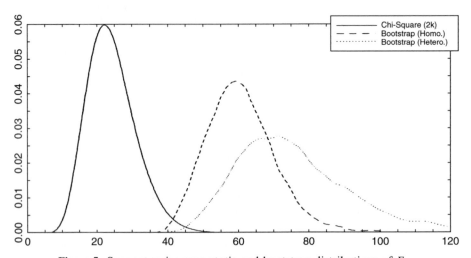

Figure 5. Sunspot series asymptotic and bootstrap distributions of F_{13}.

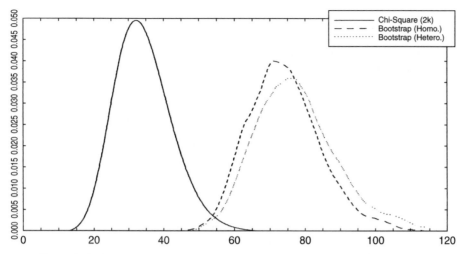

Figure 6. Industrial production asymptotic and bootstrap distributions of F_{13}.

Table 6. Bootstrap tests of SETAR(1) against SETAR(3).

		Bootstrap p-values	
	F_{13}	Homoskedastic	Heteroskedastic
Sunspots	132	0.000	0.004
Industrial production	101	0.013	0.046

7. Testing SETAR(2) against SETAR(3)

The F_{13} test does not allow the discrimination between the SETAR(2) and SETAR(3) models, and therefore is not a sufficient tool for model selection. We now consider the F_{23} test, which directly allows a comparison between these models. As in the previous section, we use bootstrap methods to evaluate the sampling distribution. We do this with some caution, because there has not yet been a demonstration that a bootstrap procedure can properly approximate the sampling distribution of F_{23} under the SETAR(2) null hypothesis. The problem is that under the null hypothesis, the model is a non-linear SETAR(2) model, and one of the parameter estimates, $\hat{\gamma}_1$, has a non-standard asymptotic distribution (see Chan (1993)).

Despite these concerns, there is no reason to expect the bootstrap to fail to achieve the correct first-order asymptotic distribution, so we proceed and describe bootstrap methods of inference. To calculate the bootstrap distribution of F_{23} under the SETAR(2) hypothesis, we need to generate simulated data from the SETAR(2) model. Given such simulated data, we can calculate the F_{23} statistic, and then repeat this procedure a large number of times to generate the bootstrap distribution.

The key feature is to generate simulated data from the SETAR(2). We use the SETAR(2) parameter estimates from Section 4.2. We first consider the homoskedastic bootstrap, which treats the errors e_t as independent draws. We implement this assumption by drawing the bootstrap errors from the empirical distribution of the SETAR(2) least-squares residuals. Then the simulated series is created according to the SETAR(2) model defined in (4).

We next consider forms of the heteroskedastic bootstrap. We consider two forms. The first assumes that the conditional heteroskedasticity is limited to a regime effect, namely, that $E(e_t^2 \mid \Im_{t-1}) = \sigma_1^2 I_{1t} + \sigma_2^2 I_{2t}$. (This is an assumption commonly made in SETAR applications.) We implement this bootstrap by first dividing the SETAR(2) residuals $\hat{e}_t$ into two groups: the n_1 errors $\hat{e}_{1t}$ for which $I_{1t} = 1$, and the n_2 errors $\hat{e}_{2t}$ for which $I_{2t} = 1$. Then when simulating the distribution of y_t^* given $\Im_{t-1}^*$, if $I_{1t}^* = 1$, we draw e_t^* randomly from $\{\hat{e}_{1t}\}$, and if $I_{2t}^* = 1$, we draw e_t^* randomly from $\{\hat{e}_{2t}\}$. We call this the Regime Heteroskedastic Bootstrap.

The second form of the heteroskedastic bootstrap we consider uses the functional form estimated for the conditional variance as reported in Table 3. This is a model of the conditional variance which has regime indicators, and is linearly a function of the squares of the regressors. Simulation from this process is similar to that described in Section 5.2. We call this procedure the General Heteroskedastic Bootstrap, since it allows for heteroskedasticity of general form.

We display in Figures 7 and 8 estimated densities of the bootstrap distributions for our two time-series applications. The $\chi^2(k)$ is also plotted for reference. We find that the bootstrap distributions for the sunspot series are quite sensitive the the specification of the error process, with an increasingly 'fat' distribution as the

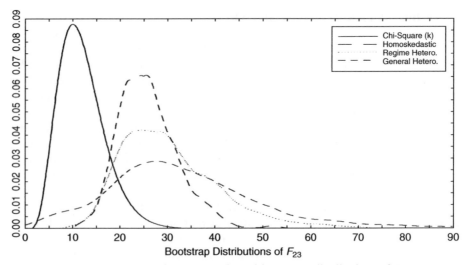

Figure 7. Sunspot series asymptotic and bootstrap distributions of F_{23}.

degree of heteroskedasticity is increased. In contrast, for the industrial production series, the bootstrap distributions are relatively insensitive to the heteroskedastic specification. This difference is likely due to our finding that the sunspot series exhibits a strong degree of heteroskedasticity, but not the industrial production series. The important message is that it is necessary to be careful about the modeling of the error process when pursuing bootstrap inference.

The bootstrap p-values for the F_{23} statistics are given in Table 7. Considering the sunspot series, the test would appear to be significant if the errors were (mistakenly) assumed to be homoskedastic, and marginally significant if the Regime Heteroskedastic Bootstrap were applied. The p-value rises to 12%, however, if we allow a general process for the error heteroskedasticity. Since this type of heteroskedasticity seems quite likely in this data, we conclude that we cannot reject the hypothesis of the SETAR(2) model against the SETAR(3) model. This suggests that an appropriate model for the sunspot series is the SETAR(2) model.

Table 7. Bootstrap tests of SETAR(2) against SETAR(3).

		Bootstrap p-values		
	F_{23}	Homoskedastic	Regime heteroskedastic	General heteroskedastic
Sunspots	50	0.001	0.044	0.126
Industrial production	27	0.828	0.808	0.856

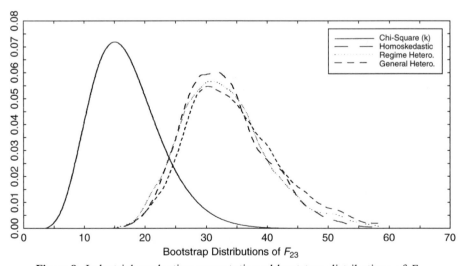

Figure 8. Industrial production asymptotic and bootstrap distributions of F_{13}.

The p-values for the industrial production series are similar across the error modeling choices, and are all far from significant, leading to the conclusion that we cannot reject the SETAR(2) model in favor of the SETAR(3) model. As for the sunspot series, we find that the evidence supports a SETAR(2) model for the industrial production series.

8. Conclusion

We have presented the theory of least-squares inference for the number of regimes in SETAR models. Least-squares estimation and test construction is conceptually and computationally straightforward. Evaluation of test significance is complicated, however, by the fact that the asymptotic distributions are non-standard and non-similar, precluding tabulation. While it is possible to calculate the asymptotic distribution in any application, it seems most prudent to report bootstrap p-values. Such bootstrap p-values can be sensitive to how the bootstrap data is generated, our suggestion is to pay careful attention to the specification of the conditional variance. A naive bootstrap which assumes independent errors can yield inaccurate inferences.

The procedures described in this chapter are not very difficult to program, and the computation requirements appear quite reasonable for applications.

We illustrated these methods with two applications, comparing SETAR(1), SETAR(2), and SETAR(3) specifications. Our tests led to the conclusion that annual sunspots and monthly U.S. industrial production are SETAR(2) processes.

While we only explicitly examine tests between SETAR(1), SETAR(2), and SETAR(3) models, the methods extend to higher-order SETAR models as well. The main caution to consider, however, is that we expect the accuracy of the bootstrap approximations to deteriorate when higher-order SETAR models are tested, due to the more complicated forms of nonlinearity.

Acknowledgements

Prepared for a special issue of the *Journal of Economic Surveys* on nonlinear modeling. This research was supported by a grant from the National Science Foundation. I thank Nikolay Gospodinov for finding an error in a previous draft, and Simon Potter for helpful comments which improved the presentation.

Notes

1. Tong (1990) calls this a SETAR$(m; p, ..., p)$.
2. $I(a) = 1$ if a is true, else $I(a) = 0$.
3. $\Im_t$ equals the Borel sigma-field $\sigma(Y_t, Y_{t-1}, Y_{t-2} ...)$.
4. This algorithm applies as well to the Andrews–Ploberger (1994) exponentially weighted and averaged test statistics.
5. The density estimates were calculated using an Epanechnikov kernel with the Silverman (1986) rule-of-thumb bandwidth. See Hardle and Linton (1994) for a description of non-parametric density estimation.

6. The main computational savings from calculating the asymptotic distribution, rather than the bootstrap, is that the moments matrices $M_n^*(\gamma, d)^{-1}$ can be stored. While the list of such matrices is relatively small for estimation of the SETAR(2), it is quite large for the SETAR(3) model, making programming and memory requirements quite prohibitive.

References

Andrews, D. W. K. (1993) Tests for parameter instability and structural change with unknown change point. *Econometrica*, 61, 821–856.

Andrews, D. W. K. (1994) Empirical process methods in econometrics. *Handbook of Econometrics, Vol IV*, 2248–2296, R. F. Engle and D. L. McFadden, eds., Amsterdam: Elsevier Science.

Andrews, D. W. K. and Ploberger, W. (1994) Optimal tests when a nuisance parameter is present only under the alternative. *Econometrica*, 62, 1383–1414.

Bai, J. (1997) Estimating multiple breaks one at a time. *Econometric Theory*, 13, 315–352.

Bai, J. and Perron, P. (1998) Estimating and testing linear models with multiple structural changes. *Econometrica*, 66, 47–78.

Brock, W. A. and Potter, S. (1993) *Nonlinear Time Series and Macroeconometrics*. In G. S. Maddala, C. R. Rao, H. D. Vinod (eds), *Handbook of Statistics*. Amsterdam: North-Holland.

Burgess, S. M. (1992) Nonlinear dynamics in a structural model of employment. *Journal of Applied Econometrics*, 7, S101–S118.

Caner, M. and Hansen, B. E. (1998) *Threshold autoregression with a near unit root.* Madison: Department of Economics, University of Wisconsin, Madison.

Cao, C. Q. and Tsay, R. S. (1992) Nonlinear time-series analysis of stock volatilities. *Journal of Applied Econometrics*, 7, S165–S186.

Chan, K. S. (1990) Testing for threshold autoregression. *The Annals of Statistics*, 18, 1886–1894.

Chan, K. S. (1991) Percentage points of likelihood ratio tests for threshold autoregresion. *Journal of the Royal Statistical Society, Series B*, 53, 691–696.

Chan, K. S. (1993) Consistency and limiting distribution of the least squares estimator of a threshold autoregressive model. *The Annals of Statistics*, 21, 520–533.

Chan, K. S. and Tong, H. (1986) On estimating thresholds in autoregressive models. *Journal of Time Series Analysis*, 7, 179–194.

Chan, K. S. and Tong, H. (1990) On likelihood ratio tests for threshold autoregression. *Journal of the Royal Statistical Society B*, 52, 469–476.

Davison, A. C. and Hinkley, D. V. (1997) *Bootstrap Methods and their Application.* Cambridge University Press.

Davies, R. B. (1977) Hypothesis testing when a nuisance parameter is present only under the alternative. *Biometrika*, 64, 247–254.

Davies, R. B. (1987) Hypothesis testing when a nuisance parameter is present only under the alternative. *Biometrika*, 74, 33–43.

Diebold, F. X. and Chen, C. (1996) Testing structural stability with endogenous break point: A size comparison of analytic and bootstrap procedures. *Journal of Econometrics*, 70, 221–241.

Galbraith, J. W. (1996) Credit rationing and threshold effects in the relation between money and output. *Journal of Applied Econometrics*, 11, 419–429.

Ghaddar, D. K. and Tong, H. (1981) Data transformation and self-exciting threshold autoregression. *Journal of the Royal Statistical Society*, C30, 238–248.

Granger, C. W. J. and Teräsvirta, T. (1993) *Modelling Nonlinear Economic Relationships.* Oxford: Oxford University Press.

Hall, P. (1992) *The Bootstrap and Edgeworth Expansion*, New York: Springer-Verlag.

Hansen, B. E. (1992) Testing for parameter instability in regressions with I(1) processes. *Journal of Business and Economic Statistics*, 10, 321–55.

Hansen, B. E. (1996) Inference when a nuisance parameter is not identified under the null hypothesis. *Econometrica*, 64, 413–430.

Hansen, B. E. (1997) Inference in TAR models. *Studies in Nonlinear Dynamics and Econometrics*, 1(2), 1–14.

Hansen, B. E. (1999a) Testing for structural change in conditional models. *Journal of Econometrics*, forthcoming.

Hansen, B. E. (1999b) Threshold effects in non-dynamic panels: Estimation, testing and inference. *Journal of Econometrics*, forthcoming.

Hardle, W. and O. Linton (1994) *Applied Nonparametric Methods*. In R. F. Engle and D. L. McFadden, (eds), *Handbook of Econometrics, Vol. IV*, pp. 2295–2339. Amsterdam: Elsevier Science.

Koop, G. and Potter, S. M. (1999) Bayes factors and nonlinearity: evidence from economic time series. *Journal of Econometrics*, 88, 251–282.

Kuo, B. S. (1998) Test for partial parameter instability in regressions with I(1) processes. *Journal of Econometrics*, 86, 337–368.

Luukkonen, R., Saikkonen, P. and Terasvirta, T. (1988) Testing linearity against smooth transition autoregressive models. *Biometrika*, 75, 491–499.

Montgomery, A. L., Zarnowitz, V., Tsay, R. S. and Tiao, G. C. (1998) Forecasting the U.S. unemployment rate. *Journal of the American Statistical Association*, 93, 478–493.

Potter, S. M. (1995) A nonlinear approach to U.S. GNP. *Journal of Applied Econometrics*, 2, 109–125.

Quandt, R. (1960) Tests of the hypothesis that a linear regression obeys two separate regimes. *Journal of the American Statistical Association*, 55, 324–330.

Rothman, P. (1991) Further evidence on the asymmetric behavior of unemployment rates over the business cycle. *Journal of Macroeconomics*, 13, 291–298.

Seo, B. (1998) Tests for structural change in cointegrated systems. *Econometric Theory*, 14, 222–259.

Shao, J. and Tu, D. (1995) *The Jackknife and Bootstrap*. NY: Springer.

Silverman, B. W. (1986) *Density Estimation for Statistics and Data Analysis*. London: Chapman and Hall.

Stinchcomb, M. B. and White, H. (1998) Consistent specification testing with nuisance parameters present only under the alternative. *Econometric Theory*, 14, 295–325.

Terasvirta, T. and Anderson, H. M. (1992) Characterizing nonlinearities in business cycles using smooth transition autoregressive models. *Journal of Applied Econometrics*, 7, S119–S139.

Terasvirta, T., Tjostheim, D. and Granger, C. W. J. (1994) Aspects of modelling nonlinear time series. *Handbook of Econometrics, Vol IV*, 2917–2957, R. F. Engle and D. L. McFadden, (eds), Amsterdam: Elsevier Science.

Tong, H. (1978) On a threshold model. *Pattern Recognition and Signal Processing*, (ed.) C. H. Chen, Amsterdam: Sijhoff & Noordhoff.

Tong, H. (1983) *Threshold Models in Non-linear Time Series Analysis. Lecture Notes in Statistics*, 21, Berlin: Springer.

Tong, H. (1990) *Non-Linear Time Series: A Dynamical System Approach*, Oxford: Oxford University Press.

Tong, H. and Lim, K. S. (1980) Threshold autoregression, limit cycles and cyclical data (with discussion). *Journal of the Royal Statistical Society*, B42, 245–292.

Tsay, R. S. (1989) Testing and modeling threshold autoregressive processes. *Journal of the American Statistical Association*, 84, 231–240.

White, H. (1980) A heteroskedasticity-consistent covariance matrix estimator and a direct test for heteroskedasticity. *Econometrica*, 48, 817–838.

4

NONLINEARITY, COMPUTATIONAL COMPLEXITY AND MACROECONOMIC MODELLING

Peter McAdam[1]

and

A. J. Hughes Hallett

1. Introduction

Economists have been generally slow to exploit the properties of non-linear models. Possible reasons for this include: the apparent lag between innovations in statistical methods and modelling practice (Wren Lewis, 1993), the difficulty of simulating and optimising non-linear systems and the fact that many models are theory- (rather than data-) led. Recent research however has focus strongly on non-linear models given that even relatively modest forms can have sophisticated properties such as multiple equilibria and chaos as well as generally better forecasting performance. That leaves us with a problem of how best to exploit the proportion of those models for analytic purposes. That is often not done, for lack of familiarity with the relevant technical literature, much of it regarded as 'peripheral' to mainstream economics.

Our concern therefore is to provide a survey and evaluation that addresses that issue: essentially solution methods and stability analysis. This is a natural concern since without reliable simulation methods, generating more non-linear models would be a wasted task. Our focus, moreover, is on *systems modelling*; the difficulties posed by single-equation or reduced form econometric non-linearity are lesser in comparison and relatively well known (e.g. Granger and Teräsvirta, 1993) although of course there is considerable complimentarity. Furthermore, given that many modelling bureaux — e.g. Bank of England (1999) and Fisher and Whitely (1998), Banca d'Italia (1999) — maintain several different model *types* (the 'suite' approach) we discuss both traditional income-expenditure macro-econometric models as well as smaller analytical models.

Although the evidence for non-linearity in macro-time series is by no means overwhelming — e.g. Neftci and McNevin (1986), Brock and Sayers (1988) — its appeal is considerable. Modellers are especially interested in non-linearity because it motivates an important concern: the analysis of business cycles. That the business cycle may be asymmetric has a long (and eclectic) lineage (Keynes, 1936, p 314, Burns and Mitchell, 1946, p 134, Friedman, 1986). However, the familiar linear modelling of the cycle — Samuelson (1939), Metzler (1941) — has the drawback that oscillations are symmetric and, if damped, require further propagation mechanisms to be introduced which seldom realistically capture the nature of the data.

Moreover, if we assume linearity between inflation and economic activity the impact of excess demand on inflation is symmetric. This gives stabilisation policy a diluted role: if policy makers do not tighten policy immediately following a negative shock, they may do so cost-lessly later. However if the economy is inherently non-linear — but controlled as if it were linear (as with simple feedback rules, e.g. Taylor rule) — the welfare costs may be non-trivial, Laxton, Rose and Tetlow (1993). Accordingly, there is a substantial literature on business-cycle non-linearity: Kaldor (1940), Goodwin (1951), Hicks (1950), Thio (1986), Blatt (1983) and a growing awareness of its inclusion in macroeconomic models, Cooke, Holly and Turner (1998), Laxton *et al.* (1998).

Furthermore, it may be optimal for agents themselves to respond asymmetrically to negative and positive shocks — e.g. with menu costs, Ball and Mankiw (1994), SS pricing (Barro, 1972). This has important implications for whether policy makers (and their models) should assume zero or (marginally) positive inflation targets.

Another form of linearity comes in quadratic adjustment costs; costs of adjustment for investment can be nested as

$$\phi \frac{\beta}{1+\beta} \left(\frac{I_t}{K_{t-1}} \right)^{1+\beta/\beta}$$

yielding the familiar Tobin's q:

$$\left(\frac{I_t}{K_{t-1}} \right) = \left(\frac{q-1}{\phi} \right)^{\beta}.$$

The Investment-Capital-q trade off therefore,

$$\frac{\beta\left(\dfrac{q-1}{\phi}\right)^{\beta}}{q-1},$$

is linear for the usual $\beta=1$ case. This is known to perform badly empirically relative to non-linear specifications, e.g. Abel and Eberly (1995) which is not unexpected given the irreversible nature of investment (e.g., Carruth, Dickerson and Henley,1999). This static rule also tends to make investment 'excessively' volatile (e.g. Roëger, 1998) unless the adjustment factor, ϕ, is scaled upwards (a common, if under-reported, practise among forecasters) or some inertia introduced. For example, in the IMF's global model (Laxton *et al.*, 1998) lags of q are used which, though aimed at smoothing investment, runs counter to the usual forward-looking interpretation of q. For any $\beta\neq1$ we eliminate this linear trade off. The Monte-Carlo simulations reported in McAdam (1998) show how β can be made consistent with the stylised facts of investment.

However, substantial nonlinearity can arise simply in other contexts. Consider the function:

$$x_{t+1}=\beta x_t(1-x_t), \quad x_0=0. \tag{1}$$

In the interval $\beta\in[0,1)$ $x^*=0$, for $\beta\in[1,3)$ we have a scale-dependent solution,

$$x^*=\frac{\beta-1}{\beta}, \frac{dx^*}{d\beta}=\frac{1}{\beta^2}$$

and at $\beta>3$ we have *bifurcation* — i.e. the point between a unique stable solution and a two cycle one. For $\beta\in(3.57,4)$ Chaos (or aperiodicity) takes hold implying seemingly random and unpredictable dynamics from a deterministic system. In such cases, initial conditions become super important limiting the use of a state-dependent linearisation. A variant on bifurcation is Catastrophe theory where substantially different time paths for variables can occur from small changes in parameters. For Economic applications: Varian (1979), George (1981), Faria (1998).

Some important lines however must be drawn between these cases and systems modelling in Economics. Whilst the same principles apply to both (i.e. sensitivity to initial conditions and the 'inappropriateness' of linearisation) important differences remain.

First, Chaos is a specialised example and is invariably limited to bi-variate cases which restricts its incorporation into large systems modelling. In that context nonlinearities in economic systems will most likely not contain aperiodic dynamics — except perhaps in models of a short run, non-optimising or experimental nature etc. Indeed, in the extreme case of chaotic dynamics, point forecasting — often a key role (and commercial justification) for modelling teams

— becomes untenable. Although the forecasting performance of macroeconomic models has been admittedly poor (e.g. Diebold, 1998) in any case.

Moreover, non-linearity brings with it the possibility of multiple equilibria — some of which may prove unstable. This creates a particular problem for forward looking systems since unless one makes specific assumptions about dynamic stability (e.g. through the imposition of saddlepaths in linear systems and terminal conditions in non-linear models etc) economically meaningless closures may result. Imposing unique stability conditions however precludes investigating cases of convergence to *different* steady states in which more than one stable saddle path exists.

Of course, the validity of these *jump* properties (of linear RE models) has long been subject to discussion — Burmeister (1980), George and Oxley (1985), Oxley and George (1994).

Second, although the concept of equilibrium notionally exists in Chaos theory (i.e. 'strange attractors'), Economists typically have strong priors about the asymptotic properties of their models. For example, in the case of macroeconomic models (congruent with say a Keynesian-Classical synthesis) equilibrium is *imposed* through integral control policy rules, error correction mechanisms, terminal conditions etc.

Third, however stochastic in appearance, chaos, bifurcation and catastrophe remain outcomes from *deterministic* systems. These concepts may be less useful in traditional macroeconomic equation systems where stochastic factors are an integral part of the modelling process.

The final difference justifies our present focus. Whereas (1) is trivial to solve, its economic interpretation and justification is open; by contrast, large non-linear economic equation systems might involve substantial numerical complexity but in general are guided by relatively straightforward theory and economic closures.

Econometricians use a variety of methods to test for the presence of non-linearity in time series such as the BDS and bi-spectrum tests (e.g. Mills, 1991) whilst tests for Chaos per se popularly include Lyapunov exponent searches and correlation dimension comparisons. Chaos testing itself (e.g. Brock, 1986) is complicated by the need for 'large' samples (typically unavailable in Economics other than financial time series where such considerations have been popular, DeGrauwe and Dewachter, 1992), and the problem near-unit root processes give in determining dimension. Consequently, we might be more assured of the presence (if not exact form) of non-linearity rather than Chaos specifically.

2. The practical importance of non-linearity: an example

Consider the following non-linear model (Laxton *et al.*, 1995).

$$PDOT_t = \beta PDOT_{t+1} + (1 - \beta)PDOT_{t-1} + \alpha_1(g^2/(g - y_t) - g)$$
$$+ \alpha_2(g^2/(g - y_{t-1}) - g)$$
$$RR_t = RS_t - \beta PDOT_{t+1} - (1 - \beta)PDOT_{t-1}$$
$$RS_t = 3PDOT_t + y_t$$
$$y_t = 0.304y_{t-1} - 0.098RR_t - 0.3151RR_{t-1} + Shock\_Y_t$$

Here inflation is a weighted average back and forward and is affected by contemporaneous and lagged excess demands; the real rate of interest is an expectation term structure. The short-run Phillips curve trade off is therefore dependent on the existing excess demand pressures and at high levels $Y > 0.03$ expansive monetary policy has far larger effects on inflation than output. Normal symbols apply.

This simple model is capable of generating significant non-linearity (i.e. asymmetry) as indicated by the output gap term in the first equation. We present three versions — the original, a linear and log-linear approximation. Note that this model is Blanchard–Kahn stable when linearised. Since this model is impulse response (with beta $= 0.414$, g $= 0.049$) the precise linearisation date is unimportant.

Some obvious points arise from Table 1 — the size of the shock does not appreciably affect simulation times in the linearised case (as expected) but does slightly affect those in the original model. The clear picture however is that the linear models trade off a substantially reduced computational burden (taking around one tenth of the time) for substantially increasing inaccuracy.

However having forward-looking elements *per se* within a model also makes linearisation problematic. For example, assume we have a reduced form model mapping policy outputs (y) to policy inputs (x) relative to a steady state base (*):

$$\left(\frac{\Delta y}{y^*}\right)_t = \sum_{i=0}^{I} \alpha_i \left(\frac{\Delta x}{x^*}\right)_{t-i} + \sum_{j=1}^{J} \beta_j \left(\frac{\Delta x}{x^*}\right)_{t+j}$$

If the model is backward looking,

$$\sum_{j=1}^{J} \beta_j = 0, \ \forall j,$$

Table 1

Model	Time-To-Solve	Accuracy
	Demand Shock $= 0.01$	
Original	38	/
Linear	5	3.2%
Log-Linear	4	3.0%
	Demand Shock $= 0.05$	
Original	39	/
Linear	5	5.1%
Log-Linear	4	4.9%
	Demand Shock $= 0.1$	
Original	42	/
Linear	5	8.5%
Log-Linear	4	8.0%

Note: Accuracy is normalised on the original (Newton) non-linear solution and shows the maximum relative difference of PDOT.

identifying the reduced form coefficient(s) is then straightforward (e.g., Ma, 1992, Bryant *et al.*, 1988). For a given shock, $\Delta X_t > 0$, $X \neq X^*$, we would generate

$$\left(\frac{\Delta y}{y^*} \right)_t$$

perturbations and so α_hat could be solved recursively as

$$\left(\frac{\Delta y}{y^*} \right)_t * \left(\frac{\Delta X}{X^*} \right)_t^{-1}$$

and subsequent multipliers as:

$$\alpha\_hat_{n-1} = \frac{\left(\frac{\Delta y}{y^*} \right)_n - \sum_{j=0}^{n-2} \left[\alpha\_hat_j \left(\frac{\Delta x}{x^*} \right)_{n-j} \right]}{\left(\frac{\Delta x}{x^*} \right)_t}$$

However, if any

$$\sum_{j=1}^{J} \beta_j$$

are non-zero we cannot identify future impacts in the same recursive manner because they are unknown. Of course, this is a particular case and there exists many methods of linearising non-linear lead models — e.g. Ma (1992), Holly and Hughes Hallett (1989). However such methods suffer from the fact that the approximation of the lead dynamics around a chosen horizon (and shock) will cease to be representative outside that neighbourhood.

Linearisations, moreover, are routinely applied in modelling with little formal justification or qualified conclusions. For example much of the empirical literature on the benefits of international policy co-operation are derived from linear (or linearised) models, and so the robustness of the conclusions to the linearisation is an open question. Given these difficulties and uncertainties, an appropriate knowledge of efficient solution and stability techniques for non-linear models is essential. That remains the subject of the remainder of this chapter.

3. Efficient solution methods for non-linear equation systems

In this section we analyse and evaluate the main contributions to non-linear solution methods. Throughout, we are keen to compare first-order and Newton methods (in both the linear and non-linear case) and to make clear, where appropriate, limiting and equivalence cases.

3.1. *First order stationary techniques: the linear case*

Consider the linear equation system

$$Ay = b \tag{2}$$

where $A \in R^{n,n}$ is a known real matrix of order n with non-vanishing diagonal elements, and where y and b are real vectors containing the unknown and predetermined parts of each equation respectively. Stationary first-order iterative techniques

$$y^{(s)} = Gy^{(s-1)} + c, \qquad s = 1, 2, \ldots \tag{3}$$

with an arbitrary start $y^{(0)}$, are routinely used to construct the numerical solution to (2) where s is the current iteration number. They are computationally efficient if A is a large, sparse or ill-conditioned matrix. They are also widely used for solving non-linear equations systems, in which case A represents the system's Jacobian matrix.

These first order methods are based on the splitting $A = P - Q$ where P is nonsingular; and they are completely consistent with (2) when $G = P^{-1}Q$ and $c = P^{-1}b$ define the iteration matrix and forcing function. The most widely used splittings are Jacobi, Gauss–Seidel and Successive Over Relaxation methods; respectively,

$$P = D \quad \text{and} \quad P = (D - L) \quad \text{and} \quad P = \alpha^{-1}D(I - \alpha D^{-1}L) \tag{4}$$

where D and L are matrices of order n such that

$$D_{ij} = \begin{cases} A_{ij} & \text{if } i = j \\ 0 & \text{otherwise,} \end{cases} \quad \text{and} \quad L_{ij} = \begin{cases} -A_{ij} & \text{if } i < j \\ 0 & \text{otherwise,} \end{cases}$$

where $U = D - A - L$, and α is a relaxation parameter to be chosen. Without loss of generality let (3) contain the normalisation $D = I$, and let $B = I - A$.[1] The rate of convergence of (3) can be increased by the one parameter extrapolation:

$$y^{(s+1)} = \gamma(Gy^{(s)} + c) + (1 - \gamma)y^{(s)} \tag{5}$$

Two particular versions of (5) are routinely used; the Jacobi over-relaxation (JOR) method with $G = I - A$ and the Fast Gauss–Seidel (FGS) method with $G = (I - \alpha L)^{-1}(\alpha U + (1 - \alpha)I)$, or incorporating its acceleration parameter, $\gamma(I - \alpha L)^{-1}(\alpha U + (1 - \alpha)I) + (1 - \gamma)I$. Note that variations can be nested within this last term with ($\alpha = 1$, $\gamma = 1$) retrieving (pure) Gauss–Seidel, ($\alpha \neq 1$, $\gamma = 1$) retrieving Gauss–Seidel plus SOR, and ($\alpha = 1$, $\gamma \neq 1$) yielding Fast Gauss–Seidel with no SOR.[2] Furthermore Fisher and Hughes Hallett (1987) suggest an optimal multiplicative α, γ search rule.

The convergence theory for first order linear iterations is well known and is summarised and referenced in appendix one. Proofs will be found in Hughes Hallett (1984a, 1986). The main result being that (3) converges iff $p(G) < 1$, where $p(\cdot)$ denotes special radius (Young, 1971) or, of a matrix, the absolute value of the largest eigenvalue of G. The number of steps to convergence in (5), given $p(H) < 1$ and a convergence criterion of

$$\max_i |(y_i^s - y_i^{s-1})/y_i^{s-1}| < \tau$$

is approximately $\log \tau / \log p(H)$. The corresponding convergence speed can be measured as its asymptotic rate $(-\log p(H))$ which, as we shall see later, implies a linear rate of convergence $(q = 0)$.

3.2. First order stationary techniques: the non-linear case

Non-stationary first-order iterations, in particular those generated by non-linear equation systems, can easily be fitted into this framework and their convergence properties handled in an analogous way. Similarly we can also treat solution techniques for (non-linear) models with forward-looking expectations within exactly the same framework; see Fisher and Hughes Hallett (1988) for example. What follows can therefore be applied to any of those cases, pari passu, within a neighbourhood of the solution.

Consider the non-stationary iteration:

$$y^{(s)} = G^{(s-1)}y^{(s-1)} + k, \qquad s = 1, 2, \dots \tag{6}$$

where the iteration matrix, $G^{(s-1)}$ is dependent on the iteration path, $y^{(s-1)} \dots y^{(0)}$. For example JOR and SOR iterations applied to the general non-linear model $f_i(y, x) = 0 \; i = 1, 2, \dots, n$ are obtained by choosing a normalisation, say $y_i = g_i(y)$, and then computing respectively,

$$y_i^{(s)} = \gamma g_i(y_1^{(s-1)} \dots Y_n^{(s-1)}) + (1 - \gamma)y_i^{(s-1)} \tag{7a}$$

or

$$y_i^{(s)} = \alpha g_i(y_1^{(s)} \dots y_{i-1}^{(s)}, y_{i+1}^{(s-1)} \dots y_n^{(s-1)}) + (1 - \alpha)y_i^{(s-1)} \tag{7b}$$

for $i = 1, \dots, n$ and $s = 1, 2 \dots$. The FGS iterates are obtained by replacing the complete vector $y^{(s)}$ from (7b) with the extrapolation $\gamma y^{(s)} + (1 - \gamma)y^{(s-1)}$ and then using the extrapolated values at the start of each step $s + 1$, i.e.

$$y_i^{(s-1/2)} = \alpha g_i(y_1^{(s-1/2)} \dots y_{i-1}^{(s-1/2)}, y_{i+1}^{(s-1)} \dots y_n^{(s-1)}) + (1 - \alpha)y_i^{(s-1)} \tag{8a}$$

and

$$y_i^{(s)} = \gamma y_i^{(s-1/2)} + (1 - \gamma)y_i^{(s-1)} \tag{8b}$$

The non-linear JOR, SOR and FGS iterations are special cases of (6) with

$$G^{(s-1)} = \gamma B^{(s-1)} + (I - \gamma)I$$
$$G^{(s-1)} = (I - \alpha L^{(s)})^{-1}(\alpha U^{(s-1)} + (1 - \alpha)I)$$
$$G^{(s-1)} = \gamma(I - \alpha L^{(s-1/2)})^{-1}(\alpha U^{(s-1)} + (1 - \alpha)I) + (1 - \gamma)I$$

respectively, where $B^{(s-1)} = (\delta g/\delta y)_{y(s-1)}$ has upper and lower triangle sub-matrices $U^{(s-1)}$ and $L^{(s-1)}$. Convergence to a fixed point, y^*, given an arbitrary start, $y^{(0)}$ within a neighbourhood of y^*, then follows if $p(G^*) < 1$ where G^* is $G^{(s-1)}$ evaluated at y^*, Ostrowski (1966). The *rate* of convergence will be linear for any of these models.

Alternatively we may use **second-order semi-iterative** techniques. These involve accelerating the whole sequence of $y^{(s)}$ iterates with the weighted sums:

$$v(s) = \sum_{k=0}^{s} d_{s,k} y^{(k)}, \quad \text{where} \quad \sum_{s=0}^{s} d_{s,k} = 1 \tag{9}$$

The optimal weights — in the sense of minimising $\| \rho_s(G) \|$ — are related through a second-order (Chebychev) recursion which, when put back into (9), produces a second-order iteration in $y^{(s)}$ with guaranteed convergence. This method requires knowledge of all the eigenvalues of G. However simplifications (or approximations) can be made (see Hughes Hallett, Ma and Ying, 1996) although how much those approximations might damage the method's convergence properties is unclear.

3.3. Newton methods

Given the non-linear[3] system:

$$f_i(y, x) = 0 \qquad i = 1, 2, ..., n \tag{10}$$

where $y \in R^n$ and $x \in R^m$ are vectors of real-valued unknown and predetermined variables respectively, and where $f(\cdot)$ is the model's functional form. The Newton solution is based on an expansion around a starting solution y^{s-1}:

$$y^s = y^{s-1} - (F^{s-1})^{-1} f(y^{s-1}, x) \tag{11}$$

Where F, the Jacobian, is the matrix of partial derivatives evaluated at the present iteration:

$$F^{s-1} = [\delta f/\delta y]_{y(s-1)} \tag{12}$$

The convergence results for Newton methods are relatively straight forward (Ortega and Rheinboldt, 1970, p. 312ff); if the form of the functional form $f(\cdot)$ is continuously differentiable over a convex set D containing the unique true solution, y^*, where $f(y^*)$ is non-singular and $f(y^*, x) = 0$ then there exists around y^* an open set C such that (11) converges at least linearly from any $y^{(0)} \in C$.

Furthermore if the Liptschiz condition,

$$\| F(y) - F(y^*) \| \leqslant d \| y - y^* \| \tag{13}$$

holds for $y \in C$ with $d > 0$ the rate of convergence becomes:

$$\| y^{(s)} - y^* \| \leqslant \delta \| y^{(s-1)} - y^* \|^{1+q} \tag{14}$$

Thus, convergence is quadratic (as opposed to linear as under First-Order systems) for $q = 1$ and $\delta > 0$. Indeed quadratic convergence rates is the norm if C is sufficiently small when $f_i(\cdot) = 0$ is twice differentiable around Y^* (Dennis and Moore, 1977). But there are a number of modified (simplified) Newton methods, discussed later, designed to reduce the huge computational burden of evaluating and inverting F^{s-1} at each step. These modifications have linear convergence rates, $q = 0$, like First Order methods. On the other hand all Newton methods have the property that convergence to y^* is *guaranteed* once the iterates (or indeed any arbitrary starts) are within the open set C — without the need for damping or acceleration parameters.

3.4. A comparison of first order and Newton methods

- **First Order methods** require an explicit normalisation and may be sensitive to equation ordering if GS variants are used. Thus simulations may converge either slowly or not at all (even when a well-defined stable solution exists[4]) depending on whatever equation ordering call exists. Normalisation itself is also important: models can be written in any number of (algebraically equivalent) ways but may fail to solve depending on whatever normalisation is employed.

  In the event of convergence difficulties (other than those simply requiring different acceleration parameters) there are a number of equation re-ordering schemes available. Some of these involve a restructuring of the system into a small block of truly simultaneous equations plus recursive blocks, Don and Gallo (1987). Others depend on restructuring the Jacobian matrix to minimise the number of non zero elements above the diagonal, or more sophisticated variants on the same theme (Hughes Hallett and Piscitelli, 1998). But all of them attempt to re-order the model's equations to reduce the spectral radius of the iteration matrix G.

  The *advantages* of first-order techniques are their relative ease of use (in terms of programming, debugging and computational burden), general suitability for most models and their straightforward application to forward looking models, Fair and Taylor (1983). The main advantage for most practising Econometricians has therefore been ease of implementation, in particular the ability to back track into the algorithm to determine where a fault or source of non-convergence may lie if the solution procedure fails. For many, that is a crucial property which cannot be reproduced so easily with Newton methods.

- The *advantages* of **Newton** methods (which require no explicit normalisation or ordering) are that (i) convergence is extremely fast (super-linear) once the iterates are within C; (ii) convergence is guaranteed for an arbitrary system given any start within C; (iii) no parameters need to be set to ensure convergence.

  The *disadvantages* are: (a) because of the derivative evaluations and matrix inversions, it is computationally expensive (even in 'small' models) without the compensating guarantee of *global* convergence (the number of calculations per step are of $0(n^3)$).[5] (b) the initial vector of 'guesses', $y^{(0)}$, might have to be a good approximation of y^* because C can be very small. Divergence is certainly possible, and simpler but slower methods may have a wider radius of convergence. (c) the inversion of the Jacobian prevents any exploitation of the sparseness of F when solving for each iterate.[6]

- **Modified Newton methods**

  The literature has thus identified several ways to reduce the computational burden of the Newton method:

  Avoiding Any Derivative Evaluations: The matrix F can be constructed using information from past iterates rather than by differentiation. Ortega and Rheinboldt (1970) suggest various schemes for this purpose. But to identify all the elements of F requires n initial iterations, and then a matrix inversion of order n, so there are no computational savings.

  Avoiding Repeated Matrix Inversions: Another suggestion is to avoid inverting F repeatedly. This involves evaluating F only every mth step. If $m = 1$, we have the original Newton method. If $m = \infty$, the same F value will be used throughout. The overall rate of convergence now falls to $(m + 1)/m$ (Ortega and Rheinboldt, 1970, p.[3] 16). So as m increases, the speed of convergence falls to that of linear first order iterations and the Newton method's advantage has been lost. An intermediate position is occupied by Becker and Rustem's (1993) N-SCE method which re-evaluates only parts of F and then only when it improves the rate of convergence. The same results must therefore apply, although the fall to linear convergence rates will of course be a little slower.

  Avoiding Matrix Inversions Altogether: Yet another method is to generate successive F^{-1} values by rank one or rank two updating schemes, rather than by function evaluations. The rate of convergence of (11) using these updates is at least linear if $f(\cdot)$ satisfies the Lipschitz condition (Dennis and More, 1977). However, the system's sparseness is not exploited and the number of calculations per step is still $0(n^2)$. With convergence slower by an order of magnitude, that means there are no computational savings.

  Sparse Matrix Techniques: Perhaps the most effective way of reducing the computational burden of Newton methods is to employ sparse techniques within each step. Duff, Erisman and Reid (1986) show that the computational complexity of solving (11) can be reduced to $0(c^2 n)$ per step, where $c = \sum n_i/n$ is the average number of nonzero entries per row of the Jacobian. This is a significant improvement; and since econometric models typically have no more than 3 or 4 endogenous variables on the right of each equation, it would leave each Newton step 3 or 4 times more expensive than its first order (e.g. Gauss–Seidel) counterpart which has a computational burden of $0(\sum n_i)$. To that comparison, we must add the cost of obtaining numerical values of the partial derivatives in F — a further n iterations at least, as noted above. Thus a sparse Newton algorithm would become competitive if it were more than, say, $3n$ times faster than its first order counterpart. Sparse matrix techniques, for example the new breed of Stacked Newton methods, could prove competitive. In practice it will depend very much on how they perform in models with forward looking variables. But it is obvious from this discussion, the choice of solution technique turns on a trade-off between the smaller number of steps to convergence with Newton methods vs. the smaller amount of computational work per step in First Order methods.

4. The sensitivity of non-linear models to starting values

For **Newton**, therefore, it is starts outside the neighbourhood of y^* defined by the set C (such as 'illegal arithmetic'; $\log(x \rightarrow 0)$) which prevents convergence. We are therefore virtually assured quadratic convergence within some neighbourhood of y^*. But that neighbourhood could be small, and we are still faced with the problem of how to find starting values $y_{(0)}$ which actually lie within C whose exact location cannot be known ex ante. By contrast, **Gauss–Seidel** will fail to converge if the system's Jacobian has eigenvalues greater than unity in real part.

How important is this likely to be in *practical* terms? It is of course rare that a model builder has *no* idea about possible starts. For example with empirical estimated macro models it is easier to guess good starting values: usually lagged historical ones. Similarly, users will tend to know something of the *logical* structure of their model. For example, various parameter restrictions — e.g. that constant-returns production function parameters sum to one — and variable constraints — e.g. non negativity in unemployment and nominal interest rates etc — can guide their choice of starting values.

However the general problem of starts searches tend to be most acute in non-linear models constructed from optimising behaviour[7]; and in models with forward looking expectations. The difficulty with forward looking expectations models is that they need starting values not only for the current period's solution but also for all future periods as well, just to get the current period's solution. If such models are solved numerically there may be insufficient information to tie down those first guesses — other than an uninformative zero solution. Nevertheless, starts may be a problem even in estimated models; for example, where users wish to test alternative dynamic paths to the steady state. In such cases, even the historical starts may be so far from the implied dynamic or equilibrium path that the solution breaks down.

With the exception of McAdam and Hughes Hallett (1999) none of the algorithm comparison exercises in the literature have focused on how to select the start values. This is an *especially important* in non-linear models since not only is the choice of initial conditions crucial in achieving convergence, but so too is handling the dynamic path resulting from the non-linearity.

5. Hybrid or switching algorithms

The major disadvantage of the basic Newton method, recall, is its computational expense. The repeated derivative evaluations and matrix inversions require calculations of the order of $sn^2(n+1)$ to reach the sth step, whereas linear first order iterations such as Gauss–Seidel require only $s \sum n_i$ (where $n_i =$ the number of unknown variables in the ith equation). The work involved per Gauss–Seidel step is typically up to an order of magnitude lower than that in the Newton method.

Thus Gauss–Seidel methods trade slower convergence for less computation per step and may therefore be strictly superior or more robust for a wide class of non-linear systems. Note that this is purely a generic argument — on any particular model or acceleration scheme either algorithm type may outdo the other, for example, Hughes Hallett and Fisher (1990) show that performance trade-off favoured the Gauss–Seidel based schemes in the context of 6 econometric models of the UK economy (see also Norman et al., 1983 for relative support of first-order techniques); Pioro, McAdam and Laxton (1996), Armstrong et al. (1998) and Juillard et al. (1998, 1999) favour Newton methods. And if Gauss–Seidel techniques have lower computation burdens than Newton, then it would pay to switch to Gauss–Seidel techniques as soon as they are convergent at sufficient speed to yield a lower overall burden.

The second, and more important point is that neither Gauss–Seidel nor Newton methods are guaranteed to converge from *any* start values. Moreover, their convergence radii are quite different. That means that, in certain circumstances, one will be convergent and the other divergent. For Newton, it is starts outside the neighbourhood of y^* defined by the set C, whose exact location of C cannot be known ex ante, which prevents convergence. By contrast, Gauss–Seidel will fail to converge if the system's Jacobian has eigenvalues greater than unity in real part. In other words, a switching mechanism could be designed to switch to the convergent algorithm automatically if the other should prove divergent.

The switching device can now be constructed as follows. At each stop define the *composite* iteration

$$y^{(S)} = w_S y_N^{(S)} + (1 - w_S) y_G^{(S)} \tag{15}$$

with initial conditions $y_N^{(0)} = y_G^{(0)} = y^{(0)}$, where $y_N^{(S)}$ and $y_G^{(S)}$ are the current iterates from $y^{(S-1)}$ by the Newton and Gauss–Seidel methods respectively. Set $w_1 = 1$, and thereafter

$$w_s = \frac{\alpha_s}{1 - \alpha_s} \quad \text{where } \alpha_s = p_s \left(\frac{\sum n_i}{2n^3 + 8n^2 + 3n} \right) \tag{16}$$

We have used the fact that each step of the Gauss–Seidel algorithm involves $\sum n_i$ arithmetic operations, and $2n^3 + 8n^2 + 3n$ in the Newton algorithm (Hughes Hallett and Fisher, 1990). If, by reordering the equations, the Newton algorithm can be confined to the feedback set of a simultaneous block then α_s in (16) will be replaced by

$$\alpha_s = p_s \left(\frac{\sum_{i=1}^{m} n_i}{2p^3 + 8p^2 + 3p + \sum_{i=1}^{m-p} n_i} \right) \tag{17}$$

Since each step of the Newton algorithm plus the remaining simultaneous block variables costs $2p^3 + 8p^2 + 3p + \sum_{i=1}^{m-p} n_i$ operations. Finally, to rule out any dependence on a divergent algorithm and to switch to Gauss–Seidel as soon as its computational burden falls below that of Newton, we must impose the following *extra* conditions on w_s:

$w_s = 1$ if $\delta_s^G \geqslant 1$ (i.e. Gauss–Seidel is diverging)

$w_s = 0$ if $w_s \leqslant \frac{1}{2}$ by (17); i.e. Gauss–Seidel is now cheaper or if $\delta_s^N \geqslant 1$,

i.e. Newton is diverging

Hughes Hallett, Ma and Ying (1996) discuss the case of a switching device for the second-order case.

Such algorithms have huge potential and we might expect them to be more widely used and available, as the complexity (i.e. non-linearity) of the models increases. Moreover, a significant development in the computational Economics field is the use of parallel systems processing (e.g. Nagurney, 1996) and Hybrid algorithms would be ideally suited to this with the system solving say a Newton routine and a first-order one simultaneously then switching across in cases of non-convergence or relative improvements in computational burden. Similarly faster performance in multicountry/regional models can be made possible where decomposition[8] can be made in terms of trading block or commodity composition and solved separately. This has been, for example, the practise with the FRB model.

6. Forward looking expectations modelling and non-linear systems

Much of Economics is associated with the modelling of expectations. The use of such anticipatory dynamics has put Economics in a singular class since other social sciences' analysis of real world systems has generally followed contemporaneous and historical causal modelling.

For **First-Order Techniques** invariably the Fair–Taylor algorithm is used — we fix the expectations terms at their baseline values and solve the system as in the conventional case period by period with normal Gauss–Seidel iterative techniques (or indeed any solution method), having done this 'Type 1' we then update the lead terms, for each variable in turn; setting them equal to their forward value. We then return to the Type 1 loop with the expectations terms updated and perform another iteration — until the tolerance between successive iteration on both loops respects the pre-set convergence criteria — which may well be set differently across loops and variables. We therefore have a two-part scheme — a Type 1 loop that solves for the current, and lagged parts of the model with fixed expectations and a Type 2 loop, which solves the model consistently. When the latter has converged the model has consistently solved subject to iteration tolerance.

To illustrate, consider the model, $Y_t = BY_{t-1} + CY^e_{t+1|t} + U_t$, which stacked over time yields:

$$
\begin{bmatrix}
I & -C & 0 & 0 \\
-B & I & -C & 0 \\
0 & -B & I & -C \\
0 & 0 & -B & I
\end{bmatrix}
*
\begin{bmatrix}
Y_t \\
\cdot \\
\cdot \\
Y_T
\end{bmatrix}
=
\begin{bmatrix}
U_t \\
\cdot \\
\cdot \\
U_T
\end{bmatrix}
+
\begin{bmatrix}
B \\
0 \\
0 \\
0
\end{bmatrix}
* Y_0 +
\begin{bmatrix}
0 \\
0 \\
0 \\
C
\end{bmatrix}
* Y_{T+1}
$$

(18)

Or $HY = b$ with b_t containing predetermined variables such as lags, residuals, exogenous terms. A solution exists iff H^{-1} is defined with the matrix H itself being unit block diagonal with upper and lower triangular sub-matrices of U^{s-1} and L^{s-1}. The lower triangle can by solved by any solution method keeping expectations fixed with the upper block triangle solved by equating expectations terms equal to their forward solution from the lower triangle.

Often modellers have sought to take advantage of this splitting by computing incomplete inner iterations. Since the solutions of Type 1 loop will be updated with every Type 2 loop, we can avoid many of the repetitive and unnecessary calculations by setting a looser convergence criteria for the type 1 which solves for the current endogenous variables, given earlier solutions for the past endogenous variables and fixed (assumed) values for the forward (expected) variables. That cuts the inner iterations loop off early since there is no point in computing accurate and detailed values for the current endogenous variables when they will be changed again when the future (forward looking) variables have their values updated at the next outer loop step. Fisher and Hughes Hallett (1988) for example and Holly et al. (1996), find that this innovation does more to speed up the rate of convergence and extend the radius of convergence of first order methods, than all of the acceleration and recording techniques discussed earlier put together.

The most recent developments in non-linear solution methods for RE models have, however, been on the **Newton** side. Stacked Newton methods are essentially a single loop Newton algorithm suitable for simulating models with rational expectations. The n time periods are 'stacked' together and the model is solved consistently for its leads by solving all time periods simultaneously. To illustrate, given the non-linear model:

$$
\mathbf{f}_t(\mathbf{y}_{t-1}, \mathbf{y}_t, E_t\mathbf{y}_{t+1}, \mathbf{x}_t) = 0
$$

(19)

Where $\mathbf{f}_t$ is a vector of n non-linear dynamic equations and $\mathbf{y}_t$ and $\mathbf{x}_t$ are vectors of endogenous and exogenous variables. Stacking the model for all time periods:

$$
\mathbf{F}(\mathbf{z}, \mathbf{x};\ t) = \begin{bmatrix} f_t(\mathbf{z}_t, \mathbf{x}_t) \\ \vdots \\ f_{t+j}(\mathbf{z}_{t+j}, \mathbf{x}_{t+j}) \\ \vdots \\ f_{t+T}(\mathbf{z}_{t+T}, \mathbf{x}_{t+T}) \end{bmatrix} = 0 \tag{20}
$$

where $\mathbf{z}_{t+j} = (\mathbf{y}_{t+j-1}, \mathbf{y}_{t+j}, E_t \mathbf{y}_{t+j+1})$. We solve this equation system by Newton given a predetermined variable $\mathbf{y}_{t-1}$ and the terminal condition $\mathbf{y}_{t+T+1}$. However for medium-to-large non-linear systems, the inversion of the Jacobian is non-trivial. Indeed it remains the biggest single disadvantage of Newton methods and can easily lead to unacceptably heavy computational burdens. If that is true of a conventional system, where the inversion will involve calculations of order n^3 across T periods, it will be even more important for stacked forward looking models where the inversion will 'cost' calculations of order $n^3 T^3$ across 1 'composite period'. For any realistic problem $n^3 T^3$ calculations will be much more than $n^3 T$. Consequently much work has gone into designing algorithms which exploit the repetitive structure of this stacked system, which is block triangular with the blocks corresponding to the different time periods (for more details see Juillard et al., 1998). By taking advantage of the sparsity within the single period blocks, the numerical and computational burden can be reduced significantly. Appendix three specifies how that can be done.

There are two members of this class: 'OLDSTACK' (see Armstrong et al., 1995) and 'NEWSTACK' (see Juillard et al., 1998). They are both single loop Stacked Newton solution methods suitable for simulating models with 'rational' (endogenous) leads. They both take advantage of sparsity within the Jacobian and its associated factored blocks. However they differ crucially in that OLDSTACK does not use any a priori knowledge about the repetitive structure of the Jacobian and so solves the model as if it were backward looking but with separately coded equations for the leads. In fact often it is generally faster than NEWSTACK for repetitive solutions (see Hollinger, 1996 for some trials), but it can be much slower the first time; given that the information on the repetitive structure of the Jacobian is not saved from one simulation task to another — although the algorithm can be made to retain information on its repetitive structure in repeated simulations, Poiro (1995).

7. A synthesis

These new Newton techniques have now been used in many important applications and qualitative evidence, however unscientific, appendix three, certainly suggests they will dominate first-order methods on a production basis;

i.e. for repeated simulations which make small changes around an existing solution. However, it is not obvious that they will do so well in simulations involving rather larger changes, or in identifying that solution in the first place when there are significant nonlinearities in the model.

Moreover the stacked Newton techniques, being 'single loop' methods, cannot take advantage of the incomplete inner loop accelerations available with first order methods — even if the sparsity in the Jacobian matrix has been fully exploited. In this regard, much of the literature comparing these various techniques — e.g. Hughes Hallett and Fisher (1990) as well as the Juillard *et al.* papers (1998, 1999) — has muddied the waters. Whilst some papers have compared accelerated first-order methods with standard Newton methods, other have compared non-accelerated first order methods with the fast Stacked Newton methods. We can get a better grip of the trade-off between the faster convergence (smaller number of steps to convergence) offered by stacked Newton methods, and the smaller computational burden per step offered by first order methods, by doing an operation count for each method. We define one multiplication and one addition to be one operation. Then a conventional first order method requires

$$S_I \sum_i^n n_i$$

arithmetic operations if it converges in s_1 steps, where there are n_ith equation and there are n equations in the simultaneous block. The standard Newton algorithm requires $S_N (2n^3 + 8n^2 + 3n)$ operations to converge in S_N steps, including the inversion of the Jacobian matrix at each step. To that we should add $S_N \sum n_i$ derivative evaluations to evaluate that matrix at each step.

Following the same idea, a first order method for a model with forward looking expectations solved over T periods — like (18) for example — will require

$$TS_0[S_I \sum n_i + \sum (l_i + f_i)] \tag{21}$$

operations, where S_I is the (average) number of iterations per inner loop step and S_0 the average number of outer loop steps. We have also written l_i and f_i as the number of lags and lead variables in the ith equation respectively. Using NEWSTACK, we get the corresponding expression:

$$S_N T[(2n^3 + 7n^2 + 3n) + (n^3 + 2n^2)] \tag{22}$$

where the $2n^3 + 7n^2 + 3n$ term is the cost of inverting the sparse Jacobian matrix in this algorithm, $(C - LM)^{-1}$, and the $n^3 + 2n^2$ term represents the cost of evaluating the derivatives in the matrix/vector pair (M, d). Comparing (21) and (22), first order methods will be cheaper computationally iff

$$S_N \geqslant \frac{S_0[S_I \sum n_i + \sum (l_i + f_i)]}{3n^3 + 9n^2 + 3n + \sum (n_i + f_i + l_i)} \tag{23a}$$

where $\sum (n_i + f_i + l_i)$ in the denominator comes from the derivative evaluations necessary to make the Newton method work.[9]

Finally let $d = \sum (n_i + f_i + l_i)/n$ be the 'density' of endogenous variables to be solved for (i.e. that contribute to) each period's solution. We then have

$$Q = \frac{S_I d}{3n^2 + 9n + 3 + d} \tag{23b}$$

and

$$\frac{\partial Q}{\partial n} = -\frac{S_I d(6n + 9)}{(3n^2 + 9n + 3 + d)^2} < 0 \tag{23c}$$

if this 'density' factor remains approximately constant across our model and the number of inner loop iterations does not vary systematically with the size of the model. The latter is clearly true: most algorithms limit the maximum number of inner loop iterations directly, or via a loose convergence test, anyway. The former is a standard feature of *structural* economics models: the number of explanatory endogenous variables (including leads and lags) in any one equation does not increase with the number of the equations in the model — even if the number of indirect linkages through those explanatory variables does. Consequently we have our first general result:

Proposition 1: The advantage of Stacked Newton methods, over First Order methods, is lost in larger systems (diminishes as the size of the system increases). The proof follows from (23c).

How does the advantage of stacked Newton techniques fare as the density of the system increases? We look at that in two points. (23a,b) implies

$$\frac{\partial Q}{\partial \sum f_i} = \frac{\partial Q}{\partial \sum l_i} = \frac{3n^3 + 9n^2 + 3n + \sum (n_i + f_i + l_i) - S_I \sum n_i}{[3n^3 + 9n^2 + 3n + \sum (n_i + f_i + l_i)]^2} \tag{24}$$

which is clearly positive if S_I is kept fairly small. Hence the importance of exploiting, and of being able to exploit, incomplete inner iterations stands revealed. Indeed the maximum value of $S_I \sum n_i$ is $S_I(n^2 - n)$; and, from (24), $9n^2 - (S_I - 1) \sum n_i \geq 9n^2 - (S_I - 1)n(n - 1)$ is clearly positive for all values of $S_I \leq 10$ whatever the value of n. The remaining terms on the top of (24) are all strictly positive. Consequently (24) is certainly positive if the number of inner loop iterations are kept below 10 per outer loop step, and probably for a much larger number of inner loop iterations as well.

Second, (23a,b) also implies

$$\frac{\partial Q}{\partial \sum n_i} = \frac{3S_I(n^3 + 3n^2 + n) + 4 \sum (l_i + f_i)}{[3n^3 + 9n^2 + 3n + \sum (n_i + f_i + l_i)]^2} \tag{25}$$

which is unambiguously positive for any S_I, n etc. Thus putting these two steps together, we have:

Proposition 2: The general rule is that Stacked Newton techniques are preferable for solving smaller, dense equation systems. First Order techniques are preferable (computationally cheaper) for large sparse systems.

Proposition 2 is unambiguously true with respect to the density and size of the system's contemporaneous Jacobian matrix. It is strictly only true for the lead and lag components of the Jacobian if the number of inner loop iterations in the first order method is limited to 10 or less; for some number above 10, the advantage of Stacked Newton methods for some smaller systems with 'dense' dynamic structures will be lost. Hence:

Proposition 3: Proposition 2 has to be qualified. It is true if the number of inner loop iterations per outer loop step is strictly limited. But if the dynamic structure gets more dense, for a given sized system, first order methods get relatively more attractive; and the advantage of incomplete inner loop iterations diminishes (the inner loop convergence criterion should be tightened).

Thus we may rationally divide models into two categories: 1) the smaller, dense (many immediate simultaneous links) and possibly more non-linear models typical of theoretical economics analysis. And the larger, sparse (as many simultaneous links, but they are indirect with more intermediate steps) and possibly less sharply nonlinear models of empirical economic analysis. Stacked Newton methods are probably more suitable for the former group, provided the dynamics are not too complex. First Order methods lend themselves to the latter group.

To confirm this separation between small, dense theoretical models, and the larger sparse empirical models, we compare computational burdens using Stacked Newton and First Order techniques for the model examined in the comparison exercises of Hughes Hallett and Fisher (1990) and McAdam and Hughes Hallett (1999). The former reference studied the performance of First Order techniques on a sequence of 6 large, sparse, forward looking empirical models; the latter the performance of Stacked Newton techniques of 4 small theoretical models (both with the restriction $S_I = 1$). We now compare their computational cost using (23). The results are in Table 2.

These results confirm our propositions. The models clearly separate into two types, with the Stacked Newton techniques being more suitable for analysing the small theoretical models and First Order methods better for the larger sparse empirical models. Nevertheless, the superiority of Newton techniques, if any, is fairly small. In reality, it would only be preferable in the Dornbusch overshooting model out of this sample of 10.

However, these comparisons do not take account of the differences in the convergence radii, and hence the possibility of non-convergence with poorly chosen starts. Newton has a convergence radius defined in terms of a

Table 2

	Model	n	$\sum (n_i + l_i + f_i)$	d	S_0	$S_0 Q$	Newton worse if $S_N \geqslant$
Group 1:	Liverpool	32	93	2.91	20.9	0.018	1
	CUBS	88	327	3.71	21.2	3.3×10^{-3}	1
	NIESR	199	634	3 18	13.1	3.5×10^{-5}	1
	B of E	490	2176	4.44	41.1	8.0×10^{-5}	1
	HNT	908	4087	4.50	50.6	9.2×10^{-5}	1
	LBS	1252	3318	2.65	7.9	4.4×10^{-6}	1
Group 2:	Inflation	4	11	2.74	61	1.86	2
	Dornbusch	11	33	3.00	716	4.59	5
	Growth	5	8	1.60	112	1.44	2
	FLSIM	4	8	2.00	85	1.91	2

Key: Liverpool University model, CUBS = City University model, NIESR = National Institute UK model, B of E = Bank of England model, HMT = UK Treasury model, LBS = London Business School model, Inflation = Inflation — output Gap model, Dornbusch overshooting model, a non-linear growth model, a forward looking IS-LM simulation model: Group 1 from Hughes Hallett and Fisher (1990); Group 2 from McAdam and Hughes Hallett (1999).

neighbourhood about the final solution, and First Order techniques are defined by the spectrum of the real parts of the roots of the Jacobian matrix. So the two methods will not always converge or diverge at the same time; and it is here that the evidence may start to favour Newton methods a little more — the convergence of Newton methods is, in certain exercises, evidently more robust than certain versions of the First Order methods (Julliard et al.,1999). But not always (McAdam and Hughes Hallett, 1999).

Finally our contention that a model's density does not increase with model size, is confirmed; as are our results that the relative advantage of Newton methods decreases with models, but rises with model density and (but less obviously) dynamic complexity.

8. Stability issues in non-linear systems: recent developments

Recent advancements in algorithm technology have done much to promote nonlinear systems modelling. However, alongside the desire to reliably simulate, optimise and control such models there is also the necessity of checking their general stability; the two motives are linked. For example, a forward looking model that failed the Blanchard Kahn (1980) eigenvalue condition would also fail the spectral radius condition required of first-order methods — see Armstrong et al. (1998). For a non-linear model, however, eigenvalues are not defined other than those generated by a state-dependent linearisation and these will only be valid within some neighbourhood which may itself be neither stable nor representative.

How do modellers check on the stability and economic interpretation of their models? Generally, they use three approaches: extended simulation analysis, building steady state analogues of their models and local linearisation.

The extended path method of Fair–Taylor (1983) provides a way of solving for the 'true' terminal (or stability) conditions in a non-linear model by iteratively extending the simulation horizon. After the types one and two layers, the solution period is extended for a set period and solved. If the percentage difference between the latest solution and the previous one within the same solution period is below a prescribed tolerance then this (Type III iteration) is building up the true terminal conditions and solving the model consistently. Although this is useful, performing Type III iterations are not common since the usual practise is to build steady state analogues of dynamic models and use these (wherever necessary) to re-code terminal conditions. A review of the issues involved in building steady state analogues of dynamic nonlinear models can be found in McAdam (1999).That deals with the first two terms.

In the next short section we examine some of the developments in the field of checking the stability of non-linear lead models with respect to linearisation and in particular the concept of variable redundancy.

Let us first derive some background. Given a simple linear difference equation, $Y_t(1 - \alpha L - \beta L^2) = V_0$, we have the general solution, $Y_t = A_1\lambda_1^t + A_2\lambda_2^t + Y^{SS}$. Where,

$$Y^{SS} = \frac{V_0}{(1 - \alpha - \beta)} \neq 0, \quad \alpha + \beta \neq 1, \quad A_i = \frac{\lambda_i}{\lambda_j - \lambda_i}(\lambda_j Y^*_- - Y^*), \quad i \neq j$$

And

$$(Y^*_-) = Y_{-1} - Y^{SS}, \quad (Y^*) = Y_0 - Y^{SS}$$

As is well known (e.g. Chiang, 1974) roots less than one without (with) imaginary components generate stable non-oscillatory (stable oscillations) dynamics towards the steady state, and one stable and unstable root without (with) imaginary components yields unstable non-oscillatory (unstable oscillatory) dynamics.

In the case of a strictly backward looking representation the stability conditions are iff $|\lambda_i, \lambda_j| < 1 \Rightarrow \text{Lim}_{t \to \infty} Y_t \to Y^{SS}$. In the forward looking case we ensure (saddle-path) stability by imposing $A_j\lambda_j = 0, |\lambda_j| > 1$ implying that Y in its unique first period 'jump' can be written as a function of historical and steady state values weighted by the *stable* root:

$$Y_0 = (1 - \lambda_i)Y^{SS} + \lambda_i Y_0.$$

After this, it evolves according to $Y^*_{t+n} = \lambda_i^{t+n+1} Y^*_-$. In both backward and forward cases therefore, the dynamics towards the steady state are driven by stable roots. In the case of imaginary components, $\sqrt{-X}$, the model generates cyclical or oscillatory dynamics. Transforming these to polar co-ordinates, $\lambda_1, \lambda_2 = h \pm iv$; $|\lambda_1| = |\lambda_2|$, they can be re-arranged as $R \cos \phi \pm i \sin \phi R$, $\text{Sin } \phi = v/R$ and $\text{Cos } \phi = h/R$. Where R, the magnitude, is the Euclidean length, $R = \sqrt{h^2 + v^2}$.

In the case of **Macro-Economic** Systems,

$$F_i(y, x) = 0, \quad i = 1, ..., N, \quad y \in R^N, \quad x \in R^K$$

linearising around a reference base, we can re-write this as:

$$By_t = Ay^* + Cx_t \tag{25}$$

Where $B_{n \cdot n}$ is a matrix of contemporaneous derivatives with a non-vanishing diagonal and $y_{n \cdot 1}(x_{k \cdot 1})$ is the vector of the contemporaneous endogenous (exogenous) variables. In a non-linear model, B is the Jacobian. $A_{n \cdot p}$ collects all the non-zero columns corresponding to leads and lags in the model residing in $y^*_{p \cdot 1}$; where p is $\max\{L + F\}$. $C_{n \cdot k}$ collects the k exogenous variables. In a backward looking model, the transformation:

$$Y_t = \psi_1 y^* + \psi_2 x_t, \quad \text{where} \quad \psi_{1n \cdot p} = B^{-1}A^{10} \quad \text{and} \quad \psi_{2n \cdot k} = B^{-1}C \tag{26}$$

is simply the reduced form. By defining new variables to account for lags and leads >1 (in Z) among the endogenous variables, we can put the linearised model into 'state-space' form:

$$Dz_{t+1} = Ez_t + Fx_t \tag{27}$$

Where the elements of the matrices D, E and F are drawn from ψ_1, and ψ_2. To illustrate for a normalised structural model:

$$Y_t = -(\Gamma_1 Y_{t+1} + \Gamma_2 + \Gamma_3 X_t) \tag{28}$$

We have

$$Z_{t+1} = \begin{bmatrix} y^a_{t+1} \\ y^b_t \end{bmatrix}, \quad Z_t = \begin{bmatrix} y^a_t \\ y^b_{t-1} \end{bmatrix}, \quad D = \begin{bmatrix} II\Gamma_1, J_1 \\ --- \\ Q_1 \end{bmatrix}, \quad E = \begin{bmatrix} -J_2, II\Gamma_2 \\ ---- \\ Q_2 \end{bmatrix}$$

$$\text{and} \quad F = \begin{bmatrix} -II\Gamma_3 \\ --- \\ 0 \end{bmatrix}$$

Where the $J(Q)$ matrices are unit vectors conforming to the current variables in Z (the coefficients relevant where the elements of Z_{t+1} are equal to those in Z_t). Where $J_j = 1$ for $Z_{t+1,i} \subset Z_{t,i}$. Y^a and Y^b are endogenous variables appearing in the model at $t-1$ and $t+1$ respectively. And where II is a triangular matrix comprising null and identity parts to eliminate equations involving static variables (i.e. with neither leads nor lags).

In a backward-looking model, $|D| \neq 0$, and the eigenvalue problem is reduced to solving for the n eigenvalues of the transition matrix, A_1:

$$Z_{t+1} = A_1 Z_t + A_2 X_t, \quad \text{where} \quad A_1 = D^{-1} * E, A_2 = D^{-1} * F \tag{29}$$

Here Z, the state vector, contains the N endogenous variable types partitioned into $N - L$ predetermined variables and L lead variables. We know (Blanchard and Kahn, 1980) that the solution will be stable and unique if the matrix A_1, has $|\lambda_i| > 1$, $i = 1, ..., L$ and $|\lambda_j| \leqslant 1$, $j = 1, ..., N - L^{11}$; additionally A_2 is assumed $|\lambda_k| < 1$, $k = 1, ..., K$.

However, this interpretation is modified in the case of structural singularities in the macro-model's dynamics, Juillard (1999). The steady state of (27) is given if the matrix $(D - E)$ is non-singular. The eigenvalues represented by this system must then satisfy, $\lambda_i Dx_i = Ex_i$; when D is non-singular and λ_i is the eigenvalue of the A_1. When the dynamical order is less than the order of D and E, D will be singular and indeed this is common in forward looking models where lead variables are connected through static relationships elsewhere in the model. The generalised real Schur decomposition of the D and E matrices allow the creation of two orthogonal matrices Q and Z such that, $D = QTZ'$ and $E = QSZ'$ where S and T are (upper) triangular matrices with the generalised eigenvalues defined as, $\lambda_i = S_{ii}/T_{ii}$. A zero, $S = 0$, $T \neq 0$, (infinite, $S \neq 0$, $T = 0$) eigenvalue implies instantaneous adjustment to a past (future) event — in both cases there is no effect on the dynamics of the system — hence the factors which cause these are *redundant* to the system. Therefore an infinite eigenvalue — although clearly >1 — should *not* be counted in the Blanchard Kahn rule; we therefore only compare the number of explosive eigenvalues with the number of *independent* leads in our evaluation of the stability of the system. The Blanchard and Kahn rule can therefore be seen as a special case of a forward-looking model *without* redundancies.

Of course care must be taken in the interpretation of explosive roots — for example a root above one in a purely recursive part of the model (such as an identity) is no threat to stability. The redundancy methodology has only been applied to a few models — Malgrange and Juillard (1996) for MULTIMOD and McAdam (1998) for Quest II.

Of course, such techniques do rely on some chosen linearisation and might therefore seem at odds with the focus of this chapter. Notwithstanding our explanation of 'redundancies' in lead models, however, considering asymptotic linearisations is the most common method for ensuring the stability (and hence solvability) of non-linear models. There are considerable difficulties in relaying on say Fair–Taylor's extended path method since the terminal conditions that result from the model (e.g. Smith and Wallis, 1995) may be economically meaningless.

9. Small optimising models: The Stochastic Growth Model

Modelling practise often extends beyond the traditional macroeconometric accounting framework to smaller analytical forms which have their own solution methods. This is not to say that the techniques discussed earlier are redundant — for example Gagnon (1990) solves the Stochastic growth model with Fair–Taylor and Pierce (1999) with Stacked Newton. However, such models tend to be *highly* non-linear and dense and so lend themselves to other specialised numerical methods. For completeness we discuss these methods briefly.

A representative example is the 'Stochastic Growth Model':

$$\text{Max}_{c} \ E_0 \sum_{t=0}^{\infty} \beta^t \frac{c_t^{1-\tau}}{1-\tau}$$

s.t.   (30)

$$c_t + k_t - (1-\delta)k_{t-1} \leqslant \theta_t k_{t-1}^{\alpha} = y_t$$

$$(1-\rho L)\ln(\theta_t) = \varepsilon_t$$

$$\varepsilon_t \sim N(0, \sigma^2)$$

$$c_t, k_t > 0, \ \forall t, \ |\rho| < 1, \ \delta, \ \alpha \in (0,1), \ \tau > 0$$

In other words a representative individual chooses his consumption and savings plan to maximise a constant relative risk aversion utility function subject to a resource constraint with capital depreciation, a logarithmic AR specification for technology (with well behaved innovations) and positive real variable quantities. E is the expectations operator and U will denote utility. Otherwise usual symbols apply.

The equilibrium of this economy (30) is given by:

$$U'(c_t) = \beta E[U'(c_{t+1})[\theta_{t+1}f'(k_{t+1}) + 1 - \delta]] \tag{31a}$$

$$k_{t+1} = \theta_t f(k_t) + (1-\delta)k_t - c_t \tag{31b}$$

Or $c_t = h(k_t, \theta_t)$ and $k_{t+1} = \theta_t f(k_t) + (1-\delta)k_t - h(k_t, \theta_t)$. In this case we must find a decision rule for c_t and k_{t+1}; given one the other follows.

As we known from L'Hôpital's rule, setting $\tau = 1$ collapses the model to logarithmic utility. Furthermore, setting $\delta = 1$ yields the closed form solution (Brock and Mirman, 1972):

$$k_{t+1} = \alpha\beta\theta_t k_t^{\alpha}$$
$$c_t = (1 - \alpha\beta)\theta_t k_t^{\alpha} \tag{32a, 32b}$$

Otherwise, numerical methods are required to find the optimal paths. Although this solution is often used as a reference point for algorithm comparisons.[12] The Taylor and Uhlig (1990) symposium compared and discuss a number of solution methods to this model without any strong recommendation. Of course, there is always a linear or log-linear approximation or linear quadratic methods — e.g. Hansen and Sargent (1991) — but this eliminates the very non-linearities of interest. Here we discuss two solution methods to this problem which appear to dominate the literature: Parameterised Expectations and Projection methods.

The method of **Parameterised Expectations (PE)** proceeds by substituting the conditional expectation in the Euler equation that emerges from the model:

$$c_t^{-\tau} = \beta E_t(c_{t+1}^{-\tau}(\theta_{t+1}\alpha k_t^{\alpha-1} + 1 - \delta)) \tag{33}$$

which is a function of the state variables — where $c_t^{-\tau}$ is the marginal utility of current consumption and $\theta_{t+1}\alpha k_t^{\alpha-1} + 1 - \delta$, the return on capital — by a parameterised function, $\Phi(X_t; \eta)$ — here $\Phi(k_{t-1}, \theta_i; \eta)$ — of these state variables assuming consistent expectations, $E_t\{V_{t+1}\} = V_{t+1}$. Where X_t is a vector of state variables and η, the set of parameters which, after repeated stochastic drawings of σ, solves the quadratic:

$$\min_{\eta} \frac{1}{2} \sum_{t=1}^{T} (V_{t+1} - \Phi(X_t; \eta))^2 \tag{34}$$

$$s.t. \sum_{t=1}^{T} (V_{t+1} - \Phi(X_t; \eta)) = 0 \tag{35}$$

The precise functional form of $\Phi(\cdot)$ is usually modelled by some power function. Den Haan and Marcet (1994) recommend a second-order logarithmic polynomial expansion:

$$\Phi(k_{t-1}, \theta_t; \eta) = \eta_0 + \eta_1 \ln(k_{t-1}) + \eta_2 \ln(\theta_t)$$
$$+ \eta_3 \ln(k_{t-1})^2 + \eta_4 \ln(k_{t-1})\ln(\theta_t) + \eta_5 \ln(\theta_t)^2 \tag{36}$$

Of course we can always justify the approximating power of high-degree polynomials by dense set considerations: Weierstrass's theorem. Thus, this algorithms boils down to a NLS estimation problem using, for example, gradient-descent identification methods for a given set of starting parameter guesses, η_{start}. It is essentially therefore a form of agent learning — once the algorithm has converged and the given functional form satisfies the Euler equation, agents have converged on rational expectations in the sense that the errors are unpredictable.

The main problem of course is to find η_{start} sufficiently and systemically within the neighbourhood of η^*. Moreover, if the state vector is large (here it is two) the possibility of multicollinearity among the state variables will inflate $var(\eta_s)$ weakening the significance tests (i.e. more Type II errors) that den Haan and Marcet (1994) advocate as a way of furthering the accuracy of the power function approximation. Inappropriate η_{start} of course increases search costs and reduces the algorithm's relative attractiveness. This ('curse-of-dimensionality'), is an important — if prosaic — argument against polynomial approximations; indeed this is why low-order polynomial expansions are mostly used in practise.

A popular alternative to polynomial expansions to solve PE problems is **Neural Networks** (NN). These were originally motivated by beliefs about cognitive processes, whereby the stimuli of input data are analysed by a network of cells described by non-linear responses. Popular applications include GDP-growth forecasting (e.g. Tkacz and Hu, 1999) and financial time-series analysis, (e.g. Hutchinson, Lo and Poggio, 1994). Algorithms optimally estimate this system although, given the black-box nature of NN, such parameters generally have no conventional interpretation (i.e. elasticities or impact multipliers).

One of the reasons for the popularity of NNs (and related methods) is its avoidance of dimensionality problems — whilst the parameters (and cross products) of ordinary polynomial functions are exponentially increasing in the number of state variables, NN use only linearly increasing numbers of parameters and so can typically proxy just as well as power function approximations with fewer parameters (Sargeant, 1993).

An encompassing network can be written as:

$$\Phi(\cdot) = \alpha_0 + \sum_{i=1}^{I} \alpha_i \Omega_{t,i} + \sum_{j=1}^{J} \beta_j x_{t,j}$$

$$\Omega_{t,i} = h(\omega_{t,i}) \tag{37}$$

$$\omega_{i,j} = \omega_0 + \sum_{j=1}^{J} \omega_{i,j} x_{t,j} + \sum_{i=1}^{I} m_i \Omega_{t-1,j}$$

Within this, we can identify representative forms. **Simple Feed Forward**,

$$\sum_{j=1}^{J} \beta_j = \sum_{i=1}^{I} m_i = 0,$$

links inputs (x) to outputs (y) via the hidden layer.

Processing is thus *parallel* (as opposed to linear and sequential); we have both a linear combination of the inputs (equation three in system 37) and a limited-domain mapping of these through a squashing function (equation two). Thus,

$$h: R \rightarrow [0,1] \lim_{\substack{\omega \to \infty, \\ w \to -\infty}} h(\omega) = \tfrac{1}{0}.$$

Popular choices for such functions include sigmoid functions (38, Figure 1):

$$\Omega_t^i = \frac{1}{1 + exp(-\omega_t^i)}, \quad i = 1, ... \tag{38}$$

as well as Tan H, Heaviside step functions etc. Such functional forms are useful: first they model representative non-linearities (e.g. Keynesian liquidity trap where 'low' interest rates fail to stimulate the economy); second, they exemplify agent learning — at extremes of non linearity, movements of economic variables (such as interest rates or asset prices) will generate a less than proportionate response to other variables, however if this movement continues, agents learn about their environment and start reacting more proportionately to such changes.

We might also have '**Jumps**',

$$\sum_{j=1}^{J} \beta_j \neq 0, \quad \sum_{i=1}^{I} m_i = 0:$$

direct links from the inputs, x, to the outputs. Although this increases the number of parameters to be estimated, the benefit is that linearity can be considered (and tested) as a special case. For example, if the true relationship is linear then only

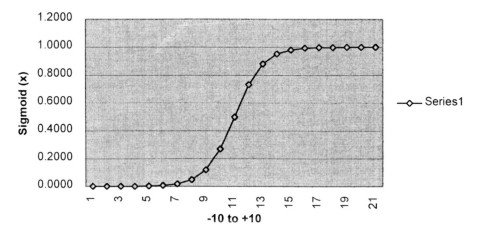

Figure 1. Sigmoid transformation $(w_i = -10, -9, \ldots, 0, \ldots, +10)$

the jump connections will be significant:

$$\sum_{j=1}^{J} \beta_j \neq 0;$$

if non-linear, then

$$\sum_{j=1}^{J} \beta_j = 0$$

whilst α and ω would be highly significant.

Finally, we have **Recurrent** networks, (Elman, 1988),

$$\sum_{j=1}^{J} \beta_j = 0, \quad \sum_{i=1}^{I} m_i \neq 0,$$

with current and lagged values of the inputs into system (memory).

Neural Networks are *highly* non-linear systems and so generally pose substantial numerical problems. Typically such systems are solved by gradient, backward propagation or genetic solution methods.

With gradient algorithms, the solution step is given by:

$$\Delta C^t = -\eta H^{-1} \frac{\delta E}{\delta C} \mid c = c^t, x \tag{39}$$

where η, the 'squeezing' parameter, may or may not be time variant (e.g. $\eta = 1 \ \forall t$; $\eta = \eta(t)$). Where C is the coefficient set and E the error function (i.e. as in 34,35).

H may be either an identity matrix (Steepest descent) or the Hessian matrix in the Newton method. Convergence however is generally quicker when using second order derivatives (White,1988) and although Hessian evaluation can be difficult (i.e. may be positive definite/non-invertible) users may apply a positive diagonal add factor or use Ricotti's approximation. Moreover the short cuts to numerical evaluation (i.e. rank updating schemes) discussed in earlier sections are equally applicable here.

The (more common) back propagation method for estimating NN,

$$\Delta C^t = -\eta H^{-1} \frac{\delta E_t}{\delta C} \mid c = c^t, x + \mu(c^t - c^{t-1}) \tag{40}$$

is similar except that the error function is evaluated at time t and not (as with gradient) for all t. There is an additional momentum adjustment parameter, μ: if $\Delta C > 0$ this will continue the adjustment in a positive direction.

For $t = 1, ..., T$, if convergence is not achieved after T iterations the process is repeated by replacing C^0 by C^T. This is known as the training epoch. For $\eta \neq 1, \mu \neq 0$ we have respectively learning and momentum. Scaling is important: too low learning makes the coefficients only adjust gradually thus extending the epoch and too large a rate leads to overshooting of the coefficients, beyond the point where the sum of squared errors can be minimised. Kuan and White (1994) show that for, $\eta \propto t^{-n}$ $(0.5 < n \leqslant 1)$ convergence is guaranteed. The learning rate itself may be endogenous:

$$\frac{\Delta \eta_k}{\eta_{k-1}} = (a - 1) \quad \text{iff } \Delta E < 0, \quad (b - 1) \text{ otherwise.} \mid a, b \tag{41}$$

The convergence criteria set is also a practical issue — too tight (loose) and NNs can over-fit in sample, missing trend and therefore forecasting badly (fail to capture the fundamental pattern of the data).

Although Back propagation methods can be improved upon — by for example expanding epoch number and acceleration strategies on the learning and momentum parameters — they tend to be slow relative to other gradient procedures that use second-order derivatives.

The problem with both methods is that global convergence is by no means guaranteed and with a large number of estimable parameters this constraint becomes more binding; hence the interest in **genetic algorithms** (GA). GA start with a population of potential C candidates which are subject to selection pressures and different genetic procedures in the search for optimum solutions. The fundamental idea — Holland (1975) — is that GA optimise on the trade off between new C searches and 'well-behaved' past C values.

Subject to a error function (34,35), we first set up a population, p, of (potentially arbitrarily chosen) C candidates (coefficient vectors) from which two pairs are chosen and evaluated for fitness (i.e. minimising the error function) and the two best (Parent) coefficient vectors proceed.

Crossover, with some given probability, is performed on each pair of the parent vectors. Following the crossover each pair of parent vectors is associated with two children coefficient vectors. With a small and declining probability each coefficient of the children vectors is subject to mutation. This is performed by the non-uniform transfer: for repeated drawings of $r1, r2 - \in [0, 1]$ — and the random numbers, $s \sim N(0, 1)$. The mutated coefficient is given by:

$$\eta = \begin{cases} \eta + s(1 - r_2^{(1 - t/T)^b}) & \text{if } r_1 > 0.5 \\ \eta - s(1 - r_2^{(1 - t/T)^b}) & \text{otherwise.} \end{cases} \quad (42)$$

Where $T(t)$ is maximum generation number and b a parameter governing the uniformity of the mutation operator. The non-uniformity shows that the algorithm is sampling increasingly in the neighbourhood of existing values. As $t \to T$ the probability that the value of the new coefficient vector value being from the current coefficient vector reduces.

After the mutation, the whole family is subject to re-evaluation and, depending on fitness score, generational replacement. This process is repeated — for replacement of the parent vectors — until the next generation is populated with p coefficient vectors.

The ELITISM stage follows, which compares new and old generations (of coefficients) and proceeds by fitness evaluation. This process is repeated for a specified number of generations, after which the coefficient vector with the best fitness initialises the (Newton) algorithm.

Of course, just as in our previous discussion a hybrid approach is feasible: we may switch off the global method after some specified point and use its last coefficient vector as input to the gradient or back propagation method. In this case however we need not necessarily switch across in divergent cases but after say a fixed number of training periods in the case of the genetic algorithm.

The final discussion is on Projection Methods. Let us return to the original Euler problem. Focusing on the Euler equation — or Euler error, (43):

$$V(\cdot) = U'(c_t) - \beta E[U'(c_{t+1})[\theta_{t+1} f'(k_{t+1}) + 1 - \delta]] \quad (43)$$

we can express the model's equilibrium as the zero of an operator, $V: A_1 \to A_2$ where A_1, A_2 are function spaces. Here the operator is simply the Euler error but it can be any generalised functional equation. Projection methods then select a finite dimensional subspace of A, which is computationally manageable and sufficiently close to the 'true' solution. Given V_hat, the approximation to V, we find an element which is a 'zero' of V. Projection methods are defined for the following algorithms, for $V(f) = 0$. We choose a degree of approximation for f:

$$f\_hat = \sum_{i=1}^{n} \eta_i \lambda_i(x) \quad (44)$$

where the choice of n determines accuracy. For η_0 compute (44) and the level residual function, $V\_hat(f\_hat)(x)$, (43) where η is chosen to minimise, as before, the weighted sum of squared residuals. For example the η may be chosen to solve the equation of projection:

$$P_i(\eta) = \langle V\_hat(f\_hat)(x), \lambda_i(x) \rangle_2 \approx 0 \quad (45)$$

Where $\langle \cdot, \cdot \rangle$ is the inner product. Common forms for $\lambda_i(x)$ include Tchebyshev polynomials (Judd, 1992, Collard and Juillard, 1999), tent functions (Coleman, 1990) or any standard polynomial.

10. Final remarks

In this chapter, we have tried to give a flavour of solution methods to typical non-linear models — both macro- and Small analytical models. Despite the number of algorithm competitions in the literature we have attempted an appraisal and synthesis of the techniques which in general have different radii of convergence and different starting properties. Indeed, we have suggested Hybrid algorithms for exploiting the convergence characteristics of algorithm types.

Often, however, these competitions leave ordinary researchers (and journal referees!) confused as to the relative robustness of different algorithms, largely due to a incoherent comparison methodology. We might therefore consider the following as 'good' practise in such comparisons:

1. **Do simulations on the same machine.** Obvious advice but not for example followed in the Taylor and Uhlig (1990) symposium. Moreover if a common technology is used, any inherent biases of that technology must be clearly spelt out. For example, a computer with a relatively large RAM will typically favour Newton Stacked algorithms over first order ones.[13]

2. **Use a portfolio of typical models.** For example in McAdam and Hughes Hallett's starts (1999), *a number* of representative models were chosen (i.e. Dornbush overshooting exchange rate model, a growth model, output gap model) rather than some single preferred test-bed — for example Juillard *et al.*, 1998 only considered MULTIMOD, Armstrong *et al.*, 1998, QPM. Such conclusions do not always appear robust: despite the favourable performance reported in Armstrong *et al.* (1998) the second author — in Poiro *et al.* (1996) found it impossible to reliably simulate MULTIMOD for this algorithm.

   However if one particular model is used for comparisons then its (linearised) dynamical properties must be made clear. For example in retrospect the structure of the Hughes Hallett, Ma and Ying (1996) resource extraction model — see the discussion in McAdam (1998) — makes it by *definition* more favourable to first order methods than two-point boundary methods such as NEWSTACK.

3. **Make the broadest possible comparison.** This would include comparisons of algorithms in accuracy, CPU time, iteration number, sensitivity to initial and terminal conditions and changes in functional forms, sensitivity of step size to perturbation size.

4. **Acceleration strategies.** Regularly solvers of non-linear economic systems take recourse to acceleration strategies and we have discussed these in this chapter. But rarely is this brought to practical use in comparisons — for example the Juillard papers did not consider the family of SOR and FGS acceleration strategies for first order algorithms nor did it investigate incomplete inner iterations (attempted with varying success in Poiro *et al.*, 1996); similarly Fisher and Hughes Hallett did not compare Newton algorithms with accelerated sparse code methods.

The introduction of non-linearity in systems modelling, as we have noted, has not generally been at the same pace in standard econometric practise. There is therefore much work to be done to improve this state of affairs. We might furthermore expect greater incorporation of non-linearity to enrich our understanding of, for example, the fiscal and monetary transmission mechanisms and propagation mechanisms within the business cycle. Without reliable solution and stability methods, this will not be possible. We hope that this chapter has motivated and contributed towards an understanding of such methods.

Notes

1. Any views expressed in this chapter are the authors and do not necessarily correspond to those of the European Central Bank.
2. The following pedagogical elaboration might help clarify this; in a first-order solution (Gauss–Seidel, Jacobi or variants) the iterative solution is of the form: $y^s = G y^{s-1} + c_t$. In Gauss–Seidel (GS) we progress by solving equations sequentially (based on first-guesses for the endogenous variables Y^{s-1} or Y^0 in the case of the first iteration) with an exogenous variable set. In other words:

$$Y_{1t}^s = \sum_{j=2}^n b_{ij} Y_{jt}^{s-1} + b_{1t}$$
$$Y_{2t}^s = b_{21} Y_{1t}^s + \sum_{j=3}^n b_{ij} Y_{jt}^{s-1} + b_{2t}$$
$$Y_{3t}^s = b_{31} Y_{1t}^s + b_{32} Y_{1t}^s + \sum_{j=4}^n b_{ij} Y_{jt}^{s-1} + b_{3t}$$
$$Y_t^s = L Y_t^s + U Y_t^{s-1} + b_t$$

Collecting terms,

$$Y_t^s = (I-L)^{-1} U Y_t^{s-1} + (I-L)^{-1} b_t$$

The iteration pattern therefore depends on values already solved for (indicated by the submatrix L for lower) and values for which there is not yet a new solution because they are solved further down in the model (indicated U for upper). This last equation can be re-written as $Y_t^s = G Y_t^{s-1} + c_t$, where $G = (I-L)^{-1} U$ and $c = (I-L)^{-1} b_t$. And so in the case of the Jacobi iteration pattern we use only past iteration values in the current iteration update whilst GS uses (where possible) the value of current iterations in solving forward. GS tends to be considered the faster of the two (Fair, 1984). However under Jacobi, convergence is independent of equation ordering.
3. For Newton, convergence is guaranteed within the first iteration of a linear model — unless un-necessary damping is applied. Damping is of the form, $y^s = y^{s-1} - \alpha (F^{s-1})^{-1} f(y^{s-1}, x)$, $\alpha \in (0, 1]$.
4. Armstrong et al. (1998) discuss cases where first-order methods (albeit a Newton-based one) fail to find a solution in a linear saddle path system.
5. This estimate of computational burden assumes matrix inversion by factorisation, see Hughes Hallett and Fisher (1990).
6. Sparseness refers to zero entries in the Jacobian, a natural consequence of the model's identification restrictions, and is given by the index, $(\sum n_i / n^2)$.
7. Strictly speaking any comparisons between Newton and First-order methods will be ambiguous in this context because they will be dependent on the arbitrary choice of start values (Hughes Hallett, 1990).

8. Almost all macro-models can be delineated as one or two huge simultaneous block and the rest pre- and post-recursive ones. For example, we found that the IMF's Multimod (Laxton *et al.*, 1998) with its 601 equations comprised 195 separate blocks comprising two truly simultaneous blocks (of order 417 and 3 equations respectively) and the rest single equation (pre- and post-) recursive ones.

9. If one of the modified Newton methods without repeated derivative evaluations is used we must divide $\sum (n_i + f_i + l_i)$ by T in (23). It is easily checked that that makes little difference to the results which follow in this section.

10. Only in extreme cases will B be singular, as with inappropriate first-guesses (see McAdam and Hughes Hallett, 1999) or if the Jacobian is near singular around the solution.

11. Additionally as Blanchard and Kahn (op. cit.) show, if $i < L$ there are an infinity number of stable roots solutions. If $i > L$ there is no solution which is non-explosive.

12. Note that here, in the stochastic growth model case, the larger the perturbation the more the polynomial approximation will dominate (in accuracy) over a Neural Network since the closed form solution is itself log linear. The polynomial expansion, is the correct functional form (although potentially over-parameterised) whereas other methods such as the neural network are only functional approximations. The results of Duffy and McNelis (1999), moreover, would suggest that this dominance appears for $\sigma \in [0.06, 1)$.

13. Although Ram considerations can limit the use of Stacked Newton methods. For example in the Quest II model, for a 'stack' of 70 years (280 periods) approximately 380 MB of RAM is required, for a simulation over 100 years (the true steady state of the model, McAdam, 1998) requires (the unavailable) 500 MB. See in't Veld (1997).

14. The problem here is essentially a two-point boundary problem accommodating initial and terminal conditions hence the 2 in '$T + 2$'.

Appendix 1

Given $p(G) < 1$ in (3) we have

LEMMA 1. (5) converges from some $\gamma > 0$ if and only if $a_j < 1, j = 1, ..., n$; where G has eigenvalues $\lambda_j = a_j + ib_j$ and $i = \sqrt{-1}$.

PROOF. Hughes Hallett (1984).

LEMMA 2. Let $r_j^2 = (a_j - 1)^2 + b_j^2$; $\beta_j = -2(a_j - 1)/r_j^2$ and $\beta = \min_j(\beta_j)$. Then, under the conditions of Lemma 1, the optimal value of γ in the one parameter extrapolation (5) is now

$$\gamma^* = \min\left(\min_k \{\gamma_k \mid \tfrac{1}{2}\beta_k < \gamma_k \leqslant \beta\}, \tfrac{1}{2}\beta_{k-1} \right) > 0$$

where $\gamma_1 = \min_{j=1,...,n}\{1 - a_j\}$ defines a_1 among the set a_j, and $\gamma_k = \min_{j>k-1}\{2(a_{k-1} - a_j)/(r_j^2 - r_{k-1}^2)\}$ defines a_k (for $k = 2, ..., n-1$). It is convergent only if $0 < \gamma < \beta$.

PROOF. Hughes Hallett (1984).

LEMMA 3. SOR is convergent for $0 < \alpha < 2$ when A is symmetric and positive definite or irreducibly diagonally dominant. Moreover SOR and JOR are both convergent, but SOR is faster for a given α, if $0 < \alpha < \beta$ and B is either a nonnegative matrix or it can be made weakly block cyclic when $\rho(B) < 1$.

PROOF. Young (1971).

Consequently the convergence (and superiority) of SOR has been established only in special cases, none of which will normally hold for a general model whose only possible restriction is that B should be real. However, we do have:

THEOREM 1: $\alpha > 0$ exists small enough such that the SOR iteration is convergent if the matrix $B = I - A$ has all eigenvalues with real parts less than unity: $\lambda_j = a_j + ib_j$ with $a_j < 1, j = 1, ..., n$, where $i = \sqrt{-1}$. But it converges only if $0 < \alpha < 2$.

PROOF: Hughes Hallett (1986).

It has been possible only to extend Lemma 3 for a few special cases; for example where A is cyclic, symmetric and positive definite, or irreducibly diagonally dominant. However much tighter convergence conditions for SOR are given in Hughes Hallett and Piscitelli (1998a,b). They are much more complicated, easy to programme but complex to manipulate analytically. Finally FGS (with SOR) can be handled by combining Lemma 2 and Theorem 1.

Appendix 2. A new Newton method for RE models: NEWSTACK

The NEWSTACK algorithm has its genesis in Laffargue (1990), Boucekkine (1995) and Juillard et al. (1998). Note Hall (1985) also attempted to treat the solution of lead non-linear models as a single large matrix inversion problem albeit with Gauss–Seidel. We can write the equations of a model as

$$f(z_t) = \begin{bmatrix} g_1(y_{t-1}, y_t, y_{t+1}, x_t, \theta) \\ \vdots \\ g_n(y_{t-1}, y_t, y_{t+1}, x_t, \theta) \end{bmatrix} \tag{46}$$

for $t - 1, 2, ..., T$ and $z_t = [y'_{t-1}, y'_t, y'_{t+1}]'$. That is to say as a stacked non-normalised equation set over time. Solving all periods simultaneously we can build up the vector of endogenous variables: $Y' = [y'_0, y'_1, ..., y'_T, y'_{T+1}]'$. We know the initial and terminal points: $f_0 = (Y_0 - Y_0^*) = f_{T+1} = (y_{T+1} - y_{T+1}) = 0$ and so the entire system forms a $(T+2)^*n$ equation system:

$$F(Y) = \begin{bmatrix} f_0(y_0) \\ f_1(z_1) \\ \vdots \\ f(z_t) \\ f_{T+1}(y_{T+1}) \end{bmatrix} = 0 \tag{47}$$

Now recall the general Newton structure, $[F^{s-1}]^{-1} \Delta Y^s = -f(y^s, x)$, which here in full matrix form becomes:

$$
\begin{bmatrix}
I & 0 & 0 & 0 & 0 & 0 & 0 \\
L_1 & C_1 & F_1 & 0 & 0 & 0 & 0 \\
0 & \cdot & \cdot & \cdot & 0 & 0 & 0 \\
0 & 0 & L_t & C_t & F_t & 0 & 0 \\
0 & 0 & 0 & \cdot & \cdot & \cdot & 0 \\
0 & 0 & 0 & 0 & L_T & C_T & F_T \\
0 & 0 & 0 & 0 & 0 & 0 & I
\end{bmatrix}
* \Delta Y = -
\begin{bmatrix}
0 \\
f_1(z_1) \\
\cdot \\
f_t(z_t) \\
\cdot \\
f_T(z_T) \\
0
\end{bmatrix}
\tag{48}
$$

where L, C and F are the partial Jacobian for lagged, contemporaneous and forward variables, i.e., $F_t = \delta f_t(z_t)/\delta y_{t+1}$ etc. The approach of NEWSTACK is to remove elements below or above the main diagonal (here we remove below but the solution is invariant to whether you end up with an upper or lower block Jacobian) and so the solution can proceed recursively either backwards or forwards. Consider the first period solution:

$$
L_1 \Delta Y_0 + C_1 \Delta Y_1 + F_1 \Delta Y_2 = -f_1(z_1)
\tag{49}
$$

Given $\Delta y_0 = 0$ this reduces to $\Delta Y_1 + M_1 \Delta Y_2 = d_1$ where, $M_1 = (C_1)^{-1} * F_1$ and $d_1 = -(C_1)^{-1} * f_1(z_1)$. For the second period:

$$
L_t \Delta Y_1 + C_t \Delta Y_t + F_t \Delta Y_{t+1} = -f_t(z_t)
\tag{50}
$$

ΔY_1 can be therefore be retrieved) and substitution Y_{t-1} for Y_1 yields:

$$
\Delta Y_t + M_t \Delta Y_{t+1} = D_t
\tag{51}
$$

where $M_t = (C_t - L_t M_t)^{-1} * F_t$ and $d_t = -(C_t - L_t M_{t-1})^{-1} * [f_1(z_1) + L_t d_{t-1}]$. We can do this for all subsequent periods but the M and d pattern is apparent. Thus the system can be recomposed as

$$
\begin{bmatrix}
I & 0 & 0 & 0 & 0 \\
0 & I & M_I & 0 & 0 \\
0 & 0 & \cdot & \cdot & 0 \\
0 & 0 & 0 & I & M_T \\
0 & 0 & 0 & 0 & I
\end{bmatrix}
* \Delta Y =
\begin{bmatrix}
0 \\
d_I \\
\cdot \\
d_T \\
0
\end{bmatrix}
\tag{52}
$$

And the value of ΔY can be retrieved through backward substitution:

$$
\Delta Y_t = d_t - M_t \Delta Y_{t+1}
\tag{53}
$$

And so in this approach it is only the M_t and d_t block, for $t = 1, 2, .., T$ which require storage. And further storage reduction can be achieved by taking into account the sparse columns of the Jacobians using conventional sparse matrix techniques — e.g. Duff *et al.* (1986), Press *et al.* (1992). As suggested operational Newton techniques often require some decomposition of the Jacobian to reduce the computational burden to manageable levels; for example in the MULTAR vintage of MULTIMOD with 466 equations and, say, 120 simulation periods we would have a Jacobian of dimension 56 852 by 56 852 (i.e., $[n^*(T+2)]^*[n^*(T+2)]$.[14] However as is shown in Laffargue (1990) the structure of this matrix is such that its triangularization can be handled recursively and so there is no need to store the entire Jacobian at any one time; the matrix stored need only in fact be of order 55 920 by 112 (i.e., n^*T by Total-Number-Of-Lead-Variables).

Appendix 3. Notes on modellers' experiences

No.	Model	Equations	Periods	Iterations	Solution Time	User Experience
1.	Faruqee *et al.* (1997)	56	180	4	1	A,C
2.	CAMOD: Mark III	92	50	5	3	B,C
3.	FR/global: Canada	161	100	7	7	D
4.	CPAM	177	100	3	156	A,C
5.	FPS	185	100	6	244	A,C
6.	Bryant (1999)	236	214	26	118	A
7.	FRB/US (1998)	280	200	5	245	A,C
8.	QPM	402	100	4	779	A,C
9.	MULTIMOD: Mark III	601	50	6	261	B,C
10.	Bayoumi et al. (1998)	625	300	7	2000	A,C
11.	DEMOD: Mark III	673	50	3	376	A
12.	ICB: Mark III	50	80	19	10	A,C
13.	Quest (1998)	1031	280	4	1373	A,C

(A) Do not currently use first-order methods because the newer breed of Newton-based algorithms are considered more efficient and reliable; (B) Occasionally use first-order and hybrid methods for highly non-linear models but mainly use the newer breed of Newton-based algorithms because they work more reliably; (C) Have experienced lots of difficulties with first-order methods in cases where Newton-based algorithms work more reliably; (D) Generally use a combination of first-order and second-order methods.
Note: We thank the respective modelling teams for their participation in this survey which is taken from Juillard *et al.* (1999).

Appendix 4. Software issues and some useful Web links

Here we include various web sites for readers interested in systems modelling and numerical analysis. These chosen packages are *by no means* exclusive — and we do not seek to make recommendations! — but they are readily used to solve typical problems. An interesting case is the NEOS Server, which freely and automatically solves non-linear problems emailed into it.

ASPEN
http://www.cs.sandia.gov/tech_reports/rjprvor/Aspen.html
GAMS
http://gams.nist.gov/
GAUSS
http://www.aptech.com/
LANCELOT
http://www-fp.mcs.anl.gov/otc/Guide/SoftwareGuide/Blurbs/lancelot.html
LBS MODEL BUILDER
http://www.lbs.ac.uk/cef/Software/software.html
MAPLE
http://www.maplesoft.com/
MATHEMATICA
http://www.wolfram.com/
MATLAB
http://www.mathworks.com/products/matlab/
MCKIBBIN SOFTWARE GROUP
http://www.msgpl.com.au/msgpl/msghome.htm
NEOS SERVER
http://www-unix.mcs.anl.gov/neos/Server/
NITSOL
http://www-fp.mos.anl.gov/otc/Guide/SoftwareGuide/Blurbs/nitsol.html
OPTIMA
http://www-fp.mcs.anl.gov/otc/Guide/SoftwareGuide/Blurbs/optima.html
SALFORD SOFTWARE
http://www.ftn95.com/offers/index.html
TROLL
http://www.intex.com/homepage/Troll.htm
WINSOLVE
http://trabbi.econ.surrey.ac.uk/winsolve/index.html

Finally, for an overview of global and regional macroeconomics models and their uses, see the comprehensive web site of Prof. Dr. Götz Uebe:
http://www.unibw-hamburg.de/WWEB/math/uebe/modelle/titelseite. html

References

Abel, A. B. and Eberly, J. C. (1995) Investment and *q* with fixed costs: an empirical analysis. mimeo, Wharton School, University of Pennsylvania.

Armstrong, J., Black, D., Laxton, D. and Rose, D. (1998) A robust method for simulating forward-looking models. *Journal of Economic Dynamics and Control*, 22, 489–501.

Ball, L. and Mankiw, G. (1994) Asymmetric price adjustment and economic fluctuations. *Economic Journal*, 104, 247–261.

Bank of England (1995) *Macroeconomic Forecasting Model, Monetary Affairs*, London: Bank of England.

Bank of England (1999) *Economic Models at the Bank of England*, London: Bank of England.

Banca d'Italia (1999) The Banca d'Italia's Quarterly Economic Model. Banca d'Italia, Mimeo.

Barro, R. (1972) A theory of monopolistic price adjustment. *Review of Economic Studies*, 34, 1, 17–26.

Bayoumi, T., Coe, D. and Laxton, D. (1998) Liberating supply: technological innovation in a multicountry econometric model. IMF Working Paper 98/95, June.

Becker, R. and Rustem, B. (1993) Algorithms for solving non-linear dynamic decision models. *Annals of Operation Research*, 44, 117–42.

Black, R. and Rose, D. (1997) The Canadian policy analysis model: CPAM. Bank of Canada Working Paper 97–16.

Black, R., Laxton, D., Rose, D. and Tetlow, R. (1994) The steady-state model: SSQPM. The Bank of Canada's New Quarterly Projection Model, Part 1, Technical Report No. 72, (Ottawa: Bank of Canada).

Black, R., Cassino, V., Drew, A., Hansen, E., Rose, D. and Scott, A. (1997) The forecasting and policy system: the core model. Research Paper No. 43 (Wellington, New Zealand: Reserve Bank of New Zealand).

Blanchard, O. and Kahn, C. (1980) The solution of linear difference equations under rational expectations. *Econometrica*, 48, 1305–11.

Blatt, J. (1983) *Dynamic Economic Systems: A Post Keynesian Approach*, New York: Armonk.

Bomfim, A., Tetlow, R., von zur Muehlen, P. and Williams, J. (1997) Expectations, learning and the costs of disinflation: experiments using the FRB/US model. Finance and Economics Discussion paper series 1997–42, Board of Governors of the Federal Reserve System (August).

Boucekkine, R. (1995) An alternative methodology for solving non linear forward looking models. *Journal of Economic Dynamics and Control*, 19, 711–34.

Brayton, F., Levin, A., Tyron, R. and Williams, J. (1997) The evolution of macro models at the Federal Reserve Board. mimeo, Federal Reserve Board.

Brayton, F. and Tinsley, P. (1996) A guide to FRB/US: a macroeconometric model of the United States, Finance and Economics Discussion paper series 1996–42, Board of Governors of the Federal Reserve System (October).

Brayton, F., Maukopf, E., Reifschneider, D., Tinsley, P. and Williams, J. C. (1997) The role of expectations in the FRB/US macroeconometric model. Federal Reserve Bulletin (April), pp. 227–245.

Brock, W. and Mirman, L. (1972) Optimal economic growth and uncertainty: the discounted case. *Journal of Economic Theory*, 4, 3, 479–513.

Bryant, R., Henderson, D. and Symansky, S. (1988) Estimates of the consequences of policy actions derived from model simulation. In Bryant, R. (ed.), *Empirical Macroeconomics for Interdependent Economies* (1989).

Bryant, R. (1999) *The Government's Budget and Economic Prosperity*, forthcoming. Washington, DC: Brookings Institution

Brock, W. and Sayers, C. (1988) Is the business cycle characterised by deterministic chaos? *Journal of Monetary Economics*, 22, 71–90.

Burns, A. and Mitchell, W. (1976) *Measuring Business Cycles*. Columbia University Press.

Burmeister, E. (1980) On some conceptual issues in rational expectations modelling. *Journal of Money, Credit and Banking*, 12, 800–16.

Carruth, A., Dickerson, A. and Henley, A. (1998) What do we know about investment under uncertainty?. University Of Kent at Canterbury, Department of Economics, Discussion Paper, 98/4.

Chiang, A. C. (1974) *Fundamental Methods of Mathematical Economics*. London: McGraw-Hill (2nd Edition).

Coletti, D. Hunt, B., Rose, D. and Tetlow, R. (1996) *The Bank of Canada's New Quarterly Projection Model*, Part 3, The Dynamic Model: QPM Technical Report No. 75 (Ottawa: Bank of Canada).

Coleman, W. (1990) Solving the stochastic growth model by policy function iteration. *Journal of Business and Economic Statistics*, 8, 27–29.

Collard, F. and Juillard, M. (1999) Stochastic simulations of forward-looking models. CEPREMAP mimeo, January.

Cooke, S., Holly, S. and Turner, R. (1998) The conduct of monetary policy when the business cycle is non-linear. University of Cambridge, mimeo.

Dennis, J. E. and More, J. J. (1977) Quasi-Newton methods: motivation and theory. *SIAM Review*, 19, 46–89.

Diebold, F. (1998) The past, present and future of macroeconomic forecasting. *Journal of Economic Perspectives*, 12, 2.

Don, F. J. H. and Gallo, G. M. (1987) Solving large sparse systems of equations in econometric models. *Journal of Forecasting*, 6, 167–80.

Dorn, W. and McCracken, D. (1972) *Numerical Methods With Fortran IV Case Studies*, New York: Wiley.

Duff, I. (1977) *A Set Of Fortran Routines For Sparse Unsymmetric Equations*, Technical Report R-8730, AERE Harwell Laboratory.

Duff, I. S., Erisman, A. M. and Reid, J. K. (1986) *Direct Methods for Sparse Matrices* Oxford: Oxford University Press.

Duffy, J. and McNelis, P. (1999) *Approximating and Simulating the Real Business Cycle Model: Parameterized Expectations, Neural Networks, and the Genetic Algorithms*, mimeo.

Elman, J. (1988) *Finding Structure in time*. University of California, mimeo.

Fair, R. C. (1979) Analysis of a macro-econometric model with rational expectations in the bond and stock market. *American Economic Review*, 69, 539–552.

Fair, R. C. and Taylor, J. B. (1983) Solution and maximum likelihood estimation of dynamic non-linear rational expectation models. *Econometrica*, 51, 1169–1186.

Fair, R. C. (1984) *Specification, Estimation and Analysis of Macroeconomic Models*. Harvard University Press.

Faria, J. (1998) The economics of witchcraft and the big eye effect. *Kyklos*, 51, 537–546.

Faruqee, H., Laxton, D. and Symansky, S. (1996) *Government Debt, Life- Cycle Income and Liquidity Constraints: Beyond Approximate Ricardian Equivalence*. IMF Working Paper 96/140 and IMF Staff Papers, Vol. 44 (September 1997), pp. 374–82 (Washington: International Monetary Fund).

Fisher, P. G. and Hughes Hallett, A. J. (1987) The convergence characteristics of iterative techniques for solving econometric models. *Oxford Bulletin of Economics and Statistics*, May 1987, 49, 2, 231–44.

Fisher, P. G. (1992) *Rational Expectations In Macro-economic Models*. Kluwer.

Fisher, P. G., Holly, S. and Hughes Hallett, A. J. (1986) Efficient solution techniques for dynamic non-linear rational expectations Models. *Journal of Economic Dynamics and Control*, 10, 139–45.

Fisher, P. G. and Hughes Hallett, A. J. (1987) The convergence characteristics of iterative techniques for solving econometric models. *Oxford Bulletin of Economics and Statistics*, 49, 231–44.

Fisher, P. G. and Hughes Hallett, A. J. (1988a), Iterative techniques for solving simultaneous equation systems: a view from the economics literature. *Journal of Computational and Applied Mathematics*, 24, 241–55.

Fisher, P. G. and Hughes Hallett, A. J. (1988b), Efficient solution techniques for linear and non-linear rational expectations models. *Journal of Economic Dynamics and Control*, 12, 635–57.

Fisher, P. G. and Whitely, J. (1998) *Macro Economic Models at the Bank Of England.* mimeo.

Friedman, M. (1986) The role of monetary policy. *American Economic Review*, 58, 1–17.

Gabay, D., Nepomiastchy, P., Rachdi, M. and Ravelli, A. (1980), *Numerical Methods.*

Gagnon, J. E. (1990) Solving the stochastic growth model by deterministic extended path. *Journal of Business and Economic Statistics*, 1990, 8, 1).

George, D. A. R. (1981) Equilibrium and catastrophies in Economics. *Scottish Journal of Political Economy*, 28, 43–61.

George, D. A. R. and Oxley, T. (1985) Structural stability and model design. *Economic Modelling*, 2, 307–316.

Gilli, M. (1992) Causal ordering and beyond. *International Economic Review*, 33, 957–71.

Gilli, M. and Pauletto, G. (1997) Non-stationary iterative methods for solving models with forward looking variables. *Journal of Economic Dynamics and Control*, 22 (8–9) (1998) 1291–1318.

Goodwin, R. (1951) The non-linear accelerator and the persistence of business cycles. *Econometrica.* 19, 1–17.

Granger, C. and Teräsvirta, T. (1993) *Modelling Non linear economic Relationships.* Oxford: Oxford University Press.

Hall, S. G. (1987) Forecasting with a large macro model incorporating pervasive consistent expectations: NIESR Model 8. *Large Scale Systems Theory and Applications*, 13, 145–55.

Hall, S. G. (1987) On the solution of large economic models with consistent expectations. *Bulletin of Economic Research*, 37, 157–61.

Hicks, J. (1950) *A Contribution to the Theory of the Trade Cycle.* Oxford University Press.

Holland, J. (1975) *Adaption in Natural and Artificial Systems.* University of Michigan Press.

Hollinger, P. (1996) The stacked-time simulator in TROLL: a robust algorithm for solving forward looking models. Paper presented at the Second International Conference On Computing in Economics and Finance, Geneva, Switzerland, June 26–28, 1996.

Holly, S. and Zarrop, M. (1983) On optimality and time consistency when expectations are rational. *European Economic Review*, 20, 23–40.

Holly, S. and Hughes Hallett, A. J. (1989) *Optimal Control, Expectations and Uncertainty.* Cambridge University Press.

Hughes Hallett, A. J. (1981) Some extensions and comparisons in the theory of Gauss–Seidel iterative techniques for solving large equation systems. In D. Charatsis (ed.), *Computer Simulation Experiments with models of Economic systems*, Amsterdam: North Holland.

Hughes Hallett, A. J. (1982) Alternative techniques for solving systems of nonlinear equations. *Journal of Computational and Applied Mathematics*, 8, 35–48.

Hughes Hallett, A. J. (1984a) Simple and optimal extrapolations for first order iterations. *International Journal of Computer Mathematics*, 15, 309–18.

Hughes Hallett, A. J. (1984b) Second order iterations with guaranteed convergence. *Journal of Computation and Applied Mathematics*, 10, 285–91.

Hughes Hallett, A. J. (1985) Techniques which accelerate the convergence of first order iterations automatically. *Linear Algebra and its Applications*, 68, 115–30.

Hughes Hallett, A. J. (1986) The convergence of accelerated overrelaxation iterations. *Mathematics of Computation*, 47, 219–23.

Hughes Hallett, A. J. (1990) A note on the difficulty of comparing iterative processes with different rates of convergence. *Computer Science in Economics and Management*, 273.

Hughes Hallett A. J. (1998) When do target zones work? An examination of exchange rate targetting as a device for co-ordinating economic policies. *Open Economies Review*, 9, 115–138.

Hughes Hallett, A. J. and Fisher, P. G. (1990) On economic structures and solution methods: or should econometricians use Newton methods for model solution? *Oxford Bulletin of Economics and Statistics*, 52, 3, 317–30.

Hughes Hallett, A. J., Ma, Y. and Ying, Y. P. (1996) Hybrid algorithms with automatic switching for solving non-linear equation systems. *Journal of Economic Dynamics and Control*, 20, pp.1051–71.

Hughes Hallett, A. J. and Piscitelli, L. (1998a), Simple reordering techniques for expanding the convergence radius of first order iterative techniques. *Journal of Economic Dynamics and Control*, 22, pp.1319–33.

Hughes Hallett, A. J. and Piscitelli, L. (1998b), A new convergence theorem for for successive over relaxation iterations. *Computational Economics*, 22, 1319–33.

Hutchinson, J. A. Lo, and T. Poggio (1994) A non parametric approach to the pricing and hedging of derivative securities via learning networks. *Journal of Finance*, 49, 851–99.

Journal of Business and Economic Statistics, The (1990, 8, 1).

Juillard, M. (1999) The dynamic analysis of forward looking models. In A. J. Hughes Hallett and P. McAdam, (eds), *Analyses in Macroeconomic Modelling*. Kluwer Academic Press.

Juillard, M., Laxton, D., McAdam, P. and Pioro, H. (1998) An algorithm competition: First-order iterations versus Newton-based techniques. *Journal of Economic Dynamics and Control*, 22 (8–9) 1291–1318.

Juillard, M., Laxton, D., McAdam, P. and Pioro, H. (1999) Solution methods and non linear forward looking models. In A. J. Hughes-Hallett and P. McAdam (eds) *Analyses In MacroEconomic Modelling*. Kluwer Academic Press.

Kaldor, N. (1940) A model of the trade cycle. *Economic Journal*, 50, 78–92.

Keynes, J. M. (1936) *The General Theory of Employment, Interest and Money*. London: Macmillan.

Kuan, C. and White, H. (1994) Artificial neural networks: an economic perspective. *Econometric Reviews*, 13, 1–91.

Laffargue, J. P. (1990) Resolution d'un Modele Macro-Economique Avec Anticipations Rationelles. *Annales D'Economie et Statistique*, 17.

Laxton, D., Meredith, G. and Rose, D. (1995) Asymmetric effects of economic activity on inflation: evidence and policy implications. *IMF Staff Papers*, 42 (June), 344–74.

Laxton, D., Rose, D. and Tambakis, D. (1998) The U.S. Phillips curve: the case for asymmetry. IMF Working Paper (forthcoming; Washington: International Monetary Fund).

Laxton, D., Rose, D. and Tetlow, R. (1993) Is the Canadian Phillips curve non-linear? Working Paper 93–7 (Ottawa: Bank of Canada, July).

Laxton, D., Isard, P., Faruqee, H., Prasad, E, and Turtleboom, B. (1998) MULTIMOD Mark III: the core dynamic and steady-state models. IMF Occasional Paper 164, IMF, Washington DC.

Levin, R. and Tryon, R. (1997) A guide to FRB/global. *Federal Reserve Bulletin*, October.

Ma, Y. (1992) Policy measurement for the dynamic linear model with expectations variables: a multiplier approach. *Computational Economics*, 5, 303–312.

Malgrange, P. and Juillard, M. (1996) Paper presented at the Second International Conference On Computing in Economics and Finance, Geneva, Switzerland, June 26–28, 1996.

McAdam, P. (1998) Dynamical analysis of economic models. Paper presented to the European Central Bank, Frankfurt, 8th December.

McAdam, P. (1999) The long run in macro economic modelling: a Guide. In A. J. Hughes Hallett and P. McAdam (eds), *Analyses In MacroEconomic Modelling*. Kluwer Academic Press.

McAdam, P. and Hughes Hallett, A. J. (1999) From here to eternity: the robustness of solution methods to imperfect starting values. In A. J. Hughes Hallett and P. McAdam (eds), *Analyses In Macroeconomic Modelling*. Kluwer Academic Press.

Metzler, L. (1941) The nature and stability of inventory cycles. *Review of Economics and Statistics*, 23, 113–29.

Meredith, G. (1998) A dynamic extension of the macroeconomic balance approach. In Exchange Rate Assessment, IMF Occasional Paper 167, IMF, Washington DC.

Meredith, G. (1998) The yen: past movements and future prospects. In *Structural Change in Japan*, B. Aghevli, T. Bayoumi and G. Meredith (eds), Washington DC, IMF.

Mills, T. (1991) Non-linear time series models in economics. *Journal of Economic Surveys*, 215–42.

Nagurney, A. (1996) Parallel computation. In *Handbook of Computational Economics*. Vol 1, (eds), H. Amman, D. Kendrick and J.Rust, Amsterdam: North Holland.

Nash, J. C. (1979) *Compact Numerical Methods for Computers*. Bristol: Adam Hilger.

Neftci, S. and McNevin, B. (1986) Some evidence on the nonlinearity of economic time series. 1892–1981. New York University mimeo.

Nepomiastchi, P. and Ravelli, A. (1978) Adapted methods for solving and optimising quasi triangular econometric models. *Journal of Economic Dynamics and Control*, 6, 555–562.

Norman, A. L., Lasdon, L. S. and Hsin, J. (1983) A comparison of methods for solving and optimising large non-linear economic models. *Journal of Economic Dynamics and Control*, 6, 3–24.

Ortega, J. M. and Rheinboldt, W. D. (1970) *Iterative Solution of Non-linear Equations*. New York: Academic Press.

Ostrowski, A. (1966) *Solutions to Equations and Systems of Equations*, New York: Academic Press.

Oxley, L. T. and George, D. A. R. (1994) Linear saddlepoint dynamics 'on their head'. The scientific content of the new orthodoxy in macroeconomics. *European Journal of Political Economy*, 10, 389–400.

Pierse, R. (1999) Winsolve tutorial: chapter three. mimeo.

Poiro, H. (1995) Faster simulation times for QPM: saving the LU decomposition indices in TROLL. Bank Of Canada, mimeo, April 4th.

Poiro, H., McAdam, P. and Laxton, D. (1996) Solving MULTIMOD with first-order and Newton based techniques. International Centre For Macroeconomic Modelling Discussion Paper No.37, University Of Strathclyde, Glasgow.

Press, W., Teukolsky, S. Vetterling, W. and Flannery, B. (1992) *Numerical Recipes in C: The Art of Scientific Computing*. Cambridge: Cambridge University Press.

Ralston, A. (1965) *A First Course in Numerical Analysis*. McGraw-Hill.

Roeger, W. (1998) Stylised facts and multi-country models. European Commission, mimeo.

Roeger, W. and Veld, J. In't (1997) QUEST Il: A multi country business cycle and growth model. Economic Papers no. 123, Directorate General for Economic and Financial Affairs, European Commission (October), Brussels.

Samuelson, P. (1939) Interaction between the multiplier analysis and the accelerator principle. *Review of Economics and Statistics*, 31, 75–8.

Smith, P. and Wallis, K. (1995) Policy simulations and long-run sustainability in forward-looking macroeconometric models. 203–221. In L. Schoonbeek, E. Sterken and S. K. Kuipers (eds), *Methods and Applications of Economic Dynamics*. Amsterdam: North-Holland.

Steward, D. V. (1962) On an approach to techniques for the analysis of the structure of large systems. *SIAM Review*, 4, 321–42.

Taylor, J. and Uhlig, H. (1990) Solving non-linear stochastic growth models: A comparison of alternative solution methods. *Journal of Business and Economic Statistics*, 8, 1.

Tkacz, G. and Hu, S. (1999) Forecasting GDP growth using artificial neural network. Bank of Canada Working Paper, 1999–3.

Thio, K. (1986) Cyclical and structural aspects of unemployment and growth in a non-linear model of cyclical growth. In R. Goodwin, M. Krueger and A. Vercelli (eds), *Non-linear Models of Fluctuating Growth*. New York: Springer Verlag, 127–45.

Varian, H. (1979) Catastrophe theory and the business cycle. *Economic Inquiry*, 17, 14–28.

In't Veld, J. (1997) Technical requirements of the Quest II model. European Commission, mimeo.

Wallis, K. and Whitely, J. (1987) Long run properties of large scale macroeconometric models. *Annales D'Economie et de Statistique*, 6/7, 207–224.

White, H. (1988) Econometric predictions using neural networks. In *Proceedings of the second annual IEEE Conference in Neural Networks, II*: 451–458, New York: IEEE Press.

Wren-Lewis, S. (1993) Macroeconomic theory and UK econometric models. International centre for MacroEconomic Modelling, University of Strathclyde, Discussion Paper No. 9.

Young, D. (1971) *Iterative Solutions to Large Linear Systems*. New York: Academic Press.

5

NON-LINEAR DYNAMICS IN THE INFINITE TIME HORIZON MODEL

Kazuo Nishimura

and

Gerhard Sorger

1. Introduction

There are two important reasons why economic growth theory became (again) a popular field during the last fifteen years. The first one is that recently developed growth theoretic models capture more aspects of economic growth than the models used in the fifties and sixties. Nowadays, models of economic growth try to explain technological progress and innovations, whereas the purpose of traditional models was mainly to describe the process of capital accumulation. The second reason for the resurrection of growth theory is that, even in its restricted sense as a theory of optimal capital accumulation, it has been found to be able to explain a much wider range of phenomena than it has previously been believed. Using results from the theory of non-linear dynamical systems, it has been shown that optimal growth theory can provide new explanations for business cycles and for international differences in growth and development. The present survey concentrates on this aspect of optimal growth theory, that is on the possibility of fluctuations and non-uniqueness in models of optimal capital accumulation. It is a selective survey on non-linear dynamics in infinite time horizon models of optimal growth, which extends and updates our earlier paper Nishimura and Sorger (1996).

The general framework for all the models discussed in this chapter is the same: one seeks a Pareto-optimal allocation in an intertemporal equilibrium model with production. The social welfare function is the discounted sum over an infinite time horizon of utility derived from consumption. The constraints of the optimization problem are given by the production technology. We discuss models with a single production sector (the aggregative model), models with separate sectors for the production of consumption goods and investment goods (the two-sector model), and general *n*-sector models. For the most part we do not allow for external effects in production, such that the models can be stated as dynamic optimization problems. In that case, our main concern is with the occurrence of optimal cycles and optimal chaos. In Sections 4 and 5, however, we introduce production externalities. This requires that the optimization models are augmented by an equilibrium condition. In the analysis of these models one is primarily interested in the possibility of non-uniqueness and indeterminacy of equilibria.

Except for Section 5 we concentrate on models that are stated in a discrete-time framework. On the one hand, some of the results we present for discrete-time models have exact analogues in continuous-time models. Discussing both versions would lead to unnecessary repetitions. On other hand, there are important differences between modelling time as a discrete variable or as a continuous variable. To obtain periodic solutions in a continuous-time model, it is necessary that the state space has at least dimension two, and to obtain chaotic dynamics the minimum dimension of the state space is three. In contrast, cycles of arbitrary length and chaos are already possible for one-dimensional difference equations. Therefore, most of the literature on complicated dynamics has used the simpler discrete-time approach and we follow this tradition.

We start in Section 2 by introducing the simplest of all optimal growth models, namely the aggregative model. Under the standard assumption of a neoclassical production function, all optimal paths converge monotonically to a unique non-trivial steady state. If one allows for increasing returns to scale at small capital-labour ratios, then there can be two steady state solutions and it depends on the initial capital-labour ratio to which steady state the economy converges. The remainder of Section 2 deals with two-sector models of optimal growth. After introducing the general framework of two-sector models, we discuss the possibility of optimal cycles and optimal chaos. The former is shown to occur in an economy in which both sectors have Cobb–Douglas production functions whereas the latter is demonstrated in an economy with technologies that are (approximately) described by Leontief production functions.

In Section 3 we consider optimal growth models in reduced form. Because these models do not specify the details of the production technologies, they have a more compact and, hence, simpler mathematical structure. We present results that characterize to a large extent the set of all possible optimal policy functions for this general class of models. Section 3.3 deals with the role of the time-preference for the occurrence of complicated dynamic phenomena. We present various results that show precisely in what sense a high time-preference rate is responsible for the optimality of complicated dynamics. A survey of some prominent examples of complicated dynamics in reduced form optimal growth models concludes Section 3.

Section 4 introduces external effects and shows how the resulting equilibrium problem can have a continuum of different solutions. Section 5 surveys a few results on optimal growth models that are formulated in continuous time. Since continuous-time dynamical systems can exhibit complicated dynamics only for a sufficiently high dimension of the state space, the results on cycles and chaos are somewhat harder to derive than in the discrete-time case. We state results on the occurrence of Hopf bifurcations and closed orbits in multi-sector optimal growth models without external effects, and on indeterminacy of equilibria in models with externalities. For both cases we use a framework with Cobb–Douglas technologies.

2. Basic models of economic growth

This section introduces one-sector and two-sector models of optimal growth. These are the most commonly used models in growth theory. We show in Subsection 2.1 that all equilibrium paths converge monotonically to a unique steady state if the production function satisfies the usual neoclassical assumptions. Subsection 2.2 shows that monotonicity still holds if the production technology exhibits increasing returns to scale for small capital-labour ratios. However, in this case there may be two steady states and the initial conditions determine to which one the economy converges. Subsection 2.3 deals with models with separate production sectors for consumption goods and investment goods. It is shown that in this class of models optimal paths may be non-monotonic and even chaotic. This result holds true even if the production functions satisfy the usual neoclassical properties.

2.1. An aggregative model with a neo-classical production function

The basic premises of the aggregative model can be described as follows: in each period t, a single homogeneous output, Y_t, is produced from the two homogeneous input factors labour, L_t, and capital, K_t. The technically efficient possibilities for production are summarized by an aggregate production function $F(K_t, L_t)$ which exhibits constant returns to scale, positive marginal utility, and decreasing marginal rate of substitution. Because of constant returns to scale, the output-labour rate $y_t = Y_t/L_t$ is given by

$$y_t = f(k_t), \tag{1}$$

where $k_t = K_t/L_t$ is the capital-labour ratio and $f(k) = F(k, 1)$. The following assumptions on the function f will be used.

A1 $f:[0, +\infty) \mapsto \mathbb{R}$ is continuous, and twice continuously differentiable on $(0, +\infty)$.

A2 $f(0) = 0$, $f(k) > 0$, $f'(k) > 0$, and $f''(k) < 0$ for all $k > 0$. Moreover, $\lim_{k \to 0} f'(k) = +\infty$ and $\lim_{k \to +\infty} f'(k) = 0$.

The labour force is assumed to be constant and the capital stock is depreciating at the positive rate δ. Per capita output may be allocated between consumption and gross investment. Denoting per capita consumption by c_t this implies

$$y_t = c_t + k_{t+1} - (1 - \delta)k_t. \tag{2}$$

The initial per capita capital stock k_0 is historically given. Social welfare over the infinite planning period is presumed to be represented by the functional

$$\sum_{t=0}^{+\infty} \rho^t u(c_t), \tag{3}$$

where $\rho \in (0, 1)$ is the discount factor. Thus, social welfare is the discounted sum of period-wise utility of per capita consumption. The utility function is assumed to be increasing and to have decreasing marginal utility.

A3 $u : [0, +\infty) \mapsto \mathbb{R}$ is continuous, increasing, and twice continuously differentiable on $(0, +\infty)$.

A4 $u'(c) > 0$ and $u''(c) < 0$ for all $c > 0$. Moreover, $\lim_{c \to 0} u'(c) = +\infty$ and $\lim_{c \to +\infty} u'(c) = 0$.

A sequence of stocks $(k_t)_{t=0}^{+\infty}$ is called a feasible path from k_0 if it satisfies the condition $0 \leqslant k_{t+1} \leqslant f(k_t) + (1 - \delta)k_t$ for all $k \geqslant 1$. For each feasible path there is a corresponding sequence of consumption rates $(c_t)_{t=0}^{+\infty}$ determined by (1) and (2). A feasible path is called an interior path if $c_t > 0$ holds for all $t \geqslant 0$, and it is called stationary if $k_t = k$ for all $t \geqslant 0$ and some constant $k \geqslant 0$. An optimal path from k_0 is a feasible path from k_0 that maximizes the objective functional in (3).

An interior path will be called an Euler path if it satisfies the discrete-time Euler equation

$$u'(c_{t-1}) = \rho u'(c_t)[f'(k_t) + 1 - \delta]. \tag{4}$$

If an interior path is optimal then it must be an Euler path. We shall outline a proof of this statement in a more general framework in Section 3 below. Under the assumptions stated above, any Euler path which satisfies the transversatility condition

$$\lim_{t \to \infty} \rho^t u'(c_t)[f'(k_t) + 1 - \delta]k_t = 0$$

is an optimal path.[1] The economic interpretation of the transversatility condition is based on the observation that, in a competitive economy, $f'(k_t) + 1 - \delta$ is equal to the interest rate and $f(k_t) - k_t f'(k_t)$ is equal to the wage rate. Using this fact it can be shown that the transversatility condition says that the present value of lifetime consumption is exactly equal to the present value of lifetime labour income plus the value of the initial capital stock.

Because we assume that the marginal utility of consumption becomes unbounded as the level of consumption goes to 0, every optimal path from a positive initial stock $k_0 > 0$ is an interior path and, consequently, it must be an Euler path. A stationary optimal path $(k, k, k, ...)$ with $k > 0$ must satisfy the Euler equation (4) and, hence,

$$\rho^{-1} = f'(k) + 1 - \delta. \tag{5}$$

We call a solution of (5) a steady state. The following theorem is the discrete-time version of a result proved by Cass (1965) and Koopmans (1965). The basic structure of the aggregative model was first laid out by Ramsey (1928).

THEOREM 1 Consider the model defined by (1)–(3). Under assumptions A1–A4 there exists a unique steady state k^*. Moreover, an optimal path from $k_0 > 0$ is a monotonic sequence converging to k^*.

2.2. An aggregative model with convex-concave production function

For this section we assume $\delta = 1$ so that the capital stock fully depreciates in one period. The production function is assumed to exhibit increasing returns to scale for sufficiently small capital stocks. Thus, assumption A2 is replaced by the following one.

A2' $f(0) = 0$, $f(k) > 0$, and $f'(k) > 0$ for all $k > 0$. There exists $k_I > 0$ such that $f''(k) > 0$ for all $k \in (0, k_I)$, and $f''(k) < 0$ for all $k \in (k_I, +\infty)$. Moreover, $\lim_{k \to 0} f'(k) \geqslant 1$ and $\lim_{k \to +\infty} f'(k) = 0$.

Recall that a steady state of the economy is a solution of $\rho f'(k) = 1$. If the condition

$$\lim_{k \to 0} f'(k) < \rho^{-1} < \max\{f(k)/k \mid k > 0\} \tag{6}$$

holds, as then there exist two steady states k_* and k^*. Without loss of generality we assume $k_* < k^*$. The aggregative optimal growth model with a production function that shows increasing returns for small capital-labour ratios and decreasing returns for large capital-labour ratios was studied by Majumdar and Nermuth (1982), Dechert and Nishimura (1983), and Mitra and Ray (1984). The following result is due to Dechert and Nishimura (1983).

THEOREM 2 Consider the model defined by (1)–(3). Under assumptions A1, A2', and A3–A4 the following is true.
  (a) The optimal path from $k_0 > 0$ is a monotonic sequence.
  (b) if (6) holds, then there exists $k_c \in (0, k^*)$ with the following property: an optimal path from $k_0 < k_c$ converges to 0 and an optimal path from $k_0 > k_c$ converges to k^*.

2.3. Two-sector models

2.3.1. The basic framework

The model we consider in this section is a discrete-time version of the two-sector optimal growth model from Uzawa (1964). There are two goods: the pure consumption good, C, and the pure capital good, K. Each sector uses both capital and labour as inputs. Capital input must be made one period prior to the production of output. Labor input is made in the same period as output is produced. Denote by $F_C(K_C, L_C)$ and $F_K(K_K, L_K)$ the production functions of sectors C and K, respectively, where K_i and L_i denote the factor inputs in sector $i \in \{C, K\}$. The production functions are assumed to have all the standard neoclassical properties.

The labour endowment of the economy is constant and time-independent. Without loss of generality we normalize it to 1. Denote by c_t and y_t the (per capita) outputs of sectors C and K, respectively, in period t. Moreover, denote by $K_{C, t-1}$ and $L_{C, t}$ the factor inputs used in sector C for the production of c_t, and by $K_{K, t-1}$ and $L_{K, t}$ those used in sector K to produce y_t, i.e.,

$$c_t = F_C(K_{C, t-1}, L_{C, t}), \tag{7}$$
$$y_t = F_K(K_{K, t-1}, L_{K, t}). \tag{8}$$

Moreover, denote by k_{t-1} the aggregate capital input, i.e.,

$$K_{C, t-1} + K_{K, t-1} = k_{t-1}. \tag{9}$$

The output of the capital good sector, y_t, represents the gross accumulation of capital, that is

$$y_t = k_t - (1 - \delta)k_{t-1}, \tag{10}$$

where $\delta \in (0, 1)$ is the rate of depreciation. Since the total labor force in the economy has been normalized to 1, we have

$$L_{C, t} + L_{K, t} = 1. \tag{11}$$

Denote by $u(c)$ the representative consumer's instantaneous utility when he consumes c units of the consumption good. With these notations, the two-sector optimal growth model is described by the maximization problem

$$\text{maximize} \sum_{t=1}^{+\infty} \rho^t u(c_t) \tag{12}$$

$$\text{subject to} \quad k_0 = k \text{ and constraints (7)–(11)},$$

where $\rho \in (0, 1)$ is the discount factor.

In order to analyze the dynamics of the above model it is convenient to express, for each given amount of capital input k, the trade-off between the two outputs by

$c = T(y, k)$, i.e.,

$$T(y, k) = \max F_C(K_C, L_C) \tag{13}$$

$$\text{subject to} \begin{cases} F_K(K_K, L_K) = y, \\ L_C + L_K = 1, \\ K_C + K_K = k. \end{cases}$$

Note that for a given amount of capital input, k_{t-1}, the relation $c_t = T(y_t, k_{t-1})$ describes the production possibility frontier in the output plane. The domain of the function T is defined as $\Omega = \{(y, k) \mid k \geqslant 0, 0 \leqslant y \leqslant F_K(k, 1)\}$. With this definition, the optimal growth model (12) can be transformed into the form

$$\text{maximize} \quad \sum_{t=1}^{+\infty} \rho^t U(k_{t-1}, k_t)$$

$$\text{subject to} \quad k_0 = k \quad \text{and} \quad k_t \leqslant F_K(k_{t-1}, 1) + (1 - \delta)k_{t-1},$$

where $U(x, z) = u(T(z - (1 - \delta)x, x))$. This is the reduced form of the two-sector optimal growth model. We shall discuss models in reduced form in detail in Section 3 below.

2.3.2. *Optimal cycles*

In the following we assume that the instantaneous utility function is linear, i.e., $u(c) = c$ and that capital fully depreciates within one period, i.e., $\delta = 1$. Then the reduced form utility function is identical to the social production function, i.e., $U(k, y) = T(y, k)$.

The Euler equation in the two-sector optimal growth model is

$$U_2(k_{t-1}, k_t) + \rho U_1(k_t, k_{t+1}) = 0, \tag{14}$$

where $U_1(k, y) = \partial U(k, y)/\partial k$ and $U_2(k, y) = \partial U(k, y)/\partial y$. The steady state k^* corresponds to a stationary solution $(k^*, k^*, k^*, ...)$ of (14). The local behaviour around k^* is determined by the roots of the characteristic equation evaluated at the steady state. This equation is

$$\rho U_{12}(k^*, k^*)\lambda^2 + [\rho U_{11}(k^*, k^*) + U_{22}(k^*, k^*)]\lambda + U_{21}(k^*, k^*) = 0. \tag{15}$$

We consider the case in which the production functions in both sectors are of the Cobb–Douglas form. Specifically, we assume

$$F_C(K_C, L_C) = K_C^\alpha L_C^{1-\alpha}, \tag{16}$$

$$F_K(K_K, L_K) = K_K^\beta L_K^{1-\beta}, \tag{17}$$

where α and β are positive numbers smaller than 1. From the first order conditions for problem (13) we can derive

$$(K_K/L_K)/(K_C/L_C) = [\beta/(1 - \beta)]/[\alpha/(1 - \alpha)].$$

Hence

$$(K_K/L_K) - (K_C/L_C) \begin{cases} >0 & \text{if } \beta > \alpha, \\ <0 & \text{if } \beta < \alpha. \end{cases} \tag{18}$$

As long as the powers in both Cobb–Douglas production functions differ from each other, no factor intensity reversal takes place. If $\beta > \alpha$, the production of consumption goods is more labour intensive than the production of capital goods, and if, $\beta < \alpha$, the converse is true. For this economy the steady state value is

$$k^* = \frac{\alpha(1 - \beta)(\rho\beta)^{1/(1-\beta)}}{\beta[1 - \alpha + \rho(\alpha - \beta)]} \tag{19}$$

and the roots of equation (15) are $\lambda_1 = (\beta - \alpha)/(1 - \alpha)$ and $\lambda_2 = (1 - \alpha)/[\rho(\beta - \alpha)]$. If $\alpha > \beta$, then both roots are negative, and if $\rho < (1 - \alpha)/(\alpha - \beta) < 1$, then the steady state is totally unstable. In this case, there exists an optimal cycle of period 2 as shown in the following theorem from Nishimura and Yano (1995b).

> THEOREM 3. Consider the economy described by the production functions (16) and (17), linear utility function $u(c) = c$, and full depreciation $\delta = 1$. If
>
> $$\rho < \frac{1 - \alpha}{1 - \beta} < 1$$
>
> then the steady state k^* given in (19) is totally unstable and there exists an optimal path which is periodic of period 2.

In two sector model with Cobb–Douglas production functions and linear utility, the sign of the cross partial derivative $U_{12}(x, y)$ is determined by the factor intensity difference of the consumption good sector and the capital good sector (see Benhabib and Nishimura (1985)). This fact together with the relation in (18) implies that

$$U_{12}(x, y) \begin{cases} >0 & \text{if } \beta > \alpha, \\ <0 & \text{if } \beta < \alpha. \end{cases} \tag{20}$$

Optimal paths in this model can be described by a difference equation of the form $k_{t+1} = h(k_t)$. The function h is called the optimal policy function and will be discussed in detail in Section 3 below. Equation (20) implies (see Theorem 14 below) that, in the case $\beta > \alpha$, the graph of the optimal policy function h is strictly increasing whenever it lies in the interior of Ω. Analogously, if $\alpha > \beta$, then the graph of h is strictly decreasing in every point in the interior of Ω. In the case of $\alpha > \beta$ the optimal policy function h becomes an unimodal map because the graph of h increases along the boundary of Ω and decreases in the interior of Ω. The global dynamics of the two sector model with Cobb–Douglas production functions is studied by Nishimura and Yano (1995b). The analysis has been extended to the case of partial depreciation by Baierl, Nishimura, and Yano (1998), from where the following result is taken.

THEOREM 4. Consider the economy described by the production functions (16) and (17), linear utility function $u(c) = c$, and depreciation $\delta \in [0, 1]$. If $\alpha > \beta$ and

$$\frac{(1 - \alpha) - (\alpha - \beta)}{1 - \beta} < \rho(1 - \delta) < \frac{1 - \alpha - \rho(\alpha - \beta)}{1 - \beta}$$

then the steady state is totally unstable and there exists an optimal path which is periodic of period 2.

2.3.3. Optimal chaos for arbitrarily weak discounting

Before we proceed, we have to discuss three possible definitions of complicated dynamics in systems of the form $x_{t+1} = h(x_t)$. Here, x_t is the state of the economy at time t (for example the capital-labour ratio) and $h : [0, 1] \mapsto [0, 1]$ is a continuous function which describes the evolution of the economy.[2]

We say that the dynamical system $x_{t+1} = h(x_t)$ exhibits ergodic chaos if there exists an absolutely continuous probability measure μ on the interval $[0, 1]$ which is invariant and ergodic under h. Here, a measure μ on the set $[0, 1]$ is said to be absolutely continuous if it has a Radon–Nikodym derivative with respect to the Lebesgue measure, and it is said to be invariant under h if $\mu(\{x \in [0, 1] \mid h(x) \in B\}) = \mu(B)$ for all measurable sets $B \subseteq [0, 1]$. The invariant measure μ is said to be ergodic if for every measurable set $B \subseteq [0, 1]$ which satisfies $\{x \in [0, 1] \mid h(x) \in B\} = B$ we have either $\mu(B) = 0$ or $\mu(B) = 1$. The most important property of a dynamical system which exhibits ergodic chaos is that the (asymptotic) statistical properties of the deterministic trajectories can be approximated by the invariant and ergodic measure μ. In other words, time averages along a trajectory $(x_0, x_1, x_2, ...)$ can be replaced by space averages in the following form:

$$\lim_{\tau \to +\infty} \frac{1}{\tau} \sum_{t=0}^{\tau-1} \phi(h^{(t)}(x)) = \int_{[0, 1]} \phi(z)\mu(dz),$$

where $h^{(t)}(x)$ is the t-th iterate of h evaluated at x, that is, $h^{(0)}(x) = x$ and $h^{(t+1)}(x) = h^{(t)}(h(x))$ for all $t \geq 1$ and all $x \in [0, 1]$. This formula, which is known as the ergodic theorem, is valid for μ-almost all initial points $x \in [0, 1]$ and for all continuous functions $\phi : [0, 1] \mapsto \mathbb{R}$.

We say that the dynamical system $x_{t+1} = h(x_t)$ exhibits geometric sensitivity if there is a real constant $\gamma > 0$ such that the following is true: for any $\tau = 0, 1, 2 ...$ there exists $\varepsilon > 0$ such that for all $x, y \in [0, 1]$ with $|x - y| < \varepsilon$ and for all $t \in \{0, 1, ..., \tau\}$ it holds that

$$|h^{(t)}(x) - h^{(t)}(y)| \geq (1 + \gamma)^t |x - y|.$$

Geometric sensitivity implies that small perturbations of the initial conditions are magnified at a geometric rate over arbitrary but finite time periods. Of course, the geometric magnification cannot last indefinitely because the state space $[0, 1]$ of the dynamical system is bounded. Note also that geometric sensitivity implies that there is no stable periodic path of the dynamical system.

Finally, we say that the dynamical system $x_{t+1} = h(x_t)$ exhibits topological chaos if there exists a p-periodic solution for all sufficiently large integers p and there exists an uncountable invariant set $S \subseteq [0, 1]$ containing no periodic points such that

$$\liminf_{t \to +\infty} |h^{(t)}(x) - h^{(t)}(y)| = 0 < \limsup_{t \to +\infty} |h^{(t)}(x) - h^{(t)}(z)|$$

holds, whenever $x \in S$, $y \in S$, and either $x \neq z \in S$ or z is a periodic point. The set S is called a scrambled set. The condition displayed above says that any two trajectories starting in the scrambled set move arbitrarily close to each other but do not converge to each other or to any periodic orbit. Thus, trajectories starting in the scrambled set are highly unpredictable over the long-run. Although the scrambled set is required to be uncountable, it can be a set of measure 0.

Let us now return to two-sector optimal growth models. Suppose that both sectors have Leontief production functions

$$F_C(K_C, L_C) = \min\{K_C, L_C\}, \tag{21}$$

$$F_K(K_K, L_K) = \mu \min\{K_K, L_K/b\}, \tag{22}$$

where $\mu > \rho^{-1}$ and $b > 1$. Note that $b > 1$ implies that the capital good sector is more labour intensive than the consumption good sector. We still assume that the utility function is linear and that capital is fully depreciated after one period. In this case the maximization problem (12) can have multiple solutions such that, in general, the solution cannot be described by an optimal policy function. Nishimura and Yano (1995a, 1996b), however, prove that optimal paths are described by an optimal policy function, if the parameter values are suitably chosen. Furthermore, they show that, under certain parameter restrictions, the optimal policy function is expansive and unimodal.[3] We are now going to describe this result. Let $\gamma = b - 1$ and define

$$h(k) = \begin{cases} \mu k & \text{if } 0 \leqslant k \leqslant 1/(\gamma + 1), \\ -(\mu/\gamma)(k - 1) & \text{if } 1/(\gamma + 1) \leqslant k \leqslant 1. \end{cases} \tag{23}$$

Under the assumption $\mu/(1 + \gamma) \leqslant 1$ the function h maps the closed interval $I = [0, \mu/(1 + \gamma)]$ onto itself. For all practical purposes, we may therefore restrict our attention to the interval I and treat h as a function from I onto itself. Nishimura and Yano (1996b) prove the following result.

THEOREM 5. Let h_I be the function defined in (23) restricted to the interval $I = [0, \mu/(1 + \gamma)]$. Suppose that the parameters μ, ρ, and γ satisfy

$$0 < \rho < 1, \qquad \gamma > 0, \qquad \rho\mu > 1 \quad \text{and} \quad \gamma + 1 > \mu. \tag{24}$$

Then it follows that optimal paths of the two-sector model with linear utility function and Leontief production functions (21) and (22) satisfy the equation $k_{t+1} = h_I(k_t)$ provided that one of the following two conditions is satisfied:

A: $\mu \leqslant \gamma$,
B: $\gamma < \mu \leqslant \min\{(\gamma + \sqrt{\gamma^2 + 4\gamma})/2, (-1 + \sqrt{1 + 4\gamma})/(2\rho)\}$.

Under condition A the decreasing portion of h_I has slope larger than or equal to -1. More specifically, if condition A is satisfied with strict inequality, then the positive fixed point of the difference equation $k_{t+1} = h_I(k_t)$ is globally asymptotically stable. If, instead, condition A is satisfied with equality, then every optimal solution from $k > 0$ converges to a period-two cycle, except for the unique path that corresponds to the positive fixed point.

Under condition B, the decreasing portion of h_I has slope smaller than -1. In this case, h_I is expansive and unimodal. It has been shown that these two properties imply that the dynamical system $k_{t+1} = h_I(k_t)$ exhibits ergodic chaos and geometric sensitivity. Nishimura and Yano (1996b) show that the set of parameter values (ρ, μ, γ) satisfying condition B and (24) is non-empty if $0 < \rho < 1/2$.

Condition B and (24) are sufficient conditions for h_I to be an optimal policy function that generates chaotic dynamics. There may be other sufficient conditions. In fact, Nishimura and Yano (1993, 1995a) provide an alternative and constructive method to find parameter values (μ, γ) for which h_I describes optimal paths and is ergodically chaotic and geometrically sensitive. This method works for any given discount factor ρ, even if it is arbitrarily close to 1. In those papers it is shown that part of the graph of the optimal policy function lies on a von Neumann facet containing the stationary state and that any optimal path is confined in a small neighbourhood of the facet. In this respect, the result is closely related to the neighbourhood turnpike theorem of McKenzie (1983), which implies that any optimal path converges to a neighbourhood of the von Neumann facet. Nishimura, Sorger, and Yano (1994) extend the results of Nishimura and Yano (1993, 1995a) to the case in which the von Neumann facet is trivial.

The above result is based on a model with Leontief production functions and a linear utility function, in which part of the graph of the optimal policy function lies on the boundary of the technology set Ω. Consequently, the consumption levels along an optimal path are at the minimum level (which is equal to 0) during the periods in which the activities lie on the boundary. In the following we demonstrate the existence of a topologically chaotic optimal policy function whose graph lies in the interior of the technology set, even if future utility is discounted arbitrarily weakly. In this case, the consumption levels are always strictly positive. For this purpose, we adopt a model with CES production functions and a utility function with a constant elasticity of intertemporal substitution. This model, which has been analyzed in Nishimura, Shigoka, and Yano (1998), contains that from Nishimura and Yano (1993, 1995a) as a limiting case. It is a parametrized model of optimal growth involving parameters $\pi = (\mu, a, b, \rho)$ that satisfy

$$\pi \in \Pi := \{(\mu, a, b, \rho) \mid b > a > 0, 1/a > \mu > 1/\rho, \mu > (b-a)/a\}.$$

In addition to those parameters we introduce a 'shift parameter' $\lambda \in [0, 1)$. We define the instantaneous utility function

$$u_\lambda(c) = \frac{1}{1 - \lambda} c^{1 - \lambda}, \tag{25}$$

and the production functions

$$F_{C, \lambda, \pi}(K_C, L_C) = [\tfrac{1}{2} K_C^{-1/\lambda} + \tfrac{1}{2}(L_C/a)^{-1/\lambda}]^{-\lambda}, \tag{26}$$

$$F_{K, \lambda, \pi}(K_K, L_K) = \mu_\lambda [\tfrac{1}{2} K_K^{-1/\lambda} + \tfrac{1}{2}(L_K/b)^{-1/\lambda}]^{-\lambda}, \tag{27}$$

where $\mu_\lambda = (1/2)^\lambda [1 + \mu^{1/\lambda}]^\lambda$. The economy defined by these functions converges to the CES economy discussed before as the parameter λ approaches 0. The following result is proved in Nishimura, Shigoka, and Yano (1998).

THEOREM 6. For any $\rho' \in (0, 1)$ there exist $\pi \in \Pi$, $\bar{\lambda} \in (0, 1)$, and $\rho \in (\rho', 1)$ such that the two-sector economy defined by (25)–(27), depreciation rate $\delta = 1$, and discount factor ρ has the following properties for all $\lambda \in (0, \bar{\lambda})$:

(a) An optimal path from $k_0 > 0$ is an interior path.
(b) Optimal paths are described by an optimal policy function which exhibits topological chaos.

3. Reduced form models in discrete time

This section deals with optimal growth models in reduced form. This means that the utility function and the sectoral production functions are not explicitly specified but that they are only implicitly given in the form of a reduced utility function and a transition possibility set. We continue to use a discrete-time framework and to exclude any external effects. The latter assumption implies that the models can be formulated as standard dynamic optimization problems. Subsection 3.1 introduces the model, discusses the assumptions, and states a few optimality conditions. Subsection 3.2 presents general results for the character-ization of the optima (equilibria) of the model, Subsection 3.3 studies the interrelation between the size of the discount factor (i.e., a measure of the time-preference of the decision maker) and the dynamic complexity of the equilibrium paths, and Subsection 3.4 discusses various examples from the literature.

3.1. Definitions, assumptions, and optimality conditions

Reduced form optimal growth models have been used by many authors because of their simple mathematical structure and their wide applicability in economics. For a comprehensive survey of methods for and applications of such models we refer to McKenzie (1986) and Stokey and Lucas (1989). In this subsection we briefly summarize the definitions and results which are needed in the remainder of this section.

At each time t the state of the economic system is described by a vector $x_t \in X$ where the state space $X \subseteq \mathbb{R}^n$ is a compact and convex set with non-empty interior. A reduced form optimal growth model consists in finding

$$V(x) = \text{Sup} \sum_{t=0}^{+\infty} \rho^t U(x_t, x_{t+1}), \qquad (28)$$

where the supremum is taken over the set of all sequences $(x_t)_{t=0}^{+\infty}$ satisfying the constraints

$$(x_t, x_{t+1}) \in \Omega \qquad t \in \{0, 1, 2, ...\} \qquad (29)$$

$$x_0 = x. \qquad (30)$$

Here, ρ is the discount factor, U is the reduced utility function, Ω is the transition possibility set, $x \in X$ is the initial state, and V is the optimal value function.

It has been illustrated in Subsection 2.3.1 how an optimal growth model in primitive form can be converted into its reduced form. We now introduce a number of assumptions that will be used in this section.

A5 $\Omega \subseteq X \times X$ is a closed and convex set such that the x-section $\Omega_x = \{y \in X \mid (x, y) \in \Omega\}$ is non-empty for all $x \in X$. The set $\cup_{x \in X} \Omega_x$ has non-empty interior.[4]

A6 $U : \Omega \mapsto \mathbb{R}$ is a continuous and concave function.

A7 $\rho \in (0, 1)$.

We shall refer to the dynamic optimization problem (28)–(30) as problem (Ω, U, ρ). Assumptions A5–A7 are standard assumptions in the relevant literature. They imply that (Ω, U, ρ) has an optimal path from any given initial state $x \in X$ and that the Bellman equation

$$V(x) = \max\{U(x, y) + \rho V(y) \mid y \in \Omega_x\}$$

holds for all $x \in X$. Moreover, a path $(x_t)_{t=0}^{+\infty}$ satisfying (29) and (30) is optimal if and only if $V(x_t) = U(x_t, x_{t+1}) + \rho V(x_{t+1})$ holds for all $t \in \{0, 1, 2, ...\}$. However, optimal paths for (28)–(30) need not be unique. To ensure that optimal paths are unique one has to add a strict concavity assumption. A very weak version of this assumption is the following.

A8 The optimal value function V is strictly concave.

If A5–A8 hold, then there exists for every $x \in X$ exactly one $y \in \Omega_x$ such that $V(x) = U(x, y) + \rho V(y)$. In other words, there exists a unique maximizer on the right hand side of the Bellman equation. Let $h(x)$ denote this maximizer, that is,

$$h(x) = \text{argmax}\{U(x, y) + \rho V(y) \mid y \in \Omega_x\}.$$

The function $h : X \mapsto X$ defined in that way is called the optimal policy function of the optimization problem (Ω, U, ρ). It maps each state $x \in X$ to its optimal successor state $h(x)$. Optimal paths are uniquely determined as the trajectories of the difference equation $x_{t+1} = h(x_t)$ with (30) as the initial condition. Under assumptions A5–A8 both h and V are continuous functions.

Assumption A8 is sometimes awkward, because it involves the optimal value function V. A sufficient (but not necessary) condition for A8 is that the function U is strictly concave. Some of the results presented below involve an assumption that is based on the concepts of α-concavity and a-convexity. If α is any real number then V is α-concave, if $x \mapsto V(x) + (\alpha/2)\|x\|^2$ is a concave function. Analogously, we say that V is α-convex, if $x \mapsto V(x) - (\alpha/2)\|x\|^2$ is convex.[5]

A9   There exist positive real numbers α and β such that V is α-concave and $(-\beta)$-convex.

In many cases the optimization problem (Ω, U, ρ) is also assumed to satisfy the following monotonicity and smoothness assumptions.

A10 If $x \leqslant \bar{x}$ then $\Omega_x \subseteq \Omega_{\bar{x}}$. The function $x \mapsto U(x, y)$ is non-decreasing and the function $y \mapsto U(x, y)$ is non-increasing.

A11 The partial derivatives $U_1(x, y)$ and $U_2(x, y)$ exist and are continuous for all (x, y) in the interior of Ω.

An optimization problem (Ω, U, ρ) which satisfies A5–A8 and A10 has a non-decreasing optimal value function V. A feasible path $(x_t)_{t=0}^{+\infty}$ for problem (Ω, U, ρ) is called an interior path if x_{t+1} is in the interior of Ω_{x_t} for all $t \geqslant 0$. It is known that under A11 an interior optimal path must satisfy the Euler equation

$$U_2(x_t, x_{t+1}) + \rho U_1(x_{t+1}, x_{t+2}) = 0$$

for all $t \geqslant 0$. This can be seen by writing the objective functional as

$$U(x_0, x_1) + \rho U(x_1, x_2) + \cdots + \rho^t U(x_t, x_{t+1}) + \rho^{t+1} U(x_{t+1}, x_{t+2}) + \cdots$$

Note that the variable x_{t+1} does not appear in any term other than those displayed above. Since $(x_t)_{t=0}^{+\infty}$ is interior and optimal, maximization with respect to x_{t+1} implies that the Euler equation holds. Conversely, if A5–A7 and A11 hold, and if a feasible path $(x_t)_{t=0}^{+\infty}$ satisfies the Euler equation as well as the limiting transversatility condition

$$\lim_{t \to +\infty} \rho^t U_1(x_t, x_{t+1}) x_t = 0,$$

then it is an optimal path.

3.2. Characterization of optimal policy functions

It has been mentioned in the previous subsection that every optimal growth model (Ω, U, ρ) that satisfies assumptions A5–A8 has a continuous optimal policy function. Thus, continuity is a necessary condition for a function to be an optimal policy function. We state this result as part (a) of the following theorem. Part (b) was proved by Mitra and Sorger (1999b) as a corollary to Theorem 10 below. It shows that by strengthening continuity to Lipschitz continuity one obtains a sufficient condition for rationalizability.[6]

THEOREM 7. (a) Let (Ω, U, ρ) be an optimal growth model satisfying assumptions A5–A8 and let h be its optimal policy function. Then h is continuous.
(b) Let $h: X \mapsto X$ be a Lipschitz continuous function with Lipschitz constant L. For every $\rho \leqslant 1/L^2$ there exists an optimization problem (Ω, U, ρ) satisfying A5–A10 such that h is the optimal policy function of (Ω, U, ρ).

Note that Lipschitz continuity of h not only guarantees the existence of a model satisfying A5–A8 with h as its optimal policy function, but that one can even require the model to satisfy the strong concavity assumption A9 as well as the monotonicity assumption A10. Weaker versions of part (b) of the above theorem (in which Lipschitz continuity is replaced by a much stronger smoothness condition) have been derived by Boldrin and Montrucchio (1986) and Neumann, O'Brien, Hoag, and Kim (1988). It has to be noted that these results as well as Theorem 7(b) have constructive proofs. In principle, it is therefore possible to find an optimal growth model for any given (sufficiently smooth) optimal policy function.

Theorem 7 shows that the set of all possible optimal policy functions contains the set of Lipschitz continuous functions but is contained in the set of all continuous functions. This obviously raises the question of how tight this characterization is. Are there continuous functions that cannot occur as optimal policy functions of optimal growth models satisfying A5–A8? Are there optimal policy functions that are not Lipschitz continuous? The answers to both of these questions are affirmative. Hewage and Neumann (1990) were the first to demonstrate that not every continuous function can be an optimal policy function of a model satisfying A5–A8. This result has been replicated in various versions by Sorger (1995), Mitra (1996b), and Mitra and Sorger (1999a). They all involve continuous functions which are defined on a one-dimensional state space and have the slope $+\infty$ at an interior fixed point. Here we present the version taken from Mitra and Sorger (1999a).

THEOREM 8. Let $h: X \mapsto X$ be a continuous function, where X is a compact interval on the real line. Assume that h has the fixed point $x = h(x) \in X$ and that there exists z in the interior of X such that $x = h(z)$. If

$$\lim \sup_{y \mapsto x} [h(y) - h(x)]/(y - x) = +\infty$$

then h cannot be the optimal policy function of an optimal growth model (Ω, U, ρ) satisfying A5–A8.

This result rules out any function as an optimal policy function which has slope $+\infty$ at a fixed point x which is either in the interior of the state space (this is the case if $z = x$ in the theorem) or can be reached along a trajectory of h emanating from the interior of X. For example, the function $h(x) = x^{1/3}$ defined on $X = [-1, 1]$ cannot be an optimal policy function of any problem (Ω, U, ρ) which satisfies A5–A8.

Now let us consider the second question posed above, namely whether every optimal policy function of a model satisfying A5–A8 is necessarily Lipschitz continuous. That this is not the case has been demonstrated by several examples. These examples also show that Theorem 8 is quite tight in the following sense: neither can any of the essential assumptions be weakened nor is the result true if one replaces the slope $+\infty$ by $-\infty$. First, it is easy to construct optimal growth models for which the optimal policy function has slope $+\infty$ at a fixed point on the boundary of X.[7] Second, an example of an optimal policy function that has slope $+\infty$ at an interior point that is not a fixed point is given in Mitra and Sorger (1999a) and, third, an example of an optimal policy function that has slope $-\infty$ at an interior fixed point is given in Mitra and Sorger (1999b).[8] Consequently, Lipschitz continuity is not a necessary condition for a function to be an optimal policy function under assumptions A5–A8.

Lipschitz continuity of h can be proved, if one adds a stronger concavity assumption. This was established under various assumptions by Montrucchio (1987, 1994) and Sorger (1994b, 1995). A version that is based on assumption A9 is presented in part (b) of Theorem 9 below (see, e.g., Sorger (1995)). If only half of the strong concavity assumption A9 is assumed, namely that V is α-concave for some positive number α (but V is not necessarily $(-\beta)$-convex), then one obtains only Hölder continuity of the optimal policy function in the interior of X. This result is stated as part (a) of the theorem (see Montrucchio (1994) and Sorger (1994b)).

THEOREM 9. Let (Ω, U, ρ) be an optimal growth model satisfying assumptions A5–A8 and let h be its optimal policy function.

(a) If there exists a positive number α such that V is α-concave, then the following is true: for every x in the interior of X there exist constants $\varepsilon > 0$ and $K \in \mathbb{R}$ such that the inequality $\| h(x) - h(y) \| \leqslant K \| x - y \|^{1/2}$ holds for for all y such that $\| x - y \| \leqslant \varepsilon$.
(b) If A9 is satisfied then h is Lipschitz continuous.

So far we have discussed the problem of characterizing the set of optimal policy functions. Now we consider briefly the characterization of the set of all pairs (h, V) consisting of an optimal policy function and the corresponding optimal value function of models (Ω, U, ρ) satisfying A5–A8. It turns out that this set can be characterized in a much more precise way. Let $W : X \mapsto \mathbb{R}$ be a concave function. The subdifferential of W at z is defined as $\partial W(z) = \{ p \in \mathbb{R}^n \mid W(y) \leqslant W(z) + p(y - z) \text{ for all } y \in X \}$. Elements of the subdifferential are called subgradients. The notion of a subgradient is one of several possible generalizations of the notion of a gradient a function which is not necessarily differentiable. If W is differentiable at z then $\partial W(z)$ contains a single element, namely the gradient. If W is not differentiable at z then $\partial W(z)$ may be empty or it may contain more than one subgradient. If z is in the interior of the domain X, then $\partial W(z)$ is necessarily non-empty. The subdifferential of a concave function may be empty at boundary points of its domain.

Let $g: X \mapsto X$ and $W: X \mapsto \mathbb{R}$ be any pair of function such that W is concave and consider the following condition $R(\rho, X; g, W)$.

$R(\rho, X; g, W)$: For every $x \in X$ such that the subdifferential $\partial W(x)$ is non-empty there exist subgradients $p_x \in \partial W(x)$ and $q_x \in \partial W(g(x))$ such that the inequality

$$W(g(x)) - W(g(y)) + q_x[g(y) - g(x)] \leq (1/\rho)[W(x) - W(y) + p_x(y - x)]$$

holds for all $y \in X$.

The following result is due to Mitra and Sorger (1999b).

THEOREM 10. Let $h: X \mapsto X$ and $V: X \mapsto \mathbb{R}$ be two given functions.

(a) If there exists a dynamic optimization problem (Ω, U, ρ) on X such that assumptions A5–A8 hold and such that h is the optimal policy function and V the optimal value function, then the following is true: h and V are continuous, V is strictly concave, and condition $R(\rho, X; h, V)$ holds.

(b) Assume that h and V are continuous, that V is strictly concave, and that there exists an open and convex set X^* containing X and a concave function $V^*: X^* \mapsto \mathbb{R}$ which coincides with V on X such that $R(\rho, X; h, V^*)$ holds. Then there exists a dynamic optimization problem (Ω, U, ρ) on X such that assumptions A5–A8 hold and such that h is the optimal policy function and V the optimal value function. If, in addition, V is non-decreasing then (Ω, U, ρ) can be chosen such that A10 holds.

Part (a) of this proposition states a condition that is necessary for the pair (h, V) to be the optimal solution of a dynamic optimization problem, whereas part (b) provides a sufficient condition. The only difference between these two conditions is that the sufficient condition requires that V can be extended as a concave function to some open set containing the state space X. Theorem 10 therefore provides an extremely tight characterization of the set of all pairs (h, V) which can arise in models satisfying A5–A8. The remaining gap between the necessary and the sufficient condition can be closed completely if one restricts the class of optimal growth models to those satisfying certain monotonicity and free disposal assumptions; see Mitra and Sorger (1999b) for details. As has already been pointed out before, Theorem 10 has several interesting consequences. The result stated in Theorem 7(b) is one of them, and others will be presented in Subsection 3.4 below.

3.3. The influence of time-preference

This subsection deals with the influence of the size of the discount factor ρ on the dynamics of optimal growth paths. There are two classes of results: turnpike theorems and minimum impatience theorems. Turnpike theory was one of the most active research areas in economic growth during the sixties and seventies and has been surveyed, for example, by McKenzie (1986). We shall therefore only state one result from this literature, just to explain the idea of a turnpike theorem. Minimum impatience theorems, on the other hand, have been derived only recently.[9] We shall discuss two such theorems, namely those which we consider as the most powerful derived so far.

Essentially, a turnpike theorem proves that, under certain conditions, optimal growth paths stay close or even converge to a unique stationary optimal growth path, which is called the turnpike. An essential assumption of most turnpike theorems is that the discount factor ρ is sufficiently close to 1.[10] Thus, turnpike theorems prove that optimal growth paths are stable and highly predictable in the long-run if the decision maker is sufficiently patient. The following result is a version of the turnpike theorem by Scheinkman (1976).

THEOREM 11. Let Ω and U be given such that A5 and A6 are satisfied and assume that U is twice continuously differentiable on the interior of Ω. Assume that there exists $\bar{x} \in X$ such that $(\bar{x}, \bar{x})$ is in the interior of Ω, $\bar{x}$ maximizes the function $x \mapsto U(x, x)$ subject to the constraint $(x, x) \in \Omega$, and from any initial state in X there exists a feasible path that reaches $\bar{x}$ in finite time. Furthermore assume that the Hessian matrix

$$\begin{pmatrix} U_{11}(\bar{x}, \bar{x}) & U_{12}(\bar{x}, \bar{x}) \\ U_{21}(\bar{x}, \bar{x}) & U_{22}(\bar{x}, \bar{x}) \end{pmatrix}$$

is negative definite and that the matrix $U_{12}(\bar{x}, \bar{x})$ is non-singular. Then there exists $\bar{\rho} \in (0, 1)$ such that the following is true for all $\rho \in (\bar{\rho}, 1)$.

(a) There exists a constant optimal growth path $(\bar{x}^\rho, \bar{x}^\rho, \bar{x}^\rho, ...)$ for the model (Ω, U, ρ).
(b) If $(x_t)_{t=0}^{+\infty}$ is an optimal growth path for problem (Ω, U, ρ) then $\lim_{t \to +\infty} x_t = \bar{x}^\rho$.

It is worth emphasizing that the critical value $\bar{\rho}$ in Theorem 11 depends in general on Ω and U. Thus, the claim that a low time-preference rate of the decision maker implies simple (i.e., asymptotically stable) behaviour of optimal paths does not hold uniformly but only for given preferences and technology.

Let us now turn to minimum impatience theorems. They are similar to turnpike theorems because they state that, in order for complicated dynamics to occur in an optimal growth model, the decision maker has to have a high time-preference rate. Minimum impatience theorems, however, are different from turnpike theorems because they do not make this statement for given fundamentals Ω and U but for a given optimal policy function, or a given class of optimal policy functions. More precisely, they state that, if a function $h: X \mapsto X$ has certain characteristics (usually related to the complexity of the dynamics it generates), then h can be an optimal policy function of a model (Ω, U, ρ) satisfying A5–A8 only if ρ is sufficiently close to 0. We shall now discuss two such results, one dealing with Li–Yorke chaos on one-dimensional state spaces and the other one dealing with dynamics with positive topological entropy on general n-dimensional state spaces. Other examples of minimum impatience theorems for specific functions h will be presented in Subsection 3.4 below.

Consider a continuous function $h: X \mapsto X$, where $X \subseteq \mathbb{R}$ is an interval. The dynamical system $x_{t+1} = h(x_t)$ is said to exhibit Li–Yorke chaos if there exists a periodic point of period 3. It is known that a one-dimensional dynamical system having this property exhibits topological chaos (see Li and Yorke, 1975). More precisely, there exists a periodic orbit for any period $p \geq 1$ as well as an uncountable scrambled set $S \subseteq X$. The importance of the existence of a point of period 3 is further demonstrated by Sarkovskii's theorem which shows that a one-dimensional dynamical system having a periodic point of period 3 has periodic points of all periods (see Sarkovskii (1964) or Block and Coppel (1992)). The following result was discovered independently by Mitra (1996a) and Nishimura and Yano (1996a).

THEOREM 12. Let $h: X \mapsto X$ be the optimal policy function of an optimal growth model (Ω, U, ρ) satisfying A5–A8 and assume that the state space X is an interval on the real line. If h exhibits Li–Yorke chaos then $\rho < (\sqrt{5} - 1)^2 / 4 \approx 0.382$. Conversely, if $\rho < (\sqrt{5} - 1)^2 / 4$ then one can find an optimal growth model (Ω, U, ρ) satisfying A5–A8 and A10 such that the optimal policy function of this model exhibits Li–Yorke chaos.

Note that a discount factor equal to 0.382 implies a discount rate approximately equal to 160%. A different way to understand the message of Theorem 12 is as follows: if the time-preference rate is 5% per year, then a discount factor of 0.382 implies that the period length of the model is roughly 20 years.

We now turn to a minimum impatience theorem that deals with the notion of topological entropy of a dynamical system. Let $h: X \mapsto X$ be a continuous map and $A \subseteq X$ a given compact and invariant subset of the state space.[11] The topological entropy $\kappa(h, A)$ of h on A measures the rate at which different trajectories of h become distinguishable by observations with finite precision as the number of observations increases. Positive topological entropy is often taken as a definition of complicated dynamics. To formally define $\kappa(h, A)$ we need a few preliminary definitions. Let T be a positive integer and $\varepsilon > 0$. We say that a subset $B \subseteq X$ is (T, ε)-separated if for any two different points x and y in B there exists $t \in \{0, 1, 2, ..., T-1\}$ such that $\| h^{(t)}(x) - h^{(t)}(y) \| > \varepsilon$.[12] Now assume that A is a compact and invariant subset of X. In that case the number

$$s_{T,\varepsilon}(h, A) = \max\{\#B \mid B \subseteq A \text{ and } B \text{ is } (T, \varepsilon) - \text{separated}\}$$

is well defined and finite. Here, $\#B$ denotes the cardinality of B. We call

$$c_+(A) = \limsup_{\varepsilon \to 0} \frac{\ln s_{1,\varepsilon}(h, A)}{-\ln \varepsilon}$$

the upper capacity of the set A (see also Brock and Dechert, 1991). It measures the growth rate of the number of ε-balls which are required to cover A as ε

approaches 0. It is clear that $c_+(A) \le n$ must hold for every compact set $A \subseteq \mathbb{R}^n$. The topological entropy of h on A is defined as

$$\kappa(h, A) = \lim_{\varepsilon \to 0} \limsup_{T \to +\infty} \frac{\ln s_{T,\varepsilon}(h, A)}{T}.$$

The positivity of topological entropy is intimately related to the sensitive dependence on initial conditions and, consequently, to the poor accuracy of long term predictions if measurements are not exact. High entropy corresponds to very sensitive dependence on initial conditions and, therefore, to the impossibility of making good long term predictions if initial states are not exactly known. For dynamical systems defined on a one-dimensional state space X there is a close relation between the topological entropy and the presence of certain periodic points. To be precise, if $\kappa(h, X) = 0$ then only periodic points of period $p = 2^i$ can occur whereas if $\kappa(h, X) > 0$ then h must have a periodic point with a period different from a power of 2 (see, e.g., Alseda, Llibre, and Misiurewicz (1993)). This shows in particular that dynamical systems exhibiting Li–Yorke chaos must have positive topological entropy. The following result was proved by Montrucchio and Sorger (1996) (see Montrucchio (1994) for an earlier version).

THEOREM 13. Let (Ω, U, ρ) be an optimal growth model satisfying A5–A8 and let $h: X \mapsto X$ be its optimal policy function. Assume that A is a compact subset of X which is contained in the interior of the state space X and which is invariant under h. Then it holds that $\kappa(h, A) \le -(\ln \rho) c_+(A)$.

This result shows that high topological entropy of the optimal policy function is only possible if ρ is close to 0. Because the upper capacity satisfies $c_+(A) \le n$, it follows from Theorem 13 that $\kappa(h, A) \le -n(\ln \rho)$. We would like to emphasize that Theorem 13 does not rule out that complicated dynamics (that is, dynamics with a positive topological entropy) can occur in optimal growth models with arbitrarily low time-preference rates. As a matter of fact, if one considers a sequence of functions $h_k: X \mapsto X$ such that $\kappa(h_k, X) > 0$ for all k and $\lim_{k \to +\infty} \kappa(h_k, X) = 0$, then it may be possible to construct a corresponding sequence of optimal growth models (Ω_k, U_k, ρ_k) satisfying A5–A8 such that h_k is the optimal policy function of (Ω_k, U_k, ρ_k) and such that $\lim_{k \to +\infty} \rho_k = 1$. Such a construction has been performed in Nishimura, Sorger, and Yano (1994) for reduced form models; see also Subsection 2.3.3 for a discussion of the construction in two-sector optimal growth models.

3.4. Examples

This subsection presents several examples of optimal growth models with cyclical or chaotic solutions. Since one can use the constructive proof of Theorem 7(b) (or its weaker version presented by Boldrin and Montrucchio (1986)) to find optimal growth models with these features, we include only examples that are interesting from a historical point of view or examples that are extremely well studied.

One of the earliest example of optimal cycles in a reduced form optimal growth model is due to Sutherland (1970). In this example the state space is $X = [0, 1]$, the transition possibility set is $\Omega = X \times X$, and the reduced utility function is

$$U(x, y) = -9x^2 - 11xy - 4y^2 + 43x.$$

There exists a unique optimal steady state $\bar{x}^\rho$ for each discount factor $\rho \in (0, 1)$. For $\rho = 1/3$ it has been shown by Sutherland (1970) that $\bar{x}^\rho = 1/2$, that $\bar{x}^\rho$ is dynamically unstable, and that the periodic path $(0, 1, 0, 1, 0, ...)$ is optimal.

Subsequently, Samuelson (1973) reported an example due to Weitzman. It was later generalized by McKenzie (1983) and Benhabib and Nishimura (1985). The state space and the transition possibility set are again given by $X = [0, 1]$ and $\Omega = X \times X$ but the utility function is of the Cobb–Douglas type

$$U(x, y) = x^\alpha (1 - y)^\beta,$$

where $\alpha > 0$, $\beta > 0$, and $0 < \alpha + \beta \leqslant 1$. Samuelson (1973) considers the case $\alpha = \beta = 1/2$, McKenzie (1983) studies the linearly homogeneous case $\alpha + \beta = 1$, and Benhabib and Nishimura (1985) analyse the general case. The optimal steady state is $\bar{x}^\rho = \rho\alpha/(\rho\alpha + \beta)$. If $\alpha \in (1/2, 1)$ and $\beta \in (0, 1/2)$ then the steady state is stable for $\rho \in (\rho_0, 1)$ and unstable for $\rho \in (0, \rho_0)$ where $\rho_0 = \beta(2\alpha - 1)/[\alpha(1 - 2\beta)]$. Under the same restrictions on α and β, Benhabib and Nishimura (1985) also prove the existence of optimal period-two cycles in this model.

In the above examples the optimal policy functions have negative slopes at the steady states. This may be checked by solving the characteristic equations of the linearized Euler equations at the steady state. A result characterizing the global monotonicity properties of the optimal policy function h in models with a one-dimensional state space is the following theorem due to Benhabib and Nishimura (1985).

THEOREM 14. Let (Ω, U, ρ) be an optimal growth model satisfying A5–A8. Assume that the state space is an interval on the real line and that U is twice continuously differentiable. Let $h: X \mapsto X$ be the optimal policy function of (Ω, U, ρ).

(a) Assume $U_{12}(x, y) > 0$ for all (x, y) in the interior of Ω. If $(z, h(z))$ is in the interior of Ω then $h(z)$ is strictly increasing at $x = z$.
(b) Assume $U_{12}(x, y) < 0$ for all (x, y) in the interior of Ω. If $(z, h(z))$ is in the interior of Ω then $h(x)$ is strictly decreasing at $x = z$.

The cross-partial derivatives of U are negative in the above examples. Thus, the optimal policy functions must be strictly decreasing by Theorem 14(b), and either no cycles at all or period-two cycles arise in these examples.

If one modifies the Weitzman example by considering the utility function

$$U(x, y) = (x - ay)^\alpha (1 - y)^\beta,$$

then more complicated dynamics may arise. This was suggested by Scheinkman (1984) and proved by Boldrin and Deneckere (1990). This leads us to examples of optimal growth models with chaotic solutions. The first to prove the possibility of chaotic optimal growth paths were Deneckere and Pelikan (1986) and Boldrin and Montrucchio (1986). In both of these papers a model with polynomial utility function was presented for which the optimal policy function is the so-called logistic map $h:[0, 1] \mapsto [0, 1]$ defined by $h(x) = 4x(1 - x)$. This is perhaps the best-known example of a chaotic dynamical system. It exhibits Li–Yorke chaos and its topological entropy is $\ln 2 > 0$. Deneckere and Pelikan (1986) used the utility function

$$U(x, y) = xy - x^2y - (1/3)y - (3/40)y^2 + (100/3)x - 7x^2 + 4x^3 - 2x^4$$

and the discount factor $\rho = 1/100$. Boldrin and Montrucchio (1986) found another example with a discount factor of about the same size. Note that $\rho = 1/100$ corresponds to 9900% discount rate. The following result shows that the logistic map cannot be an optimal policy function in any model satisfying A5–A10 with a discount factor $\rho > 1/16$. Moreover, it is shown that this is a tight discount factor restriction.

THEOREM 15. Let $h: X \mapsto X$ be defined by $h(x) = 4x(1 - x)$, where $X = [0, 1]$. Moreover, let $\rho \in (0, 1)$. The following two conditions are equivalent:

(a) There exists a transition possibility set Ω and a utility function U such that the model (Ω, U, ρ) satisfies A5–A10 and such that h is the optimal policy function of (Ω, U, ρ).
(b) The discount factor satisfies $\rho \in (0, 1/16]$.

Note that the logistic map is Lipschitz continuous with Lipschitz constant $L = 1/4$. The implication (b) $\Rightarrow$ (a) is therefore an immediate corollary of Theorem 7(b). The converse implication was shown by Montrucchio (1994) and can also be derived as a non-trivial implication of Theorem 10 (see Mitra and Sorger, 1999a).

Another prominent example of chaotic dynamics is the tent map $h(x) = 1 - |2x - 1|$ defined on $X = [0, 1]$. This function has properties very similar to the logistic map: it exhibits Li–Yorke chaos, its topological entropy is $\ln 2 > 0$, and it is topologically equivalent to the logistic map.[13] The tent map, however, can arise as an optimal policy function in models with larger discount factors as shown by the following result (taken from Mitra and Sorger, 1999a).

THEOREM 16. Let $h: X \mapsto X$ be defined by $h(x) = 1 - |2x - 1|$, where $X = [0, 1]$. Moreover, let $\rho \in (0, 1)$. The following two conditions are equivalent:

(a) There exist a transition possibility set Ω and a utility function U such that the model (Ω, U, ρ) satisfies A5–A8 and such that h is the optimal policy function of (Ω, U, ρ).
(b) The discount factor satisfies $\rho \in (0, 1/4]$.

4. External effects and indeterminacy

So far we have considered models without any externalities. The presence of external effects may have a substantial influence on the dynamic properties of equilibrium paths. Most notably, it may render equilibrium paths indeterminate. By indeterminacy we understand the existence of a continuum of equilibrium paths sharing a common initial condition. Thus, indeterminacy is a particularly strong form of non-uniqueness. This section first introduces external effects and indeterminacy by a simple example of a one-sector economy and then discusses a number of results from the literature concerning indeterminacy.

Consider the aggregate optimal growth model discussed in Subsection 2.1 above but assume that there is a production externality implying that output of each firm depends on its own capital stock and on the average capital stock of all firms. Formally, we suppose that period-t output of the representative firm is given by $f(x_t, \bar{x}_t)$, where x_t denotes its own capital stock and $\bar{x}_t$ is the average capital stock. Given any sequence $(\bar{x}_t)_{t=0}^{+\infty}$ an equilibrium relative to $(\bar{x}_t)_{t=0}^{+\infty}$ is a solution to the following dynamic optimization problem:

$$\text{maximize} \sum_{t=0}^{+\infty} \rho^t u(c_t) \tag{31}$$

subject to

$$c_t + x_{t+1} \leqslant f(x_t, \bar{x}_t), \qquad c_t \geqslant 0, \qquad x_0 = x. \tag{32}$$

Maximization is carried out with respect to sequences of consumption $(c_t)_{t=0}^{+\infty}$ and capital $(x_t)_{t=0}^{+\infty}$ taking $(\bar{x}_t)_{t=0}^{+\infty}$ as given. Since x_t is the capital stock of the representative firm and $\bar{x}_t$ is the average capital stock, in equilibrium it must hold that $x_t = \bar{x}_t$ for all t. Defining the reduced utility function $U(x, y; \bar{x}) = u(f(x, \bar{x}) - y)$ and the transition possibility set $\Omega(\bar{x}) = \{(x, y) \mid x \geqslant 0, 0 \leqslant y \leqslant f(x, \bar{x})\}$ one can rewrite the optimization problem (31)–(32) in reduced form as

$$\text{maximize} \sum_{t=0}^{+\infty} \rho^t U(x_t, x_{t+1}; \bar{x}_t)$$

$$\text{subject to} \quad (x_t, x_{t+1}) \in \Omega(\bar{x}_t), \qquad x_0 = x.$$

Writing down the optimality conditions for an interior solution and using the externality condition $x_t = \bar{x}_t$ one obtains

$$U_2(x_t, x_{t+1}; x_t) + \rho U_1(x_{t+1}, x_{t+2}; x_{t+1}) = 0, \tag{33}$$

$$\lim_{t \to +\infty} \rho^t U_1(x_t, x_{t+1}; x_t) x_t = 0. \tag{34}$$

Let us start by assuming that the Euler equation (33) has a stationary solution x^* and that the initial state $x = x_0$ coincides with x^*. Since (33) is a second-order equation, different choices of x_1 lead to different trajectories of the Euler equation. If x^* is a locally asymptotically stable solution of (33), that is, if the linearization of (33) around x^* has two roots inside the unit circle, then it follows that every value x_1 sufficiently close to x^* generates a trajectory that converges to x^*. It is obvious that the transversatility condition (34) is satisfied along all of these trajectories and one can conclude that there exists a continuum of equilibrium paths. The characteristic equation of the linearization of (33) around x^* is

$$\lambda^2 + \lambda \left(\frac{U_{22}^*}{\rho U_{12}^*} + \frac{U_{11}^* + U_{13}^*}{U_{12}^*} \right) + \frac{1}{\rho} + \frac{U_{23}^*}{\rho U_{12}^*} = 0,$$

where U_{ij}^* denotes $U_{ij}(x^*, x^*; x^*)$. A necessary and sufficient condition for both roots of this equation to be inside the unit circle is that the following three inequalities hold:

$$\frac{1}{\rho} + \frac{U_{23}^*}{\rho U_{12}^*} < 1,$$

$$\frac{1 + \rho}{\rho} + \frac{U_{23}^* + U_{22}^*}{\rho U_{12}^*} + \frac{U_{11}^* + U_{13}^*}{U_{12}^*} > 0, \tag{35}$$

$$\frac{1 + \rho}{\rho} + \frac{U_{23}^* - U_{22}^*}{\rho U_{12}^*} - \frac{U_{11}^* + U_{13}^*}{U_{12}^*} > 0.$$

If there is no external effect, then $U_{13}^* = U_{23}^* = 0$ and it follows that the first inequality cannot be satisfied because $\rho \in (0, 1)$. Thus, externalities are necessary to generate the kind of indeterminacy we have described above. If one allows for externalities, then the conditions in (35) can easily be satisfied. For example, if $\rho = 3/4$, $U_1^* = 8/3$, $U_2^* = -2$, $U_{11}^* = -34/9$ $U_{12}^* = 4/3$, $U_{13}^* = 16/3$, $U_{22}^* = -1$, and $U_{23}^* = -1$ then the Euler equation (33) as well as the stability conditions in (35) hold. Primitives u and f which generate a reduced utility function with these properties are, for example, all functions satisfying $u'(1) = 2$, $u''(1) = -1$, $f(1, 1) = 2$, $f_1(1, 1) = 4/3$, $f_2(1, 1) = -1$, $f_{11}(1, 1) = -1$, and $f_{12}(1, 1) = 2$.[14] In this example, which is due to Kehoe (1991), the external effect is negative because $f_2(1, 1) < 0$. Boldrin and Rustichini (1994) show that in the case of a positive externality (that is, if $f_2(x^*, x^*) \geq 0$), any stationary solution x^* is locally unique such that indeterminacy cannot occur.

The production externality in the above example is modelled by assuming that the average capital stock influences output. This is the most commonly assumed form of an external effect in models of capital accumulation (especially in the literature on endogenous growth). Examples of indeterminacy in the case of slightly different production externalities have been constructed by Spear (1991) and Kehoe, Levine, and Romer (1991). The former paper assumes that aggregate savings of all agents affect the production of output. This implies that tomorrow's aggregate capital stock appears as an argument of the production function for today's output. Kehoe, Levine, and Romer (1991), on the other hand, assumed that average consumption influences output.

Models with positive external effects of the kind discussed above have been used extensively in the endogenous growth literature, because they can help to explain positive long-run growth of per-capita output. Equilibria along which per-capita output, consumption, and capital are growing at constant rates are termed balanced growth paths. Boldrin and Rustichini (1994) have shown that balanced growth paths are determinate in a one-sector model if certain reasonable assumptions on the production function and the utility function hold. If negative externalities are allowed, then again indeterminacy can arise.

Although the discussion so far has focussed on one-sector models, the issue of indeterminacy is even more relevant for multi-sector models of capital accumulation. Boldrin and Rustichini (1994) prove that indeterminate equilibria may exist in two-sector models under standard assumptions on preferences and technology even in the case of positive externalities. They deal with indeterminacy of stationary solutions and balanced growth paths. The main reason why indeterminacy occurs in their model is that the social production function exhibits increasing returns to scale. Benhabib, Nishimura, and Venditti (1999) and Nishimura and Venditti (1999) show that, in a multi-sector optimal growth model with positive externalities, indeterminacy may even arise under constant or decreasing returns to scale. The result on constant returns to scale technologies is a discrete-time analogue of a corresponding result for continuous-time models by Benhabib and Nishimura (1998a) (which we will discuss in Section 5 below).

Externalities may also be a cause of chaotic dynamics. Boldrin, Nishimura, Shigoka, and Yano (1999) derived a set of conditions under which equilibrium paths in an endogenous growth model are indeterminate and behave chaotically.

Indeterminate equilibria have been found in a variety of other models, too. Models with overlapping generations (Kehoe and Levine, 1985), models with finance constraints (Woodford, 1986 or Sorger, 1994a), and money-in-the-utility-function models (Matsuyama, 1990) are just a few examples. We shall further discuss indeterminacy in the following section using a continuous-time framework.

5. Continuous-time models

So far we have concentrated on models which are formulated in discrete time. Some of the results that we have presented do only hold in this framework whereas others have continuous time counterparts. In this section we briefly discuss some of the work that has been done on infinite horizon models in continuous time. In one-sector growth models optimal paths converge to an unique steady state (see Cass, 1965 and Koopmans, 1965). This result holds in the continuous-time model as well as the discrete-time model. In the two-sector growth model with a unique steady state, optimal paths converge to the steady state in the continuous time framework, while optimal paths may be chaotic in the discrete-time framework. The global convergence in the continuous-time framework was proved by Shrinivasan (1964) and Uzawa (1964).

The main obstacle in constructing continuous-time economic models which generate complicated dynamics is the necessity of a high-dimensional state space.

Whereas cycles of arbitrary length and chaos are possible for one-dimensional difference equations, they are not possible in one-dimensional differential equations. As a matter of fact, a differential equation defined on a one-dimensional state space can only have monotonic solutions (at least if solutions are unique). For cycles to be possible a dimension of at least two is required, and for chaotic dynamics one needs at least a three-dimensional system.

Another difficulty is the lack of simple sufficient conditions for the existence of chaotic dynamics. Existence theorems for periodic solutions, on the other hand, are easier to verify. In particular one can apply the Hopf bifurcation theorem, which basically only requires that a pair of complex conjugate eigenvalues crosses the imaginary axis as one of the model parameters is varied. The first application of this theorem in the context of an infinite horizon optimal growth model was presented in Benhabib and Nishimura (1979). In the framework of multi-sector capital accumulation models they studied general conditions for a Hopf bifurcation to occur. We shall present the multi-sector model with Cobb–Douglas technologies to illustrate the source of complex dynamics.

5.1. Basic framework

The material presented in this subsection is taken from Benhabib and Nishimura (1979). We consider an economy with one consumption good sector and n capital good sectors. The production inputs are the n capital goods as well as labour. The total supply of labour in the economy at time t, $x_0(t)$, is constant and normalized to 1, that is $x_0(t) = 1$ for all t. A representative agent optimizes an additively separable utility function with discount rate $\rho > 0$. The objective functional is therefore

$$\int_0^{+\infty} e^{-\rho t} u(y_0(t)) \, dt, \tag{36}$$

where u is a twice continuously differentiable, concave, and increasing instantaneous utility function, and $y_0(t)$ denotes the consumption rate at time t. The constraints of the problem are

$$y_j(t) = e_j \prod_{i=0}^{n} x_{ij}(t)^{\beta_{ij}} \qquad j = 0, 1, ..., n, \tag{37}$$

$$\frac{dx_i(t)}{dt} = y_i(t) - \delta x_i(t) \qquad i = 1, 2, ..., n, \tag{38}$$

$$\sum_{j=0}^{n} x_{ij}(t) = x_i(t) \qquad i = 0, 1, ..., 2n. \tag{39}$$

Here, $x_i(t)$ is the stock of the i-th capital good if $i \in \{1, 2, ..., n\}$, and $x_0(t) = 1$ is the labour supply. Moreover, $x_{ij}(t)$ is the allocation of input factor i to the production of the j-th good for all $j = 0, 1, ..., n$ and all $i = 0, 1, ..., n$. The constant $\delta > 0$ is the depreciation rate. To begin with, e_j is assumed to be constant for all j. In a later subsection we shall introduce a production externality by assuming that e_j depends on the variables $x_{ij}(t)$. The parameters β_{ij} are assumed to be non-negative with $\sum_{i=0}^{n} \beta_{ij} = 1$ such that all production functions have constant returns to scale.

Equations (38) describe the accumulation of the n capital goods $x_i(t)$. The initial values of the stocks at time 0, $x_i(0)$, are given. The optimization is with respect to the inputs $x_{ij}(t)$ for all $i, j \in \{0, 1, ..., n\}$ and all $t \geqslant 0$. The Hamiltonian function associated with problem (36) is

$$H = u\left(e_0 \prod_{i=0}^{n} x_{i0}^{\beta_{i0}} \right) + \sum_{j=1}^{n} p_j \left(e_j \prod_{i=0}^{n} x_{ij}^{\beta_{ij}} - \delta x_j \right) + \sum_{i=0}^{n} w_i \left(x_i - \sum_{j=0}^{n} x_{ij} \right).$$

Here p_j and w_i are costate variables and Lagrange multipliers, representing the utility prices of the capital goods and their rentals, respectively. The first order conditions for the maximization of the Hamiltonian function are

$$w_s(t) = p_j(t)\beta_{sj}e_j x_{sj}(t)^{-1} \prod_{i=0}^{n} x_{ij}(t)^{\beta_{ij}}$$

$$= u'(y_0(t))\beta_{s0}e_0 x_{s0}(t)^{-1} \prod_{i=0}^{n} x_{i0}(t)^{\beta_{i0}} \tag{40}$$

for $j = 1, 2, ..., n$, all $s = 0, , ..., n$, and all $t > 0$.

From now on we shall assume that the utility function is linear, i.e., $u(y_0) = y_0$. It can be shown shown that under this assumption and under a constant returns Cobb–Douglas technology, the static efficiency conditions given by (40) imply that factor rentals and outputs are uniquely determined by output prices, and that outputs can be expressed as a function of aggregate stocks and prices. Therefore, taking the consumption good as the numeraire, we can express factor rentals as $w_i(p)$ and outputs as $y_i(x, p)$, where $x = (x_1, x_2, ..., x_n)$ and $p = (p_1, p_2, ..., p_n)$. The necessary conditions for the optimal solution of problem (36) are given by the following equations of motion:

$$\frac{dx_i(t)}{dt} = \partial H/\partial p_i(t) = y_i(x(t), p(t)) - \delta x_i(t) \qquad i = 1, 2, ..., n, \tag{41}$$

$$\frac{dp_i(t)}{dt} = \rho p_i(t) - \partial H/\partial x_i(t) = (\rho + \delta)p_i(t) - w_i(p(t)) \qquad i = 1, 2, ..., n. \tag{42}$$

It is straightforward to show that under our assumptions the system (41)–(42) has a unique steady state (x^*, p^*). Linearizing around the steady state we obtain

$$
\begin{bmatrix} dx(t)/dt \\ dp(t)/dt \end{bmatrix} = \begin{bmatrix} \left[\dfrac{\partial y(x^*, p^*)}{\partial x}\right] - \delta I & \left[\dfrac{\partial y(x^*, p^*)}{\partial p}\right] \\[3ex] [0] & -\left[\dfrac{\partial w(p^*)}{\partial p}\right] + (\rho + \delta)I \end{bmatrix} \begin{bmatrix} x(t) - x^* \\ p(t) - p^* \end{bmatrix}
$$

$$
= J \begin{bmatrix} x(t) - x^* \\ p(t) - p^* \end{bmatrix}. \tag{43}
$$

We note that the matrix J is quasi-triangular, so that its roots are the roots of

$$
\left[\frac{\partial y(x^*, p^*)}{\partial x}\right] - \delta I \quad \text{and} \quad -\left[\frac{\partial w(p^*)}{\partial p}\right] + (\rho + \delta)I.
$$

Let B be the $n \times n$ matrix defined by

$$
B = [\beta_{ij} - \beta_{0j}\beta_{i0}/\beta_{00}]
$$

where the constants β_{ij} are the powers from the Cobb–Douglas production functions. Moreover, let W denote the $n \times n$ diagonal matrix with diagonal elements $w_i(p^*)$, $i = 1, 2, ..., n$. Similarly let P denote the $n \times n$ diagonal matrix with diagonal elements p_i^*, $i = 1, 2, ..., n$. One can show that

$$
\left[\frac{\partial y(x^*, p^*)}{\partial x}\right] = P^{-1}B^{-1}W \quad \text{and} \quad \left[\frac{\partial w(p^*)}{\partial p}\right] = W(B')^{-1}P^{-1}.
$$

Furthermore, one can show that the roots of the matrices B and

$$
\left[\frac{\partial y(x^*, p^*)}{\partial x}\right]
$$

have the same sign structure. It follows from this property that the roots of J come in pairs of the form $(\mu_i - \delta, -\mu_i + \rho + \delta)$.

5.2. The Hopf bifurcation

In a three sector model with Cobb–Douglas production functions the steady state can be totally unstable and limit cycles may occur. The intuition for this result is as follows. From the form of the eigenvalues of J mentioned at the end of the previous subsection it follows that the steady state of system (43) is necessarily saddle point stable if $\rho = 0$. If ρ increases, then the steady state may lose the saddle point stability and become totally unstable. In Benhabib and Nishimura (1979) the three sector model with depreciation rate $\delta = 0.1$ and the following parameters is studied:

$$e_0 = 10.2425 \qquad \beta_{00} = 0.9524 \qquad \beta_{01} = 0.9723 \qquad \beta_{02} = 0.3941$$

$$e_1 = 1.5084 \qquad \beta_{10} = 0.0017 \qquad \beta_{11} = 0.0265 \qquad \beta_{12} = 0.5635$$

$$e_2 = 3.0266 \qquad \beta_{20} = 0.0459 \qquad \beta_{21} = 0.0012 \qquad \beta_{22} = 0.0423$$

The Jacobian at the steady state of this system has four complex roots when $\rho = 0.148$. The real parts of two of them change sign from negative to positive and the real parts of the other two roots remain positive when ρ crosses the value 0.148 from below. Thus, a Hopf bifurcation takes place at $\rho = 0.148$ and periodic optimal paths exist for discount rates close to 0.148.

5.3. A multi-sector model with externalities

Recently there has been a renewed interest in the possibility of indeterminacy and sunspots or, put differently, in the existence of a continuum of equilibria in dynamic economies with some market imperfections. Much of the research in this area has been concerned with the empirical plausibility of the conditions that lead to indeterminacy in economies with external effects or monopolistic competition, in which the sectoral production functions exhibit some degree of increasing returns. While the early results on indeterminacy relied on relatively large increasing returns and high markups, more recently Benhabib and Farmer (1996) showed that indeterminacy can also occur in two-sector models with small sector-specific external effects and very mild increasing returns. Benhabib and Nishimura (1998a) demonstrated that indeterminacy can occur in a standard growth model with constant social returns, decreasing private returns, and small or negligible external effects. Furthermore Benhabib and Nishimura (1998b, 1998c) provide a systematic method of treating multi-sector models with externalities.

In this subsection we consider the case that the coefficients e_j of the production functions are given by

$$e_j(t) = \prod_{i=0}^{n} x_{ij}(t)^{b_{ij}}.$$

Therefore, the social production functions are

$$y_j(t) = \prod_{i=0}^{n} x_{ij}(t)^{\beta_{ij} + b_{ij}} \qquad j = 0, 1, ..., n.$$

The representative agent, however, is not aware of the dependence of $e_j(t)$ on his choice variables. Instead, he treats $e_j(t)$ as an exogenous function of time. Thus, there is an external effect. The static first order conditions for the representative agent's problem are therefore given by (compare with (40))

$$w_s(t) = p_j(t)\beta_{sj}x_{sj}(t)^{-1} \prod_{i=0}^{n} x_{ij}(t)^{\beta_{ij}+b_{ij}}$$

$$= u'(y_0(t))\beta_{s0}x_{s0}(t)^{-1} \prod_{i=0}^{n} x_{i0}(t)^{\beta_{i0}+b_{i0}}$$

for $j = 1, 2, \ldots, n$, all $s = 0, 1, \ldots, n$, and all $t \geqslant 0$. We assume again that the utility function is given by $u(y_0) = y_0$. Following exactly the same procedure as in the case without externalities, one can derive the equations of motion from the necessary optimality conditions and linearize them around the steady state. This yields again

$$\begin{bmatrix} dx(t)/dt \\ dp(t)/dt \end{bmatrix} = \begin{bmatrix} \left[\dfrac{\partial y(x^*,p^*)}{\partial x}\right] - \delta I & \left[\dfrac{\partial y(x^*,p^*)}{\partial p}\right] \\ [0] & -\left[\dfrac{\partial w(p^*)}{\partial p}\right] + (\rho + \delta)I \end{bmatrix} \begin{bmatrix} x(t) - x^* \\ p(t) - p^* \end{bmatrix}$$

$$= J \begin{bmatrix} x(t) - x^* \\ p(t) - p^* \end{bmatrix}.$$

In the case of externalities, however, the submatrices of J are

$$\left[\frac{\partial y(x^*,p^*)}{\partial x}\right] = [a_{ij} - a_{0j}a_{i0}/a_{00}]^{-1} \quad \text{and} \quad \left[\frac{\partial w(p^*)}{\partial p}\right] = [\hat{a}_{ij} - \hat{a}_{0j}\hat{a}_{i0}/\hat{a}_{00}]^{-1},$$

where $a_{ij} = x_{ij}^*/y_j^*$ is the i-th input coefficient of the j-th output and $\hat{a}_{ij} = a_{ij}(\beta_{ij} + b_{ij})/\beta_{ij}$ is an adjusted value of a_{ij} to reflect the externality. The roots of J are related to the input coefficient matrices. Moreover, one can show that

$$[a_{ij} - a_{0j}a_{i0}/a_{00}] = W^{-1}BP$$

and

$$[\hat{a}_{ij} - \hat{a}_{0j}\hat{a}_{i0}/\hat{a}_{00}] = P\hat{B}'W^{-1},$$

where B and $\hat{B}$ are $n \times n$ matrices given by

$$B = [\beta_{ij} - \beta_{0j}\beta_{i0}/\beta_{00}]$$

and

$$\hat{B} = [(\beta_{ij} + b_{ij}) - (\beta_{0j} + b_{0j})(\beta_{i0} + b_{i0})/(\beta_{00} + b_{00})].$$

In the two sector case the matrices $\hat{B}$ and B reduce to scalars. They reflect the factor intensities defined by the Cobb–Douglas exponents with and without the external effects, respectively. We may therefore say that the capital good is labor intensive from the private perspective if $\beta_{11}\beta_{00} - \beta_{10}\beta_{01} < 0$, but that it is capital intensive from the social perspective if $(\beta_{11} + b_{11})(\beta_{00} + b_{00}) - (\beta_{10} + b_{10})(\beta_{01} + b_{01}) > 0$. The expressions above allow us to state the following result taken from Benhabib and Nishimura (1998a).

THEOREM 17. In the two-sector model, if the capital good is labour intensive from the private perspective, but capital intensive from the social perspective, then the steady state is indeterminate.

Acknowledgements

We thank Donald George, Michael McAleer and Les Oxley for many helpful comments.

Notes

1. It has to be noted that this sufficient optimality condition depends crucially on the concavity assumptions stated in A2 and A4. In the following subsection we shall modify A2. In that case the Euler equation with the transversatility condition will no longer provide a sufficient optimality condition.
2. For simplicity we assume that $x_t \in [0, 1]$ holds for all t, although the definitions hold more generally.
3. A function $h : [A, B] \mapsto [A, B]$ is called unimodal if there exists $\bar{x} \in [A, B]$ such that h is strictly increasing on $[A, \bar{x}]$ and strictly decreasing on $[\bar{x}, B]$. Moreover, h is called expansive if it is piecewise differentiable with $|h'(x)| > 1$ for all x at which h is differentiable.
4. The assumption that $\cup_{x \in X} \Omega_x$ has non-empty interior in X is satisfied whenever Ω has non-empty interior in $X \times X$. The converse is not true as can be seen by simple examples.
5. For a discussion of these concepts we refer to Vial (1983). Some authors (e.g. Montrucchio (1994)) use the term concavity-α instead of $(-\alpha)$-convexity.
6. The function $h : X \mapsto X$ is called Lipschitz continuous if there exists a constant $L > 0$ such that $\| h(x) - h(y) \| \leqslant L \| x - y \|$ for all $x, y \in X$. The number L is called a Lipschitz constant for h. It is obvious that Lipschitz continuity implies continuity but not vice versa.
7. Choose, for example, $X = [0, 1]$, $\Omega = \{(x, y) \mid x \in X, 0 \leqslant y \leqslant \sqrt{x}\}$ and $U(x, y) = ax - y$, where $a > 0$ is a sufficiently large real number. With the exception of A9 all assumptions from Subsection 3.1 hold. Moreover, the optimal policy function is $h(x) = \sqrt{x}$ which has the properties claimed in the text.
8. The existence of these examples was proved by applying Theorem 10(b) below.
9. The first minimum impatience theorems were presented in Sorger (1992a, 1992b).
10. There are also a few turnpike theorems that hold independently of the size of the discount factor, e.g. Araujo and Scheinkman (1977). These results, however, depend on quite strong structural assumptions and will not be discussed in this chapter.
11. A subset A of the state space X is called invariant (under h) if for every $x \in A$ it holds that $h(z) \in A$. The reader should not confuse this concept with the invariance of a measure μ under h, discussed in Subsection 2.3.3 above.
12. As before $h^{(t)}(x)$ denotes the t-th iterate of h evaluated at $x \in X$.

13. Two maps $h_1: X_1 \mapsto X_1$ and $h_2: X_2 \mapsto X_2$ are called topologically equivalent if there exists a homeomorphism $f: X_1 \mapsto X_2$ such that $f(h_1(x)) = h_2(f(x))$ for all $x \in X_1$.

14. In this case, $x^* = 1$ is the steady state value.

References

Alseda, L., Llibre, J. and Misiurewicz, M. (1993) *Combinatorial Dynamics and Entropy in Dimension One*, World Scientific, Singapore.

Araujo, A. and Scheinkman, J. A. (1977) Smoothness, comparative dynamics, and the turnpike property. *Econometrica*, 45, 601–620.

Baierl, G., Nishimura, K. and Yano, M. (1998) The role of capital depreciation in multi-sectoral models. *Journal of Economic Behavior and Organization*, 33, 467–479.

Benhabib, J. and Farmer, R. E. (1996) Indeterminacy and sector specific externalities. *Journal of Monetary Economics*, 37, 397–419.

Benhabib, J. and Nishimura, K. (1979) The Hopf bifurcation and the existence and stability of closed orbits in multisector models of optimal economic growth. *Journal of Economic Theory*, 21, 421–444.

Benhabib, J. and Nishimura, K. (1985) Competitive equilibrium cycles. *Journal of Economic Theory*, 35, 284–306.

Benhabib, J. and Nishimura, K. (1998a) Indeterminacy and sunspots with constant returns. *Journal of Economic Theory*, 81, 58–91.

Benhabib, J. and Nishimura, K. (1998b) Indeterminacy under constant returns to scale in multisector economies. mimeo.

Benhabib, J. and Nishimura, K. (1998c) Indeterminacy arising in multisector economies. mimeo.

Benhabib, J., Nishimura, K. and Venditti, A. (1999) Indeterminacy and cycles in two sector discrete-time models. mimeo.

Block, L. S. and Coppel, W. A. (1992) *Dynamics in One Dimension*. Springer-Verlag, Berlin.

Boldrin, M. and Deneckere, R. (1990) Sources of complex dynamics in two-sector growth models. *Journal of Economic Dynamics and Control*, 14, 627–653.

Boldrin, M. and Montrucchio, L. (1986) On the indeterminacy of capital accumulation paths. *Journal of Economic Theory*, 40, 26–39.

Boldrin, M., Nishimura, K., Shigoka, T. and Yano, M. (1999) Chaotic equilibrium dynamics in endogenous growth models. *Journal of Economic Theory*, forthcoming.

Boldrin, M. and Rustichini, A. (1994) Growth and indeterminacy in dynamic models with externalities. *Econometrica*, 62, 323–342.

Brock, W. A. and Dechert, W. D. (1991) Non-linear dynamical systems: instability and chaos in economics. In *Handbook of Mathematical Economics IV* (Hildenbrand, W. and H. Sonnenschein, eds.), North-Holland, Amsterdam, pp. 2209–2235.

Cass, D. (1965) Optimum growth in an aggregative model of capital accumulation. *Review of Economic Studies*, 32, 233–240.

Dechert, W. D. and Nishimura, K. (1983) A complete characterization of optimal growth paths in an aggregated model with a non-concave production function. *Journal of Economic Theory*, 31, 332–354.

Deneckere, R. and Pelikan, S. (1986) Competitive chaos. *Journal of Economic Theory*, 40, 13–25.

Hewage, T. U. and Neumann, D. A. (1990) Functions not realizable as policy functions in an optimal growth model. Discussion Paper, Bowling Green State University.

Kehoe, T. J. (1991) Computation and multiplicity of equilibria. In *Handbook of Mathematical Economics: Vol IV* (Hildenbrand, W. and H. Sonnenschein, eds.), North-Holland, Amsterdam, pp. 2049–2144.

Kehoe, T. J. and Levine, D. (1985) Comparative statics and perfect foresight in infinite horizon economies. *Econometrica*, 53, 433–454.

Kehoe, T. J., Levine, D. and Romer, P. (1991) On characterizing equilibria of economies with externalities and taxes as solutions to optimization problems. *Economic Theory* 2, 43–68.

Koopmans, T. C. (1965) On the concept of optimal growth. In *The Econometric Approach to Development Planning*, North-Holland, Amsterdam.

Li, T. and Yorke, J. A. (1975) Period three implies chaos. *American Mathematical Monthly*, 82, 985–992.

Majumdar, M. and Nermuth, M. (1982) Dynamic optimization in non-convex models with irreversible investment: monotonicity and turnpike results. *Zeitschrift für Nationalökonomie*, 42, 339–362.

Matsuyama, K., (1990) Sunspot equilibria (rational bubbles) in a model of money-in the-utility-function. *Journal of Monetary Economics*, 25, 137–144.

McKenzie, L. (1983) Turnpike theory, discounted utility, and the von Neumann facet. *Journal of Economic Theory*, 30, 330–352.

McKenzie, L. (1986) Optimal economic growth, turnpike theorems and comparative dynamics. In *Handbook of Mathematical Economics: Vol III* (Arrow, K. and M. Intriligator, eds.), North-Holland, Amsterdam, pp. 1281–1355.

Mitra, T. (1996a) An exact discount factor restriction for period-three cycles in dynamic optimization models. *Journal of Economic Theory*, 69, 281–305.

Mitra, T. (1996b) On the nature of policy functions of dynamic optimization models. Working Paper, Cornell University.

Mitra, T. and Ray, D. (1984) Dynamic optimization on a non-convex feasible set: some general results for non-smooth technologies. *Zeitschrift für Nationalökonomie* 44, 151–175.

Mitra, T. and Sorger, G. (1999a) On the existence of chaotic policy functions in dynamic optimization. *Japanese Economic Review*, forthcoming.

Mitra, T. and Sorger, G. (1999b) Rationalizing policy functions by dynamic optimization. *Econometrica*, 67, (1999), 375–392.

Montrucchio, L. (1987) Lipschitz continuous policy functions for strongly concave optimization problems. *Journal of Mathematical Economics*, 16, 259–273.

Montrucchio, L. (1994) Dynamic complexity of optimal paths and discount factors for strongly concave problems. *Journal of Optimization Theory and Applications*, 80, 385–406.

Montrucchio, L. and Sorger, G. (1996) Topological entropy of policy functions in concave dynamic optimization models. *Journal of Mathematical Economics*, 25, 181–194.

Neumann, D., O'Brien, T., Hoag, T. and Kim, K. (1988) Policy functions for capital accumulation paths. *Journal of Economic Theory*, 46, 205–214.

Nishimura, K., Shigoka, T. and Yano, M. (1998) Interior optimal chaos with arbitrarily low discount rates. *Japanese Economic Review*, 49, 223–233.

Nishimura, K. and Sorger, G. (1996) Optimal cycles and chaos: a survey. *Studies in Nonlinear Dynamics and Econometrics*, 1, 11–28.

Nishimura, K., Sorger, G. and Yano, M. (1994) Ergodic chaos in optimal growth models with low discount rates. *Economic Theory*, 4, 705–717.

Nishimura, K. and Venditti, A. (1999) Intersectoral externalities and indeterminacy. mimeo.

Nishimura, K. and Yano, M. (1993) Optimal chaos when future utilities are discounted arbitrarily weakly. In *Nonlinear Analysis and Mathematical Economics*, Lecture Note Series, Institute of Mathematical Analysis, Kyoto University.

Nishimura, K. and Yano, M. (1995a) Nonlinear dynamics and optimal growth: an example. *Econometrica*, 63, 981–1001.

Nishimura, K. and Yano, M. (1995b) Non-linearity and business cycles in a two-sector equilibrium model: an example with Cobb–Douglas production functions. In *Nonlinear and Convex Analysis in Economic Theory* (Maruyama, T. and W. Takahashi, eds.), Springer-Verlag, Berlin, pp. 231–245.

Nishimura, K. and Yano, M. (1996a) On the least upper bound of discount factors that are compatible with optimal period-three cycles. *Journal of Economic Theory* 69, 206–333.

Nishimura, K. and Yano, M. (1996b) Chaotic solutions in dynamic linear programming. *Chaos, Solitions and Fractals*, 7, 1941–1953.

Ramsey, F. (1928) A mathematical theory of saving. *Economic Journal*, 38, 543–559.

Samuelson, P. A. (1973) Optimality of profit, including prices under ideal planning. *Proceedings of the National Academy of Sciences of the United States of America* 70, 2109–2111.

Sarkovskii, A. N. (1964) Coexistence of cycles of a continuous map of a line into itself. *Ukrainian Mathematical Journal*, 16, 61–71.

Scheinkman, J. A. (1976) On optimal steady states of n-sector growth models when utility is discounted. *Journal of Economic Theory*, 12, 11–20.

Scheinkman, J. (1984) General equilibrium models of business fluctuations. mimeo, University of Chicago.

Shrinivasan, T. N. (1964) Optimal savings in a two-sector model of growth. *Econometrica*, 32, 358–373.

Sorger, G. (1992a) *Minimum Impatience Theorems for Recursive Economic Models.* Springer-Verlag, Heidelberg.

Sorger, G. (1992b) On the minimum rate of impatience for complicated optimal growth paths. *Journal of Economic Theory*, 56, 160–179.

Sorger, G. (1994a) On the structure of Ramsey equilibrium: cycles, indeterminacy, and sunspots. *Economic Theory*, 4, 745–764.

Sorger, G. (1994b) Policy functions of strictly concave optimal growth models. *Ricerche Economiche*, 48, 195–212.

Sorger, G. (1995) On the sensitivity of optimal growth paths. *Journal of Mathematical Economics*, 24, 353–369.

Spear, S. E. (1991) Growth, externalities, and sunspots. *Journal of Economic Theory*, 54, 215–223.

Stokey, N. L. and Lucas, R. E. (1989) *Recursive Methods in Economic Dynamics.* Harvard University Press, Cambridge.

Sutherland, W. A. (1970) On optimal development in a multi-sectoral economy: the discounted case. *Review of Economic Studies*, 37, 585–589.

Uzawa, H. (1964) Optimal growth in a two-sector model of capital accumulation. *Review of Economic Studies*, 31, 1–24.

Vial, J. P. (1983) Strong and weak convexity of sets and functions. *Mathematics of Operations Research*, 8, 231–259.

Woodford, M. (1986) Stationary sunspot equilibria in a finance constrained economy. *Journal of Economic Theory*, 40, 128–137.

6

UNDECIDABILITY, COMPUTATION UNIVERSALITY AND MINIMALITY IN ECONOMIC DYNAMICS*

K. Vela Velupillai

Dedicated to the Memory of *Daniel Vaz*, a Friend and a Gentleman.

1. Introduction

> The unpredictable and the predetermined unfold together to make everything the way it is. ... It's the best possible time to be alive, when almost everything you thought you know is wrong. (Valentine to Hannah, Sc. 4, *Arcadia* by Tom Stoppard).

In this chapter I explore the connection between recursion theoretic formalisms and issues in economic dynamics. Questions of dynamics from traditional areas in microeconomics, behavioural economics and macroeconomics are viewed from a recursion theoretic-algorithmic-viewpoint.

Algorithms are intrinsically dynamic objects. Interesting algorithms encapsulate nonlinear dynamics in novel ways. This makes it possible to ask *decidability* questions and obtain *effective* answers. This is what I try to focus on, in the ensuing pages.

The chapter is organised as follows. In the next section, starting from the open-endedness implied by Sonnenschein-Debreu-Mantel theorems for microdynamics, an attempt is made to be more precise about algorithmic issues in the theory of computable general equilibrium modelling. The fact that algorithms are intrinsically dynamic objects makes it possible to frame questions and obtain answers in terms of economic dynamics.

* I am greatly indebted to Dr Cassey Lee for constructive comments on an earlier version of this chapter. Alas, he is not responsible for the remaining infelicities.

In Section 3 one aspect of behavioural economics is considered: adaptive behaviour. Recursion theoretic formalism for adaptive behaviour lead to the possibility of suggesting that it is completely consistent with the definition of 'rationality' in the sense in which that term is used in economics.

Methodological themes in macroeconomics are the topics that are given a recursion theoretic formalism in terms of a minimal nonlinear dynamical system called a *Generalized Shift*. This is done in Section 4. As a result notions that have traditionally been given an 'underworld' status — instability, disequilibria and nonprobabilistic inference — are viewed in a positive light.

The concluding section is simply an attempt to draw the threads together and to see whether it is possible to weave a tapestry for the future of *undecidable economic dynamics* — the basic, underlying, theme of the chapter.

I have used a couple of the more famous results from classical recursion theory in the proof sketches. In particular, Rice's Theorem and the theorem of the undecidability of the Halting Problem for Turing Machines. I conjecture that they will become, in the years to come, as much a part of the standard repertoire of tools in the arsenal of the analytical economist as the Maximum Principle, the Bellman Equation, the Poincaré-Bendixson theorem, Sarkowskii's theorem, the Brouwer and Kakutani fix point theorems and other famous results of classical analysis.

To aid the absolute novice in the basics of these results from classical recursion theory, I append a brief *mathematical appendix* with a summary of the relevant material. It is not a substitute for a good book, of which there are so many that any particular indication would be too subjective. The interested reader — that elusive creature — will find many such references in the appendix to Velupillai (1999), from which I have extracted relevant sections for this appendix.

2. Microeconomics: undecidability of Tâtonnement

A description of the consumer side of the economy for the purposes of the general equilibrium model, is adequately provided by the market excess demand functions. (Scarf and Shoven, 1984, p. 4.).

Standard results from 'the consumer side of the economy' imply the following fundamental statements:

(i) Market excess-demand functions are homogeneous of degree zero in prices:

$$\mathbf{z}(\lambda \mathbf{p}) = \mathbf{z}(\mathbf{p}), \ \lambda \in \Re^+ \tag{1}$$

where, $\mathbf{z}$: the vector of market excess-demands
   $\mathbf{p}$: the vector of prices

(ii) Market excess-demand functions satisfy the Walras Law:

$$\mathbf{p}.\mathbf{z}(\mathbf{p}) = 0 \tag{2}$$

(iii) Market excess-demand functions are continuous over their (appropriately dimensioned) domain of definition:

$$S_n^+ \equiv \{ \mathbf{p} \mid \mathbf{p} \in \Re_{n+1}^+ \quad \text{and} \quad \| \mathbf{p} \| = 1 \} \tag{3}$$

To these fundamental statements let us append a fourth statement which has, clearly, more of an ad-hoc character to it than (1)–(3):

(iv) Market excess-demand functions underpin the *tâtonnement* process:

$$\mathbf{p} = \mathbf{z}(\mathbf{p}) \tag{4}$$

Now, since prices have been normalized to lie in the (positive orthant) of the unit sphere, the Walras Law can be given the geometric interpretation given in Figure 1.

In other words, geometrically viewed, the market excess-demand vector, $\mathbf{z}(\mathbf{p})$, is tangent to S_n^+ at $\mathbf{p}$. Thus, by (iii), $\mathbf{z}(\mathbf{p})$ defines a continuous vector-field on S_n^+. Then, in view of the Sonnenschein-Debreu-Mantel (S-D-M) theorems (Sonnenschein, 1972, 1973; Debreu, 1974; Mantel, 1974), the solution to the *tâtonnement* process (4) lies on the vector-field induced by $\mathbf{z}(\mathbf{p})$ on S_n^+. This means that any arbitrary — but sufficiently smooth — curve on S_n^+ will be compatible with some consistent exchange economy. Conversely given an arbitrary exchange economy defined by a collection of individual excess-demand functions, $z_i(\mathbf{p})$, and an initial price vector, $\mathbf{p}$, there does not exist enough structure in the system to discipline the dynamics of the *tâtonnement* process to be of use:

(a) Either, in proving the existence of an exchange equilibrium as the attractor of the dynamics;

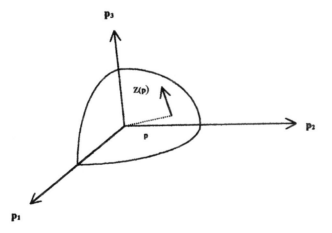

Figure 1. Inducing a vector-field on the price simplex.

(b) Or, in using the dynamics as the adjustment process towards an independently demonstrated configuration of equilibrium prices;

However, this very indeterminacy also has its blessings: it allows a new lease of life for the applicability of the *correspondence principle*. For example, restrictions on the divergence of the induced vector field on S_n^+ translate into standard properties on the demand functions that allow meaningful comparative static analysis to be undertaken.

My aim, on the other hand, is to exploit the indeterminacy due to S-D-M theorems to suggest that there may be some unwarranted enthusiasm in the claims implicit in, and made explicit by, *computable general equilibrium* (CGE), models.

The background against which my suggestion is to be viewed is the following. The basic strategy in CGE exercises has been to devise an algorithm for *approximating* a fixed point of a continuous mapping of S_n^+ into itself. Somewhere, behind the scenes, lies Uzawa's result on the equivalence between the theorem of existence of equilibrium prices for an exchange economy and Brouwer's fixed point theorem (Uzawa, 1962). This result is implicitly or explicitly invoked whenever a fix-point approximating algorithm is used in CGE exercises.

Suppose, now, that the economic equilibrium existence theorem results in a vector of equilibrium prices, say $\mathbf{p}^*$, which are *nonrecursive reals*. How, then, are we to interpret any approximating algorithm for a fix-point that is a nonrecursive real? We can attempt coherent answers in at least one of the following ways:

(a) Find an approximate recursive real, say $\mathbf{p}_{rr}^*$ to the nonrecursive real $\mathbf{p}^*$ and construct an exact algorithm to determine $\mathbf{p}_{rr}^*$;
(b) Restrict the $z_i(\mathbf{p})$ to be defined over the domain of computable reals and determine their solution algorithmically to get an exact $\mathbf{p}_{rr}^*$;
(c) Restrict the $z_i(\mathbf{p})$ to the class of functions for which there are exact algorithms to compute the equilibrium solutions;

Unfortunately, both (a) and (b) involve significant undecidabilities. A sketch of their nature is outlined in the form of two formal propositions. On the other hand, (c) is too trivial an exercise for serious analytical considerations. More importantly, by a metamathematical consideration of Rice's Theorem, it can be shown that there are no effective procedures to 'restrict the class of functions for which there are exact algorithms to compute the equilibrium solutions'.

PROPOSITION 1. Assume that the market excess-demand functions are computable and, therefore, continuous (hence satisfying (iii), above), on a suitable subset of $S_n^+ \times T$ (T: time axis). Then, there exist exchange economies such that the solution to the associated *tâtonnement* process:

$$\dot{\mathbf{p}}(t) = \mathbf{z}(\mathbf{p}(t), t) \tag{5}$$

is uncomputable inside a nontrivial domain of $z(p(t), t)$.

REMARK 1. Rewrite (5) in the classic integral form:

$$\mathbf{p}(t) = \int_0^t \mathbf{z}(x, \mathbf{p}(x)dx) \tag{6}$$

What is being claimed in Proposition 1 is that the computable transformation[1] on the RHS of (6) gives rise to an uncomputable fix point.

REMARK 2. Another way to look at the 'startling' implications of Proposition 1 is the following. Take the standard, elementary, exposition of the initial value problem to an ODE. I follow the lucid exposition in Coddington (1961, ch. 5). Find solutions to the equation

$$y' = f(x, y) \tag{7}$$

$$R: |x - x_0| \leqslant a, |y - y_0| \leqslant b, (a, b,)0) \tag{8}$$

where f is any continuous real-valued function defined on some rectangle in the real (x, y)-plane. The idea is to show that on some interval I containing x_0, there exists a solution φ of (7) s.t.:

$$\phi(x_0) = y_0 \tag{9}$$

In other words: $\exists$ a real-valued, differentiable function ϕ satisfying (9) s.t.

$$(x, \phi(x)) \in R, \quad \text{and} \quad \phi'(x) = f(x, \phi(x)), \forall x \in I \tag{10}$$

ϕ is then called a solution to the initial value problem (ivp)

$$y' = f(x, y), \ y(c_0) = y_0 \ (\text{on } I) \tag{11}$$

When we use the method of successive approximation to demonstrate the existence of solutions for an ivp we begin by showing its equivalence to the following integral equation:

$$y = y_0 + \int_{x_0}^x f(t, y)dt \quad (\text{on } I) \tag{12}$$

Again, by a solution to (12) on I, we mean $\exists \phi$, continuous and real-valued on I s.t.

$$(x, \phi(x)) \in R, \forall x \in I \quad \text{and} \quad \forall x \in I \Rightarrow \phi(x) = y_0 + \int_{x_0}^x f(t, \phi(t))dt \tag{13}$$

Now, in solving (13), we consider, as a first approximation to a solution:

$$\phi_1(x) = y_0 \tag{14}$$

Obviously (14) satisfies the initial condition given in (11). '*Compute*':

$$\phi_1(x) = y_0 + \int_{x_0}^x f(t, \phi_0(t))dt = y_0 + \int_{x_0}^x f(t, y_0)dt \tag{15}$$

If the space on which the 'flow' takes place allows '*contraction*' we can expect ϕ_1 to be a closer approximation to the final solution than ϕ_0. If we continue this process we get:

$$\text{(again):} \qquad \phi_0(x) = y_0 \tag{14}$$

and

$$\phi_{n+1}(x) = y_0 + \int_{x_0}^{x} f(t, \phi_n(t))dt \tag{16}$$

$$n = 1, 2, ...$$

Again on a suitable space on which the 'flow' takes place we might take limits s.t.:

$$\lim_{n \to \infty} \phi_n(x) = \phi(x) \tag{17}$$

and: ((13) again):

$$\phi(x) = y_0 + \int_{x_0}^{x} f(t, \phi(t))dt \tag{13}$$

The functions $\phi_0, \phi_1, \phi_2, ...$, defined by (16), are the successive approximations to the ivp or to a solution to (12). At this point Coddington gives a suggestive picture to describe or explain the method of successive approximations. Here I follow him quite literally:

> One way to picture the successive approximations is to think of *a machine S* (for solving)[2] which converts functions ϕ into new functions $S(\phi)$ defined by
>
> $$S(\phi)x = y_0 + \int_{x_0}^{x} f(t, \phi(t))dt.$$
>
> A solution to the initial value problem [(11)] would then be a function ϕ which moves through the *machine* untouched, that is, a function satisfying $S(\phi) = \phi$. Starting with $\phi_0(x) = y_0$, we see that S converts ϕ_0 into ϕ_1, and then ϕ_1 into ϕ_2. In general, $S(\phi_k) = \phi_{k+1}$, and ultimately we end up with a ϕ such that $S(\phi) = \phi$. (ibid, pp. 201–2; emphasis added).

Now let us to grant the *ivp* all that is granted by the conventional mathematician — and the economists. Then let us ask whether the *S-machine* can get 'jammed'; enter a loop; or even break down when, finally, ϕ is its input. The answer is in the affirmative and that is what is stated in the above proposition. The problem is that 'we will never end up with a ϕ such that $s(\phi) = \phi$'.

REMARK 3. The proof of Proposition 1 is far too lengthy to be given here. It is, in any case, a simple adaptation of a standard technique in computable analysis (cf. Pour-El and Richards, 1989).

PROPOSITION 2. Assume that the (individual) market excess-demand functions are restricted to be defined on the domain of computable reals. Suppose also that there are, given, an arbitrary exchange economy satisfying (i)–(iii) and a $\mathbf{p}^*$. Then, given any algorithm, initialised at the configuration of the given arbitrary exchange economy, it is undecidable whether it will terminate at $\mathbf{p}^*$.

PROOF. Direct application of *Rice's theorem* (or, alternatively, the *undecidability of the halting problem for Turing Machines*).

DISCUSSION. Microeconomic formalisms have invoked recursion theoretic concepts, ideas and frameworks without being too careful about assumptions on the domain of definition. Thus Patinkin's thought experiment for the construction of excess-demand functions used the suggestive metaphor of the rational agent as a 'utility computer' (Patinkin, 1965, p. 7); Arrow-Hahn had a Walrasian 'super-auctioneer' implementing the tâtonnement as an algorithm (Arrow-Hahn, 1971, p. 264ff); and then there is the whole subject of CGE. Some years ago Arrow conjectured that:

> The next step in analysis ... is a more consistent assumption of computability in the formulation of economic hypotheses. This is likely to have its own difficulties because, of course, not everything is computable, and there will be in this sense an inherently unpredictable element in rational behaviour. (Arrow, 1986, p. S398).

In this section I have tried to introduce, consistently, computability assumptions 'in the formulation of economic hypotheses'. Novel indeterminacies are the result, as conjectured by Arrow.

3. Behavioural economics: computation universality in adaptive behaviour

> ... [S]erious models of adaptation are inevitably nonlinear. ... [N]onlinear dynamics is a prerequisite for adaptation ... (Farmer and Packard, 1986, p. vii)

By 'behavioural economics' I mean the heterogeneous collection of tools, concepts and methodologies subsumed under *adaptive*, *evolutionary* and *experimental* economics.

If behaviour in an economic context is 'always adaptive' (Lucas, 1986, p. S408), then its 'trajectory' must also always represent *transition dynamics* to a steady state. If, moreover, behaviour is assumed to be rational, then it must be characterised by the steady states of the dynamical system which corresponds to the above 'trajectory'. It is, therefore, legitimate to ask whether we can characterise rational behaviour as it is normally understood and defined in economic theory, in terms of the limit sets of a dynamical system. Next, one may ask whether the limit sets are computationally viable. Answers to these questions may suggest an observational fact: the persistence of adaptive behaviour. These themes circumscribe the nature and scope of this section.

Lucas (op. cit) discusses a dynamic characterization of rational behaviour by suggesting that 'all behaviour is adaptive' in that traditional demand functions are decision rules' and these, in turn are 'steady states of some adaptive process' (p. S402), 'which are arrived at after a process of deliberate experimentation and assessment of outcomes' (p. S410). The assessment of outcomes is by means of the traditional formalism of preferences. Thus, Lucas seems to be making explicit the *implicit dynamics* underlying formalisms of rational behaviour. Lucas, in fact, states explicitly:

> The behaviour implied by these decision rules is 'rational' in the sense that economists use that term. But not only is it consistent with *adaptive*, trial-and-error *behaviour*; the experiment designed to discover this rationality assumes that, if it exists, it is the outcome of some (unspecified) *adaptive process*. (ibid, p. S410; italics added).

To explore the recursion theoretic characterizations and implications I shall work with the following three equivalences:

(a) Adaptive processes will be *assumed* to be dynamical systems (in the strict technical sense of the term);
(b) Dynamical systems capable of *computational universality* can be constructed from Turing Machines (TM);
(c) Rational behaviour by an economic agent is equivalent to the computational behaviour of a Turing Machine;

I should add that at least (b) and (c) are demonstrated with a certain amount of completeness and rigour in Velupillai (1999). With these equivalences at hand it will be possible to ask recursion theoretic questions about the 'steady states of ... adaptive processes'; i.e., steady states of dynamical systems or the halting configuration of Turing Machines which, by (c) depicts appropriate rational choice. The assumption of the equivalence in (a) is quite standard and is, indeed, implied in Lucas's suggestive descriptions.

Recall that, in a precise sense, every Turing Machine is also a Universal Turing Machine (UTM); i.e., such a machine can be programmed to compute any theoretically feasible computation and mimic the action of any arbitrary Turing Machine. For ease of reference in the results to be stated as theorems and proved I need two simple, synthetic, definitions.

DEFINITION 1. A dynamical system — discrete or continuous — is said to be *capable of computation universality* if, using its initial conditions, it can be programmed to simulate the action of any arbitrary Turing Machine; in particular, that of a Universal Turing Machine.

DEFINITION 2. A dynamical system capable of computation universality will be called a *Universal Dynamical System.*

I can now return to Lucas's suggested connection between adaptive behaviour and rationality and state two precise results.

THEOREM 1. Only adaptive processes capable of computation universality are consistent with rationality 'in the sense that economist's use that term'.
PROOF. Recall (cf. Velupillai, op. cit, ch. III) that the rational agent can be modelled as a Turing Machine and that the rational behaviour of the economic agent is equivalent to the appropriate computing behaviour by a Turing Machine (equivalence (c), above). Also that equivalences (a) and (b) are assumptions (although (b) is also shown in Velupillai (op. cit), ch. IV). Then, by Kramer's result on *finite* automata (Proposition 3.4, in Velupillai, *ibid*) we know that such, restricted, Turing Machines are inconsistent with rationality 'in the sense that economists use that term'. Thus, it follows that any dynamical system modelled by automata not *capable of computation universality* is similarly inconsistent and, hence, only adaptive processes *capable of computation universality* are consistent with rationality 'in the sense that economists use that term'.

THEOREM 2. There is no effective procedure to decide whether given classes of decision rules are 'steady states of (some) adaptive process'.

PROOF. Note, first of all, from the above discussions, assumptions and results, that 'steady states of adaptive processes' are 'steady states of dynamical systems'. Thus, given a class of decision rules, to ask whether they correspond to steady states of dynamical systems is equivalent to asking whether they belong to the basin of attractions of (some) such dynamical system. However, by the previous theorem, the dynamical system in question must be capable of computation universality; i.e., a universal dynamical system. For, if not, the steady states will violate some form of the rationality postulate.
Next, I claim that the basin of attraction of universal dynamical systems are *recursively enumerable but not recursive.* That they are recursively enumerable follows from the simple fact that trajectories belonging to it can be effectively listed by trying out initial conditions systematically.
    On the other hand, suppose they are recursive. Then *the halting problem for Turing Machines* would be solvable. For, given the basin of attraction and arbitrary initial points, this will mean that the dynamics will effectively answer questions of membership. Since this is a universal dynamical system it means that a query whether a Universal Turing Machine will halt, for arbitrary inputs, at a particular configuration or not can be answered. This contradicts the unsolvability of the *halting* problem. Hence, by Rice's theorem, there is no

effective procedure to decide whether any given class of decision rules is the
steady state of (some) adaptive process (or not).

These results, in a nutshell, state that there are no systematic procedures,
available *a priori*, to study and characterize long-run properties of *interesting
dynamical systems*. By 'interesting dynamical systems' I mean those that can
encapsulate fully-rational behaviour. Any economic dynamics that leads to limit-
sets that are only limit points (nodes, foci, saddle-points, even limit cycles) cannot
represent fully-rational behaviour in a very precise sense. It is an aspect of this
precise sense that I have attempted to capture in the above two theorems.

To put it another way, economic dynamics not capable of computation
universality will be incompatible with the no-arbitrage hypothesis: there will be
unexploited profitable opportunities in the limit. This is clearly one of the key
reasons for the need to supplement simple dynamics with *ad-hoc shockeries* in, for
example, growth and cycle theories (cf. next section).

But, as always, these seemingly negative results have positive aspects. After all,
these results only negate the feasibility of universally utilizable *effective procedures*
to answer *systematic* questions about (dynamically) rational choice. They do not
assert that *special-purpose procedures* do not exist, or cannot be found, to study
the *processes of rational choice*.

For example, even although Lucas suggests that 'all behaviour is adaptive' and
that decision rules, such as demand functions, are 'steady states of some adaptive
process', he also seems to have had in mind a study of special-purpose dynamics:

> In general terms, we view or model an individual as a collection of decision
> rules (rules that dictate the action to be taken in given situations) and a set of
> preferences used to evaluate the outcomes arising from particular situation-
> action combinations. These decision rules are continuously under review and
> revision, new decision rules are tried and tested against experience, and rules
> that produce desirable outcomes supplant those that do not. I use the term
> 'adaptive' to refer to this trial-and-error process through which our modes of
> behaviour are determined. (ibid, p. S-401).

Surely, this must mean that the neoclassical closure is inadequate for the study of
dynamically rational behaviour — a theme tirelessly propagated by Clower,
Leijonhufvud, Nelson, Simon, Winter, Day and other pioneers of behavioural,
evolutionary and experimental economics for many years.

4. Macroeconomics: minimal dynamical systems

> Indeed virtually any 'interesting' question about dynamical systems is — in
> general — undecidable. (Stewart, 1991, p. 664).

Dynamical systems compatible with some underlying optimization hypothesis at
the individually rational level, and capable of generating multiple equilibria are
dominant in endogenous macroeconomics. By endogenous macroeconomics I
refer to nonstochastic aggregate growth, development and business cycle theories.

There has been, in recent years, a resurgence of interest in the capabilities inherent in nonlinear dynamical systems to encapsulate the stylized facts of endogenous macroeconomics.

An older set of desiderata in macrodynamic modelling, now enshrined in the folklore of the subject, comes down from the Cowles Foundation tradition in macroeconometrics and what can be called the Fisher-Frisch-Metzler-Samuelson tradition in macrodynamics. The former is 'dogmatic' about the genesis of macroeconomic facts; the latter about the necessity of stable dynamical systems to model aggregate growth, development and cycle theories. Real business cycle theorists have been increasingly sceptical about the former dogma; (Kydland and Prescott, 1990) Samuelson himself raised queries about the latter dogma (Samuelson, 1974, esp. p. 10). In a sense the 'dogma of stability' (Samuelson, op. cit, p. 10) was etched in the collective vision and framework of macroeconomics in Samuelson's polemical question in the *Foundations* on the observable impossibility of 'an egg standing on its head'.

However recent research, in applied mathematics and economics, seems to have assigned less negative roles to unstable equilibria, multiple equilibria and disequilibria — in addition to pattern recognition in aggregate data without postulating an underlying probability model. Results in experimental economics show that unstable regimes, if calibrated carefully, are observable. The kind of development theory pioneered by Rosenstein-Rodan as the 'big-push' theory, by Myrdal as the 'theory of cumulative and circular causation', by Rostow as the 'stages theory' and so on have been modelled in terms of nonlinear dynamical systems with multiple equilibria. Many years ago, now approaching half-a-century, Leontief suggested that 'we may utilize dynamical systems that are unstable throughout' and cited capitalism as a paradigmatic example.

These diverse desiderata seem never to have been resolved in any uniform way. In this section I want to suggest a framework where all of the dissonances inherent in the above apparently irreconcilable desiderata are removed. In other words I am looking for a minimal — or parsimonious — dynamical system satisfying the following criteria:

(a) It must be capable of extracting patterns inherent in aggregate data, without assuming that such data have been generated by an underlying probability model;
(b) It must be capable of generating multiple equilibria;
(c) It must be capable of persistent (or observably) unstable equilibria;
(d) It must be consistent with the fundamental individually rational principle of no arbitrage;
(e) It must be capable of encapsulating rational disequilibria;
(f) It must be capable of non-maximum rational dynamics;

The main results of this section are the following:

(i) Only dynamical systems capable of computation universality can satisfy all five criteria simultaneously.

(ii) Generalized shifts are one class of minimal dynamical systems capable of computation universality (and, hence, satisfy all five criteria simultaneously).

I shall state these results in terms of a series of theorems, characterizations and remarks, after describing a particular Generalized Shift constructed by Moore (1990, 1991).

DEFINITION. Generalized Shift (GS) Map

$$\Phi: \wp \to \sigma^{F(\wp)}[\wp \oplus G(\wp)] \tag{18}$$

where, $\wp$: symbol sequence;
F: mapping from a finite subset of $\wp$ to the integers;
G: mapping from a finite subset of $\wp$ into $\wp$
σ: shift operator;

The given 'finite subset of $\wp$' on which F and G operate is called a *domain of dependence* (DOD). *Description of the mode of operation of (18):*
Let the given symbol sequence be:

$$\wp \equiv \{\ldots p_{-1} \, p_0 \, p_{+1} \ldots\} \tag{19}$$

Then, $\wp \oplus G(\wp) \Rightarrow$ replace DOD by $G(\wp)$.
And, $\sigma^{F(\wp)} \Rightarrow$ shift the sequence left or right by the amount $F(\wp)$.
   In practice GS is implemented by denoting a distinct position on the initially given symbol sequence as, say, p_0 and placing a 'reading head' over it. It must also be noted that $p_i \in \wp, \forall i = 1, 2, \ldots$ could, for example, denote whole words from an alphabet, etc., although in practice it will be 0, 1 and . (dot). The 'dot' will signify that the 'reading head' will be placed on the symbol to the right of it.
   Hence the first row operations will be:

Step 1: $\wp \oplus G(\wp) \Rightarrow 0.00$ is replaced by 0.11
Step 2: $\sigma^{F(\wp)} \Rightarrow -1 \equiv$ shift right $\Rightarrow 1.10$

Characterizing GS

1. Any GS is equivalent to a piecewise linear map of the plane;

Example of a GS Map (DOD = 3 terms centered around the 0-suffixed term)

$\ldots p_{-1} \, p_0 \, p_{+1}$	F	G
0.00	−1	0.11
0.01	+1	1.01
0.10	+1	1.11
0.11	−1	0.00
1.00	+1	0.01
1.01	−1	0.10
1.10	+1	0.11
1.11	−1	0.01

2. The dynamics of a GS is equivalent to the computing activities of a Turing Machine (TM). Hence, by the Church-Turing thesis, to the processes defined in an algorithm.

REMARKS.
1. GS are more general than conventional Cellular Automata (CA);
2. GS are more general — capable of more complex behaviour — than known chaotic maps; for example unpredictability is not only due to Sensitive Dependence on Initial Conditions (SDIC);
3. In view of the equivalence between any GS and a TM, the dynamics of G can persist for arbitrary long periods in metastable states — i.e., states lying on the borderline between the basins of qualitatively different attractors. In particular, 'at the edge of chaos'.

For quantitative measures characterizing the dynamics of a GS (topological entropy, Lyapunov exponent, etc), cf. Moore (op. cit).
Properties I and II can now be restated as the following theorems.

THEOREM 3. Any GS is a nonlinear (in fact, piecewise linear) dynamical system capable of computation universality; hence, they are universal dynamical systems in analogy with a Universal Turing Machine.

PROOF. Essentially by construction. For the first part see Moore (1991); for the second part see Moore (1990), esp. p. 2356.

THEOREM 4. No path of a GS when initialised to process recursively enumerable sets that are not recursive can nontrivially correspond to a maximum problem.

PROOF. By 'nontrivially' I mean the formal sense contained in the Rice or Rice-Shapiro-theorems (cf. Velupillai, ibid, Mathematical Appendix). Now, suppose, on the contrary, that any such path can be related to some solvable maximum problem. Then, every TM can be appropriately initialised to solve the halting problem effectively, which is impossible.

Property (f), therefore, is encapsulated in Theorem 4. Property (b) is a trivial implication of the fact that GS is a universal dynamical system. Properties (a) and (d) are also immediate consequences of a GS being capable of computation universality — if we define no arbitrage behaviour as exhausting all 'extractable' profitable opportunities. Properties (c) and (e) are more delicate and will require complex and tedious constructions. Heuristic motivations, and suggestions, however, can be stated against the backdrop provided by Theorem 4.

Now, equilibria in economics correspond to solvable maximization (or minimization) problems. This means, in the case of a dynamical system, determination of variables and parameters that characterize at least its basin of attraction. But these are, in general, recursively enumerable sets that are not recursive (cf. Theorem 2, in the previous section). Hence, except by flukes, any GS will persist in states that do not correspond to a maximum configuration. But even more disturbingly, it is recursively undecidable whether a GS has, in fact, entered the basin of attraction of a dynamical system's maximum configuration.

DISCUSSION. Every interesting — i.e., nonlinear — dynamical system that has been utilized in endogenous macroeconomics can be encoded appropriately and shown to be equivalent to some TM. It is a more difficult task to construct a one-one mapping from TMs to GS. However, one can exploit the fundamental result of classical recursion theory, that every TM is also capable of acting as a UTM, to use any GS to model and study the behaviour of any endogenous macroeconomic model of growth, development or business cycles. It will not be an easy task; but it will be an interesting and challenging exercise.

5. Concluding notes: in praise of unstable, disequilibrium and nonmaximum economic dynamics

The motivations [for this study] are not about the economy, they are about economics and the underlying principles of economics we use as tools to understand the economy. ... *Unstable equilibria can exist in markets.* They exist at the intersection of demand and supply, as do other classical market equilibria. (Plott and Smith, 1999, pp. 406–7; italics added).

Recursion theoretic formalisms are about intrinsically dynamic objects. Characterizations of dynamic objects tend to focus on the time profile of their behaviour. Questions about these characterizations emphasize decision problems rather than optimization exercises. Consequently, effective decidability becomes the central issue and undecidability results are not infrequent. Undecidability results have positive aspects in the same sense in which Arrow's impossibility theorem fertilized social choice theory. They alter the nature and scope of economics as a policy-oriented subject: less categorical, more modest.

If the no-arbitrage principle encapsulates rational behaviour at the individual and institutional level, as I believe it does, then dynamic objects that implement the principle must reside in that delicate border region between a stable and a strange attractor. Only then would it have sufficient flexibility to explore and evolve; to persist and adapt.

Dynamic objects that are characterized by stable, equilibrium and maximum configurations are incapable of computation universality. They are, thus, inconsistent with the *no arbitrage* principle. A dynamical system with a classical attractor as its limit set will not be able to process patterns in the data that characterize events and structures that are complex in a precisely definable way. In the language of classical recursion theory, they are finite automata that are less powerful than the (Universal) Turing Machine. Hence, the need to supplement growth theories, formalized in terms of dynamical systems with limit points as attractors, with *ad-hoc shockeries*.[3] Unstable equilibria in the microeconomics of exchange economies, disequilibrium dynamics in adaptive behavioural economics and nonmaximum dynamics in macroeconomics encapsulate undecidabilities because, being based on the *no arbitrage* principle for their rationality underpinnings, they must be capable of computation universality. Conversely, any object capable of computation universality must be intrinsically dynamic and capable of persistently unstable, disequilibrium and nonmaximum behaviour about which effective questions will receive incomplete answers.

Mathematical appendix: some recursion theoretic heuristics

By ratiocination, I mean computation. (Hobbes: *On the Body*, pt. I, ch. IV).

Description definitions and conventions

DESCRIPTION A.1. *A Turing Machine* consists of the following inter-linked parts:

(i) A movable control mechanism which at any given point in time is in one of a finite number of possible STATES;
(ii) A sensor, attached to the movable control mechanism, that can scan the symbols on an infinite tape, interpret the symbols, erase them and, also, write symbols on the tape;
(iii) The tape, infinite to the left and right, is divided into (scannable) cells in each one of which one symbol from a fixed alphabet can be written.

One of the many possible ways of depicting the essence of such a Machine is the following (see Figure 2):

CONVENTION 1.
(a) The sensor can scan exactly one cell at a time;
(b) Only a finite number of cells of the infinite tape are nonempty at any given point in time;
(c) The sensor is placed scanning the leftmost nonempty cell when it is initialised;
(d) The fixed alphabet consists of the three symbols: $\langle 0, 1, \emptyset \rangle$ (where $\emptyset$: denotes the symbol 'blank' and is different from the numeral zero, 0).

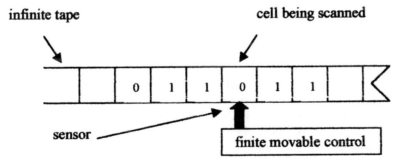

infinite tape   **cell being scanned**

| | 0 | 1 | 1 | 0 | 1 | 1 | |

sensor _____

finite movable control

Figure 2.

Denote:

Q: finite set of states;
$q_0 \in Q$:   a pre-specified initial state;
$q_T \in Q$:   a pre-specified terminal state;
δ: a partial function (i.e., not defined over the whole of its domain);

and:

$$\delta: Q \times \Lambda \to Q \times \Lambda \times \{L, R, \gamma\}$$

where, Λ: symbol set (alphabet)-$\langle 0, 1, \emptyset \rangle$ in our case;
          L: a Leftward movement of the movable control;
          R: a Rightward movement of the movable control;
          γ: No movement of the movable control;

$\delta(q_T, \alpha)$ is not defined, $\forall \alpha \in \Lambda$: i.e., if the movable control is in, or reaches, the terminal state, T, the actions of the Turing Machine cease.

DEFINITION A.1. *Turing Machine*

Given the fixed alphabet Λ, a *Turing Machine* is a quadruple: $\text{TM} \equiv \langle Q, \delta, q_0, q_T \rangle$

REMARK A.1. Many elements of the description and the convention have been chosen with a view to making the definition seem 'natural'. Not all of the elements are necessary. I have not sought a minimal set of elements for the description and the definition.

Enumerability, recursive functions and sets: some definitions and theorems

Consider the following three functions which can be accepted, unambiguously, as intuitively computable in the sense that it is easy to construct Turing Machines to compute them:

(i) The *zero function*: $z(x) = 0$, $\forall x \in N$
    This function assigns the same value, zero, to each natural number as argument.
    i.e., $z(0) = z(1) = z(2) = \cdots = 0$
(ii) The *identity function*: Id $(x) = x$, $\forall x \in N$.
     This function assigns to each natural number as argument its own value as output.
     i.e., $\text{Id}(0) = 0$; $\text{Id}(1) = 1$; $\text{Id}(2) = 2$; ...
(iii) The *successor function*: $S(x) = x + 1$, $\forall x \in N$.
(iv) The *projection function*:

$$\text{Pr}_i^k : N^k \to N$$

Defined by 'projecting' the i-th coordinate of a k-dimensioned domain as:

$$\mathrm{Pr}_i^k(x_1, x_2, ..., x_i, ..., x_k) = x_i \qquad \forall x_1, x_2, ..., x_k \in N$$

DEFINITION A.2. *The Basic Functions*

The collection of intuitively computable functions given by (i)–(iv) are the *Basic Functions*.

Next, consider the following two *operations* that are to be applied to given computable functions — again, in the sense that it is easy to construct Turing Machines to do them:

(α). *Composition of Computable Functions*

If f and $g_i(i=1, 2, ..., m)$ are computable functions of m and n arguments, respectively then h is obtained by *composition* from f and $g_i(i=1, 2, ..., m)$ as follows: $h(x_1, ..., x_n) = f(g_1, (x_1, ..., x_n), g_2(x_1, ..., x_n) ... g_m(x_1, ... x_n))$.

(β). *Primitive Recursion of Computable Functions*

Given the computable functions:

$$\varphi: N^{n-1} \to N \qquad \text{and} \qquad \theta: N^{n+1} \to N$$

the computable function Y: $N^n \to N$ is obtained from φ and θ by primitive recursion whenever:

$$\phi(0, x_2, ..., x_n) = \varphi(x_2, ..., x_n)$$

and

$$\phi(x+1, x_2, ..., x_n) = \theta(x, \phi(x_1, x_2, ..., x_n), x_2, ..., x_n).$$

DEFINITION A.3. *Primitive Recursive Functions*

The set $\mathcal{P}$ of primitive recursive functions are those that are closed with respect to (finite applications of) composition and primitive recursion on the Basic Functions.

Unfortunately, they do not exhaust the class of intuitively computable functions. The classic intuitively computable function from $N \times N \to N$ defined by Ackerman *grows faster than* any member of P. Ackerman's famous function is:

$$A(0, n) = n + 1$$
$$A(m + 1, 0) = A(m, 1)$$
$$A(m + 1, n + 1) = A(m, A(m + 1, n))$$

Now, since Ackerman's function is intuitively computable the class $\mathcal{P}$ of primitive recursive functions will have to be enlarged. On what basis can this enlargement be executed so that exactly the intuitively computable functions are included in it? We have accepted that all the Turing Machine computable functions are intuitively computable. Are there, conversely, intuitively computable computable functions that are not Turing Machine computable? Answers to these questions are summarized as the *Church-Turing thesis*. But to get to that a few more definitions and details are necessary:

DEFINITION A.4. *Partial Function and Total Function*

A function $f: X \rightarrow Y$ but where f may not be defined on the entire domain X is called a *Partial Function*. Correspondingly, a *Total Function* is defined on its entire domain.

(γ). *Minimalization of Computable Functions*

The function h of n arguments is obtained by the following operation — called *minimalisation* — from the computable total function f of $n+1$ arguments:

$$h(x_1, ..., x_n) = \begin{cases} \text{The smallest } y \text{ for which } f(x_1, ..., x_n, y) = 0, \text{ if any;} \\ \text{Undefined if } f(x_1, ..., x_n, y) = 0 \text{ for no } y \end{cases}$$

The qualification 'if any' and 'for no y' introduce elements of effective undecidability to elementary computability theory. We may keep on trying, in some definite order, different values of y till $f(x_1, ..., x_n, y) = 0$ There is no guarantee, except for trivial functions, that failure to find such a y after billion or trillion trials means that it will not be found in the next, say, 18 attempts. The same ambiguity applies to the activity of locating 'the smallest y'. This operation of minimalization ties up recursive functions with the real activity of computation. A computer (i.e., a Turing Machine) may *fail to terminate* for some inputs; a function h may be *undefined*.

DEFINITION A.5. *Partial Recursive Functions*

The set of functions PRC that are closed with respect to the (finitely applied) operations of composition, primitive recursion and minimalization on the Basic Functions are the partial recursive functions.

The Church-Turing thesis

A partial function is computable if and only if a Turing Machine can be constructed to compute it.

This is a thesis and not a theorem. It is entirely possible that some future Alan Turing will find a way to tame the monstrous growth rates inherent in uncomputable functions, as presently defined. There are distinguished recursion theorists, philosophers and mathematicians (Laszlo Kalmar, Ludwig Wittgenstein and Steve Smale, respectively, come immediately to mind) who feel that there is more to be said on these issues.

DEFINITION A.6. *Recursive Sets*

A set $X \subseteq N$ of natural numbers is *recursive* if, and only if, there is a partial recursive function φ such that $\forall n$, $n \in X$ if, and only if, $\varphi(n) = 0$.

DEFINITION A.7. *Decidable Sets*

A set if *decidable* if, and only if, there is an effective (i.e., computable) method to characterize any member of the set.

Thus, since every partial recursive function is computable, every recursive set is decidable. In other words, there is an effective method — an algorithm — to *decide* whether or not an arbitrary n is a member of X.

DEFINITION A.8. *Recursively Enumerable Sets*

A set $X \subseteq N$ of natural numbers is *recursively enumerable* (R.E) if, and only if, it is either empty or the range of a partial recursive function.

There is an open-endedness in the definition of R.E sets that is absent in the definition of recursive sets. The definition of R.E sets entails the existence of a partial recursive function (or, equivalently — by the Church-Turing thesis — a Turing Machine) which can systematically output members of such sets. Thus, the open-endedness comes from the fact that an arbitrary $n \in N$ may not, say, till the billionth try, be the output of a PRC; but it may well be the next, after the billionth try, output. We can only keep on trying, without any guarantee of a definite answer, either way.

Some elementary and immediate implications of the above three definitions are the following:

PROPOSITION A.1. If a set is recursive then its complement is also recursive.

PROPOSITION A.2. A recursive set is also recursively enumerable. (In other words, a decidable set is listable (enumerable)).

PROPOSITION A.3. If a set and its complement are both recursively enumerable, then the two sets are also recursive.

THEOREM A.1. *The Undecidability of the Halting Problem for Turing Machines*

There is no algorithm to decide whether or not any given Turing Machine enters the terminal state for arbitrary input configurations on the tape.

Any standard textbook on recursion theory will, normally include a discussion of this theorem and, of course, complete proofs. The reason for stating this theorem at this particular juncture is the following. According to this theorem there is no effective method (i.e., again, there is no algorithm) to decide whether or not a Turing Machine for an arbitrary program card will enter its terminal state. An immediately relevant question will be: can it be decided whether a Turing Machine exhibits some particular input — output behaviour.

Armed with a knowledge of the undecidability of the Halting Problem it will not be surprising that the answer is in the negative. *Rice's theorem* summarizes the result.

THEOREM A.2. *Rice's Theorem*

Denote by $\varphi_i\colon N \to N$ the partial recursive function computed by Turing Machine, TM_i. If $X \subseteq N$ is recursive, then $\exists i, j$ such that $i \in x$ and $j \in N - X$ and:

$$\varphi_i = \varphi_j$$

In other words, there are distinguishable Turing Machines, TM_i and TM_j, that compute the same partial recursive functions. Thus, if D_i is a decidable property possessed by TM_i and not possessed by TM_j, then simply by observing their input-output behaviour it is not possible to tell which is which, so to speak. Another, and more succinct way of stating the import of the theorem is as follows:

Any nontrivial input-output property of programs is *undecidable*.

This can be interpreted — exactly — to mean that only the properties of the empty set and the universal set are effectively decidable. Now, Rice's theorem characterizes recursive sets. The natural extension of Rice's theorem would be an analogous result for recursively enumerable sets. Such a result is encapsulated in the following:

THEOREM A.3. *The Rice-Shapiro Theorem*

Consider the set $\mathscr{C}$ of partial recursive functions such that:

$$\mathscr{R} = \{x\colon \varphi_x \in \mathscr{C}\} \text{ is R.E.}$$

Then, for any partial recursive function ψ:

$$\psi \in \mathscr{C}, \text{ if, and only if, } \exists \theta \subseteq \psi \text{ with finite domain and } \theta \in \mathscr{C}.$$

Now, every finite input-output configuration defines a recursive set. Going, therefore, from Rice's theorem to the Rice-Shapiro theorem would be akin to finding an extension of some finite input-output configuration to define recursively enumerable sets. Thus, according to the Rice-Shapiro theorem, a class of partial recursive functions is recursively enumerable if, and only if, each member of this class is defined by the extension of some finite input-output configuration in a recursively enumerable set of such configuration.

I have not even scratched the proverbial surface of *classical recursion theory* — let alone the more modern higher order theories. I leave it to the reader to judge how much more insight and understanding awaits the more competent dynamic economic analyst, who is also a master of higher order recursion theory.

Notes

1 Integration is a computable process.
2 Could the S-machine be a Turing Machine? The answer is: in general NO; or not necessarily. If it is not a Turing Machine what can it be? A non-algorithmic machine!
3 This felicitous phrase was coined by Richard Day (1992), p. 180.

References

Arrow, K. J. (1986) Rationality of self and others in an economic system. *Journal of Business*, 59, S.385–S.400.

Arrow, K. J. and Hahn, F. H. (1971) *General Competitive Analysis*. San Francisco: Holden-Day Inc.

Coddington, E. A. (1961) *Introduction to Ordinary Differential Equations*. New York: Dover Publications.

Day, R. H. (1992) Models of business cycles: A review article. *Structural Change and Economic Dynamics*, 3, 177–182.

Debreu, G. (1974) Excess demand functions. *Journal of Mathematical Economics*, 1, 15–21.

Farmer, J. D. and Packard, N. H. (1985) Evolution, games and learning: Models for & application in machines and nature. *Physica D*, 22D, 1–3, October–November, vii–xii.

Kydland, F. E. and Prescott, E. C. (1990) Business cycles: Real facts and a monetary myth. *Federal Reserve Bank of Minneapolis — Quarterly Review*, Spring, 3–18.

Lucas, R. E. (1986) Adaptive behaviour in economic theory. *Journal of Business*, 59, S.401–S.426.

Mantel, R. R. (1974) On the characterization of aggregate excess demand. *Journal of Economic Theory*, 9, 348–53.

Moore, C. (1990) Unpredictability and undecidability in dynamical systems. *Physical Review Letters*, 64, 20, May, 2354–57.

Moore, C. (1991) Generalized shifts: Unpredictability and undecidability in dynamical systems. *Nonlinearity*, 4, 199–203.

Patinkin, D. (1965) *Money Interest and Prices* (2nd edition). London: Harper & Row.

Plott, C. R. and Smith, J. (1999) Instability of equilibria in experimental markets: Upward sloping demands, externalities and fad-like incentives. *Southern Economic Journal*, 65, 3, January, 405–26.

Pour-El, M. B. and Richards, J. I. (1989) *Computability in Analysis and Physics*. Berlin: Springer-Verlag.

Samuelson, P. A. (1974) Remembrances of Frisch. *European Economic Review*, 1, 5, 7–22.

Scarf, H. and Shoven, J. B. Editors (1984) *Applied General Equilibrium Analysis*. Cambridge: Cambridge University Press.

Sonnenschein, H. (1972) Market excess demand functions. *Econometrica*, 40, 549–63.

Sonnenschein, H. (1973) Do Walras' identity and continuity characterize the class of community excess demand functions? *Journal of Economic Theory*, 6, 345–54.

Stewart, I. (1991) Deciding the undecidable. *Nature*, 352, 22 August, 664–5.

Uzawa, H. (1962) Walras' existence theorem and Brouwer's fixed point theorem. *Economic Studies Quarterly*, XIII, 1, 59–62.

Velupillai, K. (1999) *Computable Economics*. Oxford: Oxford University Press.

INDEX